The Realist Tradition an
International Relations

Realism is commonly portrayed ...uces International Relations to pure power politics. M... illiams provides an important re-examination of the Realist tradition and its relevance for contemporary International Relations. Examining three thinkers commonly invoked as Realism's foremost proponents – Hobbes, Rousseau, and Morgenthau – the book shows that, far from advocating a crude realpolitik, Realism's most famous classical proponents actually stressed the need for a restrained exercise of power and a politics with ethics at its core. These ideas are more relevant than ever at a time when the nature of responsible responses to international problems is at the centre of contemporary political debate. This original interpretation of major thinkers will interest scholars of International Relations and the history of ideas.

MICHAEL C. WILLIAMS is Senior Lecturer in the Department of International Politics at the University of Wales, Aberystwyth. He has published widely in both International Relations theory and security studies, including articles in *International Organization* and *International Studies Quarterly*.

CAMBRIDGE STUDIES IN INTERNATIONAL RELATIONS: 100

The Realist Tradition and the Limits of International Relations

Cambridge Studies in International Relations is a joint initiative of Cambridge University Press and the British International Studies Association (BISA). The series will include a wide range of material, from undergraduate textbooks and surveys to research-based monographs and collaborative volumes. The aim of the series is to publish the best new scholarship in International Studies from Europe, North America and the rest of the world.

CAMBRIDGE STUDIES IN INTERNATIONAL RELATIONS

100 *Michael C. Williams*
The Realist Tradition and the Limits of International Relations

99 *Ivan Arreguín-Toft*
How the Weak Win Wars
A Theory of Asymmetric Conflict

98 *Michael Barnett and Raymond Duvall (eds.)*
Power in Global Governance

97 *Yale H. Ferguson and Richard N. Mansbach*
Remapping Global Politics
History's revenge and future shock

96 *Christian Reus-Smit (ed.)*
The Politics of International Law

95 *Barry Buzan*
From International to World Society?
English School Theory and the Social Structure of Globalisation

94 *K. J. Holsti*
Taming the Sovereigns
Institutional Change in International Politics

93 *Bruce Cronin*
Institutions for the Common Good
International Protection Regimes in International Society

92 *Paul Keal*
European Conquest and the Rights of Indigenous Peoples
The Moral Backwardness of International Society

91 *Barry Buzan and Ole Wæver*
Regions and Powers
The Structure of International Security

90 *A. Claire Cutler*
Private Power and Global Authority
Transnational Merchant Law in the Global Political Economy

89 *Patrick M. Morgan*
Deterrence Now

Series list continued after index

The Realist Tradition and the Limits of International Relations

Michael C. Williams
University of Wales, Aberystwyth

PUBLISHED BY THE PRESS SYNDICATE OF THE UNIVERSITY OF CAMBRIDGE
The Pitt Building, Trumpington Street, Cambridge, United Kingdom

CAMBRIDGE UNIVERSITY PRESS
The Edinburgh Building, Cambridge, CB2 2RU, UK
40 West 20th Street, New York, NY 10011–4211, USA
477 Williamstown Road, Port Melbourne, VIC 3207, Australia
Ruiz de Alarcón 13, 28014 Madrid, Spain
Dock House, The Waterfront, Cape Town 8001, South Africa

http://www.cambridge.org

First published 2005

Printed in the United Kingdom at the University Press, Cambridge

Typeface Palatino 10/12.5 pt. *System* LaTeX 2_ε [TB]

A catalogue record for this book is available from the British Library

ISBN 0 521 82752 3 hardback
ISBN 0 521 53475 5 paperback

Contents

Acknowledgements

This book has been a long time in the making, and along the way I have benefited from the guidance, advice, and friendship of many people. I was first introduced to thinking about the relationship between political theory and International Relations as an undergraduate by R. B. J. Walker, and have continued to learn from him ever since. I suspect that there is a great deal in this book that he would disagree with, but I hope that the result does at least some justice to the inspiration. During my time as a graduate student, Paul Evans consistently tried (and failed) to convince me that there was more to Realism, and to Morgenthau in particular, than my blinkered view allowed. I am happy to acknowledge that, in the end, he was right.

For the past five years, I have been lucky enough to work with a remarkable group of colleagues in the Department of International Politics at Aberystwyth. The Department has supplied both a stimulating and convivial environment, as well as a generous sabbatical provision that greatly facilitated the completion of the project.

Many people have read and commented on different parts of the analysis, in a variety of different forms. I wish to thank in particular Asher Horowitz, Jef Huysmans, Oliver Juttersönk, Keith Krause, Jennifer Mitzen, Ross Rudolph, Anders Tjalve, and Alex Wendt for their comments on many of the individual chapters. Alexandra Gheciu, Lene Hansen, and Vibeke Schou Pedersen were kind enough to read the manuscript in its entirety, and their astute criticisms and insights greatly improved the final product. Randall Germain offered sage advice and great friendship throughout, as he has for so many years. I am also indebted to the editor of Cambridge University Press's British International Studies Association series, Steve Smith, for his guidance and remarkable support throughout the entire process.

Finally, two individuals Richard Wyn Jones and, particularly, Rita Abrahamsen displayed great fortitude and patience, sharing their time and advice with remarkable generosity. Without their help I doubt that the seemingly endless process of finishing this book would ever actually have come to a conclusion.

Introduction

Few claims are as enduring, powerful, and controversial in the study of world politics as that of being a Realist. To some, being a Realist represents the height of wisdom: the mark of a clear-sighted ability to understand the world the way it is, a willingness to confront the dynamics of power and interest that are held to govern world politics. To others, Realism is a mark of failure: morally obtuse and historically anachronistic, it represents a lack of political understanding and imagination that is misleading at best, pernicious and destructive at worst. Yet whatever stance one takes, there is little doubt that despite continual declarations of its irrelevance or imminent demise, Realism remains at the heart of theoretical and political dispute in world politics, constituting a continuing reference point against which competing positions consistently define themselves and a conceptual and rhetorical fulcrum around which both analytic and political debates revolve.

Throughout the 1990s, Realism seemed on the defensive. The end of the Cold War, it was widely argued, demonstrated its limitations all too clearly, while emerging dynamics – from state fragmentation, to globalisation, to environmental degradation – presented challenges that Realism was ill equipped to analyse, and even less well suited to address. Even amongst its supporters, the question 'Is Realism Finished?'[1] seemed to emerge with new urgency; and although they almost invariably answered their rhetorical question with a rather predictable 'no', the frequency with which it was asked illustrated the pervasiveness of the challenge and the breadth and sophistication of Realism's critics.

[1] Fareed Zakaria, 'Is Realism Finished?' *The National Interest* (Winter 1992–3).

These debates have by no means disappeared,[2] but it is difficult to avoid a sense that in the twenty-first century Realism is resurgent. Given increased impetus by the events of September 11, 2001, but driven more generally by a concern with American power and foreign policy in an era of seemingly unprecedented primacy, a series of influential writers have sought to reassert Realist truths supposedly obscured by the 'liberal' euphoria that dominated the previous decade. The hard realities of power politics, of the tradition of realpolitik, are once again being touted as lessons that must (yet again) be learnt and imperatives that must be followed. It is not difficult to discern a degree of mythologisation in these calls for a return to Realism. Casting the 1990s as a period of naïve liberalism bears suspicious signs of an attempt to reinvoke the 'twenty years' crisis' of the interwar period, and to draw on the still powerful symbolic legacy bequeathed by previous Realist assaults on well-meaning but profoundly misguided visions of world politics.[3] Be this as it may, there is no doubting Realism's resurgence. Books such as Robert Kaplan's *Warrior Politics* and Robert Kagan's *Of Paradise and Power* have made considerable impacts on the broad intellectual setting within which policy is debated, each arguing forcefully for a return to Realist principles even as they challenge previous understandings of what Realism is and how it should be applied.[4]

One of the most notable dimensions of Realism is its appeal to history, and particularly to a legacy of Realist thinking stretching back centuries, if not millennia. It is thus not surprising to find familiar references to a 'Hobbesian' international system in Kagan's account of the imperatives of power, and Kaplan's mining of the history of political thought for inspiration (while certainly refreshing in a popular book on world politics) is by no means out of the ordinary. On the contrary, the claim that there exists an identifiable 'Realist tradition' stretching across the ages and illustrating the 'timeless wisdom'[5] of a vision of world politics centred upon the principles of power politics and the dictates of

[2] See, for example, Jeffrey W. Legro and Andrew Moravcsik, 'Is Anybody Still a Realist?' *International Security* 24:2 (1999), and the responses in Peter D. Feaver, et al., Correspondence: Brother Can You Spare a Paradigm (Or, Was Anybody Ever A Realist?)', *International Security*, 25:1 (2000).

[3] For a broad survey, see David Long and Peter Wilson (eds.), *Thinkers of the Twenty Years' Crisis: Interwar Idealism Reassessed* (Oxford: Clarendon Press, 1995).

[4] Robert Kaplan, *Warrior Politics: Why Leadership Demands a Pagan Ethos* (New York: Vintage Books, 2002); Robert Kagan, *Of Paradise and Power* (London: Atlantic Books, 2003).

[5] Barry Buzan, 'The Timeless Wisdom of Realism?', in *International Theory: Positivism and Beyond*, ed. Steve Smith, Ken Booth, and Marysia Zalewski (Cambridge University Press, 1996).

international anarchy is one of the central aspects of International Relations theory. Renditions of this tale pervade the study of International Relations, informing everything from standard introductions to Realism for new students of the subject, to sophisticated scholarly and popular discussions of theoretical alternatives currently on offer. The protagonists in these stories are familiar: Thucydides and his account of the rivalry between Athens and Sparta in the Peloponnesian War; Machiavelli, with his advice to the Prince in the Italian city-states of the Renaissance; Thomas Hobbes' stark portrayal of the state of nature as a 'war of each against all'; Jean-Jacques Rousseau and his telling analogy of the stag-hunt illustrating the logic of international distrust and competition; Hans Morgenthau, with his assault upon the naïvetés of interwar 'liberalism' and his powerful restoration and reaffirmation of the principles of power politics as the basis for a revived study of International Relations in the wake of the Second World War, all play prominent roles in evocations and invocations of the Realist tradition as a bedrock for understanding world politics.[6]

The idea of a Realist tradition has a powerful impact on the study of international politics, as these figures and the tradition which they are held to comprise have become central elements in the narrative which the discipline of International Relations tells about itself, its history, and its conceptual foundations. Equally importantly, claims about the Realist tradition function as forms of legitimation, confirming the continuing validity of 'Realist' principles throughout history, and appropriating the authority of classical figures in political theory in their support. Indeed the claim that there is a Realist tradition is a key component of claims about the continuing salience and wisdom of Realism itself. The appeal of the idea of such a tradition is, therefore, hardly mysterious.

[6] For a powerful recent restatement of this position, see John Mearsheimer, *The Tragedy of Great Power Politics* (New York: Norton, 2001), pp. 17–27, 365–6. For diverse appraisals of Realism see, Michael Doyle, *Ways of War and Peace* (New York: Norton, 1997), Stefano Guzzini, *Realism in International Relations and International Political Economy: Continuing Story of a Death Foretold* (London: Routledge, 1998); David Boucher, *Political Theories of International Relations: From Thucydides to the Present* (Oxford University Press, 1998); Jack Donnelly, *Realism in International Relations* (Cambridge University Press, 2000); Johnathan Haslam, *No Virtue Like Necessity: Realist Thought in International Relations since Machiavelli* (New Haven: Yale University Press, 2002), Ashley Tellis, 'Reconstructing Political Realism: The Long March to Scientific Theory', in *Roots of Realism*, ed. Benjamin Frankel (London: Frank Coss, 1996). A major study that unfortunately arrived too recently to allow me to do it full justice is Richard Ned Lebow, *The Tragic Vision of Politics* (Cambridge University Press, 2003). See also Joseph M. Grieco, 'Realist International Theory and the Study of World Politics', in *New Thinking in International Relations*, ed. Michael Doyle and John Ikenberry (Boulder, Colo.: Westview, 1997).

This book arose from a deep dissatisfaction with the ways in which key figures in the history of political thought have been appropriated in much of International Relations, and the visions of Realism that have been associated with them. The more I looked at these thinkers, the more convinced I became that Realism had generally done little justice to those figures it claimed as its own. In fact, the more I looked, the more I came to suspect that the positions of key thinkers in the Realist canon not only bore remarkably little resemblance to their roles within standard renditions of the Realist tradition in International Relations, but that they often stood in direct opposition to the claims attributed to them. Far from supporting contemporary Realism, it seemed to me, a fuller engagement with the legacy it claimed actually undermined its authority.

The first two chapters in this study – on Thomas Hobbes and Jean-Jacques Rousseau – were the initial results of these suspicions. In each, I argue that far from supporting claims about International Relations as an inevitable 'state of nature', or a realm of realpolitik, these thinkers actually develop understandings of International Relations that profoundly challenge many of the dominant claims which they are today used to support.[7] But I also gradually became convinced that revisiting claims about a Realist tradition could go beyond just challenging conventional appropriations and misappropriations of these thinkers. In particular, it seemed that by taking the thought of these canonical figures more seriously, and reopening the questions with which they struggled, it might be possible to contribute to a reconstruction of a Realist tradition in ways that both brought out their historical concerns and altered their contemporary significance. In short, was there not another Realism – within the existing 'tradition' – that could be brought into view by challenging contemporary claims about both the nature of Realism and the positions of classical thinkers within its tradition?

[7] In this regard, these analyses support other critiques of the interpretation and appropriation of classical political thinkers within International Relations in general, and within Realism in particular. In addition to those cited above see, for example, the treatments of Thucydides by Richard Ned Lebow, 'Thucydides the Constructivist', *American Political Science Review*, 95:3 (2001), Daniel Garst, 'Thucydides and Neo-Realism', *International Studies Quarterly*, 33:2 (1989), and Stephen Forde, 'International Realism and the Science of Politics: Thucydides, Machiavelli, and Neorealism', *International Studies Quarterly*, 39:2 (1995); of Machiavelli by R. B. J. Walker, *Inside/Outside: International Relations as Political Theory* (Cambridge University Press, 1993); of Carr in Michael Cox (ed.), *E. H. Carr: A Critical Appraisal* (London: Palgrave, 2000), and Charles Jones, *E. H. Carr and International Relations: A Duty to Lie* (Cambridge University Press, 2000).

This agenda was further stimulated by an engagement with another canonical figure in the Realist tradition: Hans Morgenthau. Morgenthau, I had long assumed (largely on the basis of my own very limited reading and the assurances of numerous cursory, secondary accounts), was a remarkably crude, if surprisingly influential figure, whose theory of power politics based in a universal *animus dominandi* represented everything that a sophisticated theory of International Relations – whatever its stripe – should leave behind as rapidly as possible. As in the cases of Hobbes and Rousseau, it did not take long to discover that this view bore little resemblance to reality. Indeed, it soon became apparent that Morgenthau's thinking reflected a deep engagement with – and a clear and sophisticated understanding of – many of the issues at work in the understandings of international politics that could be found in Hobbes and Rousseau. At this point, I decided to move away from the narrower (albeit safer) theme of simply engaging with individual thinkers and providing critiques of their interpretation within the discipline of International Relations, toward the broader goal of reconstructing an understanding of Realism that would bring out (and bring together) the concerns of these thinkers and illustrate what I increasingly came to believe was their profound challenge to contemporary understandings of the Realist tradition and its place in International Relations theory today.

This book seeks to outline this understanding of the Realist tradition, a tradition that I call 'wilful Realism'. The vision of wilful Realism as I try to present it here has three defining features. The first lies in its relationship to *scepticism*. Wilful Realism is characterised by a rational questioning of the limits of reason. It is not a denial of knowledge, or of rationality, and it insists upon the importance of empirical and historical knowledge. It is, however, deeply sceptical – and often harshly critical – of modern empiricism and rationalism as adequate bases for political knowledge, and of the broader tendency to model knowledge after the lead of Enlightenment science. These concerns are not abstract: they are driven by the conviction that questions of knowledge and belief are crucial elements in the construction and evaluation of action and order. The sense of limits arising from this scepticism does not yield resignation or nihilism; on the contrary, it is taken as a challenge requiring the active construction of political and social order, leading wilful Realism to a continual concern with the relationship between knowledge and politics, the politics of knowledge, and a strong advocacy of the need for a politics both informed and suitably chastened by an understanding of the limits of knowledge.[8]

A second key component is *relationality*. Wilful Realism does not assume that the nature of either the self or political order is fixed or given. It focuses instead on the construction of subjectivity and political order through relational processes of self and other, at the level of both individuals and communities. This concern with relationality is historical and sociological, examining processes of constitution, maintenance, and transformation within and between political orders. It is also conceptual and philosophical. By focusing on the importance of knowledge in the construction of action wilful Realism seeks to ensure that the inescapability of relationality – of, for example, the self gaining identity in relation to others, or of concepts gaining meaning in relation to their antitheses – does not devolve into dualism: into understandings of identity or knowledge as defined wholly by opposition. This makes the concern with relationality more than just analytic: it is also part of a political and ethical sensibility in which the relationship between self and other has significance as a political principle, and constitutes one of the most important differences between wilful Realism and forms of rigidly oppositional power politics.

The third dimension can, more familiarly, be termed *power politics*. Power is central to any understanding of Realism, and wilful Realism is no exception. At the centre of wilful Realist analysis is an engagement with the multiple forms of power at work in politics, including those involved in knowledge claims, forms of subjectivity, and structures of authority and action (including those that allow the effective mobilisation and exercise of material power). Beyond these analytic issues, however, there again lies a broader set of political and ethical imperatives. Politics is in this vision identified by its specific duality: an indeterminacy that makes it at one and the same time a realm of power and inevitable struggle, *and* a realm of openness and self-determination. As a sphere of contest over the determination of values and wills, politics is an undetermined realm in which the struggle for power and domination is potentially limitless. Yet politics is also the sphere of activity uniquely concerned with the consideration, generation, and

[8] For broader overviews of scepticism, see R. Popkin, *The History of Skepticism from Erasmus to Spinoza* (Berkeley: University of California Press, 1979); M. Burnyeat, *The Skeptical Tradition* (Berkeley: University of California Press, 1983) and his 'The Sceptic in His Place and Time', in *Philosophy in History*, ed. Richard Rorty, J. B. Schneewind, and Quentin Skinner (Cambridge University Press, 1984).

transformation of common interests and understandings: the sphere where the fundamental meanings and values of social life are contested and determined. The lack of fixed understandings of the good and the true is the condition of modern politics, and the basis of its distinctiveness as a realm of freedom, creativity, and change. Wilful Realism is deeply concerned that a recognition of the centrality of power in politics does not result in the reduction of politics to pure power, and particularly to the capacity to wield violence. It seeks, on the contrary, a politics of limits that recognises the destructive and productive dimensions of politics, and that maximises its positive possibilities while minimising its destructive potential.

This understanding of the Realist tradition clearly stands at some distance from many – indeed most – understandings of Realism today. The first three chapters seek to establish my claims by exploring the significance of each of these dimensions in the thinking of Hobbes, Rousseau, and Morgenthau. I argue, for example, that the concept of 'Hobbesian anarchy' is both more complex and more challenging as a foundation for thinking about International Relations than has usually been recognised. The significance for International Relations of what Stephen Holmes has called the 'Hobbesian moment' in political thought lies less in Hobbes' stress on human mendacity, or a presentation of the objective 'logic of anarchy', than in his use of the state of nature as a powerful metaphor underlining the role of knowledge and belief in political action, and the centrality of the politics of knowledge in political order. One of Hobbes' most interesting, and perhaps important, contributions to thinking about international politics thus lies in his engagement with scepticism and the limits of political order, and his attempt to provide a renewed understanding (and cultural practice) of subjectivity and sovereignty that would allow a maximum degree of autonomy – while providing stability, peace, and order – both within and between states.

Like Hobbes, Rousseau has achieved a canonical status in International Relations. His parable of the stag-hunt, so influentially drawn upon by Kenneth Waltz,[9] has become a staple model and powerful metaphor conveying the structural 'logic of anarchy' in the international system. Yet Rousseau's thinking also emerges from sources considerably different from those which have been invoked in his name

[9] Kenneth Waltz, *Man, the State and War* (New York: Columbia University Press, 1959), pp. 167–71.

within International Relations. Beginning with the relationship between knowledge and politics, Rousseau develops an account of the historical development of subjectivity, grounded in the relationship between self and other, that provides him with both an explanation of the emergence of realpolitik, and a vision for moving beyond it. Far from being a quintessential theorist of the logic of anarchy, one of Rousseau's primary goals is to demonstrate how such a view systematically misunderstands politics; and far from revelling in a discovery of the deterministic laws of international anarchy, he provides a penetrating critique of the logic of realpolitik and seeks to overcome its dilemmas through an understanding of sovereignty as a politics of right formed within states, but extending beyond them.

Finally, one of the most fundamental and yet misunderstood elements of Morgenthau's Realism lies in his struggle with the nature of 'politics' itself. Morgenthau is often accused of initiating a Realist tradition that marginalised, or even excluded, the role of ideas in international politics, and of having an almost incomprehensibly narrow and simplistic concept of politics itself. I argue that a deeper enquiry into Morgenthau's understanding of politics reveals in his Realism a sophisticated interrogation of the relationship between knowledge claims, political order, social mobilisation, and political power. Far from reducing politics to power, Morgenthau's Realism recognises both the destructive and productive potential of politics, and attempts to construct an understanding of domestic politics and foreign policy that restrains modernity's worst potentials while retaining its principled and productive possibilities.

Each of these thinkers is fully aware of the destructive possibilities of modern politics, and their ideas reflect a direct concern with the politics of power, violence, and conflict. The relationship between knowledge and politics that is at the centre of Hobbes' engagement with scepticism, for example, is for him no abstract question: he sees it at the heart of the bloody conflict of the English Civil War. For Rousseau, the brutal degradation he sees in civil society, and the violent state of war he observes between sovereigns, is a direct consequence of the distorted forms that the process of relationality and the evolution of reason have undergone. Morgenthau's apparently abstruse interest in the concept of 'politics', similarly, is not an esoteric philosophical excursion: it arises directly from his attempt to oppose the violently oppositional vision of the 'concept of the political' developed by the 'crown jurist of the Nazi party', Carl Schmitt, and from his attempt to construct a viable liberal politics in the light of the collapse of Weimar and the catastrophic rise of fascism. Recognising the conflictual dimensions of politics is thus undeniably a key part of what makes these thinkers recognisably 'Realist' in the more conventional meaning of the term. But what makes them realistic in a much deeper and more significant sense is their refusal to retreat from the dilemmas bequeathed by modern politics into a reliance upon tradition, a facile fatalism, or a narrow power politics. Their 'wilfulness' resides in their unflinching attempts to construct a viable, principled understanding of modern politics, and to use this understanding to avoid its perils and achieve its promise.

The core of this Realist tradition thus does not lie in the concepts of anarchy and rationality as they have come to dominate International Relations theory. It lies instead with questions of the construction of social action and political orders, with the conditions of stable and legitimate political authority, and with the consequences of different, particular, and historically contingent resolutions to these broad political challenges. The Realism I explore in this study is not a rationalist theory of anarchy that presupposes certain forms of knowledge, subjectivity, states, and anarchy. It is a reflection on the politics of the construction of knowledge. It does not lack, or assume, a theory of subjectivity – a rational actor: it is a reflection on the constitution and limitations of precisely such a construction *of* subjectivity. It does not lack or assume a theory of domestic politics: it *is* a theory of domestic politics, a theory of the political at its most basic level, providing a sophisticated attempt to understand politics at both the domestic and international levels.

From past to present

A recovery of this tradition of Realist thinking has significant implications for International Relations theory today. Most obviously, it challenges the use of these classical thinkers as foundations for a Realist tradition of international 'anarchy' stretching across the centuries. Yet its implications extend well beyond the use and abuse of Hobbes, Rousseau, and Morgenthau. To take seriously the legacy of these thinkers presents a direct challenge to many of the conceptual foundations, categorical distinctions, and doctrinal divisions that structure contemporary International Relations theory. Chapter four explores some of these implications by looking at three key distinctions and divisions: those between Realism and liberalism, Realism and constructivism, and modernism and postmodernism.

The division between Realism and liberalism is one of the most long-standing conceptual oppositions in International Relations. However, a fuller appreciation of this relationship has been constrained by the tendency either (traditionally) to reduce liberalism to an amorphous form of 'idealism', or (more recently) to identify it with a fairly narrow form of rationalism. Treating Realism as emerging within the broader problematic of political modernity, by contrast, shows that the relationship between Realism and liberalism is much closer and more complex.[10] In fact, far from being opposed to liberalism as a whole, the Realist tradition I seek to reconstruct here has fundamental affinities with a form of non-rationalist liberalism that Richard Flathman has called 'willful liberalism'.[11] It is in part to highlight the importance of this relationship that I have chosen the term 'wilful Realism', and I will argue that it is essential to recognise that in some very important senses Realism is not opposed to liberalism: it is a form of liberalism.

If the division between Realism and liberalism represents one of the most long-standing theoretical distinctions in International Relations, one of the more pervasive recent categorisations is that which presents Realism and constructivism as clearly defined theoretical alternatives. In opposition to this tendency, I argue that wilful Realism shares many of the sensibilities of contemporary constructivism, while at the same time presenting important challenges to it. More broadly still, I suggest that one of the most significant and paradoxical implications yielded by an engagement with wilful Realism is that the divide between constructivism and rationalism that is sometimes now presented as the most basic theoretical distinction in the field, is fundamentally misconceived. Seen from the perspective of wilful Realism, rationalism *is* a construction – an historical outcome of the attempt to construct social and political order in modernity: to oppose rationalism and constructivism thus

[10] The connections between scepticism, liberalism, and 'classical' Realism have increasingly been noted in sophisticated assessments of Realism. See, for example, the interesting analysis of scepticism in Guzzini, *Realism in International Relations*, especially the Conclusion; and the excellent treatment which addresses many themes – particularly liberal modernity – common to this study, in Nicholas J. Rengger, *International Relations, Political Theory and the Problem of Order* (London: Routledge, 2000). A broad and important philosophical treatment remains R. N. Berki, *On Political Realism* (London: Dent, 1982).

[11] See Richard Flathman, *Willful Liberalism* (Ithaca: Cornell University Press, 1992), and also his *Toward a Liberalism* (Ithaca: Cornell University Press, 1989), particularly chapter 1; and his reading of Hobbes in *Thomas Hobbes: Scepticism, Individuality and Chastened Politics* (London: Sage, 1993) which I also draw upon in chapter one. A somewhat analogous view of divergent liberalisms is explored by John Gray in *Two Faces of Liberalism* (Cambridge: Polity Press, 2000).

provides a fundamentally misleading account of the theoretical alternatives available.

Finally, placing the evolution of Realism in the context of the nature of politics in modernity has implications for debates between modern and postmodern positions. In much of International Relations, postmodernism has been accused of standing outside the 'Western rationalist tradition', and thus beyond the limits of theoretical dialogue. An engagement with wilful Realism, however, shows how many of the issues raised by postmodernism do not come from outside the Western rationalist tradition, or even from outside the Realist tradition itself.[12] Indeed they find clear echoes in wilful Realism's long engagement with the rationalist tradition in modern politics, a fact that provides a possible opening for a more substantial dialogue between Realist, postmodern, and other 'critical' positions. In all three of these cases, in fact, an engagement with wilful Realism does more than challenge contemporary theoretical divides. It provides a means of loosening the overly restrictive and distortive theoretical divides that have tended to dominate International Relations over the past two decades, and can contribute toward a more productive and engaged dialogue between and across positions that are too often presented as irreconcilably opposed.

The final chapter examines two of Realism's most central and contested concepts: the ethic of responsibility and the national interest. Contrary to conventional interpretations of Realism's ethics, I argue that the ethic of responsibility employed in wilful Realism is more than a prudential principle. Rather than a simple expression of an ethic of consequences, it is part of an attempt to construct subjects and political cultures capable of reflecting upon, and exercising, responsibility. This in turn has implications for understanding the meaning of the national interest. Returning to focus on Morgenthau, I demonstrate that for him the national interest functions as a self-reflexive concept, and a sophisticated analytic and rhetorical device attempting to mobilise civic virtue and support a politics of limits. This understanding of the ethic of responsibility and the national interest has continued resonance in contemporary world politics. In particular, wilful Realism's deep concern with the politics of modernity has important connections to neoconservative visions of US foreign policy, while at the same time providing fundamental challenges to many of neoconservativism's

[12] This point has often been argued by thinkers such as Richard Ashley and James Der Derian; it is also noted in Guzzini, *Realism in International Relations*, p. 216, and in Rengger, *International Relations, Political Theory and the Problem of Order*.

central claims. In this way a recovery of the wilful Realist tradition is much more than an exercise in intellectual history; it speaks to some of the most controversial and important issues in contemporary world politics

Questions and interpretations

Undertaking a study of this kind presents several challenges. It early on seemed clear to me that this enquiry must either be quite brief or very long. I have chosen the former, in part, I confess, since I have often wished that authors who have chosen the latter had done otherwise. This strategy comes at a cost: the thinkers I engage are all subjects of complex conceptual and interpretive debates (and sub-debates) to which it is scarcely possible to do justice in this setting. Undoubtedly much more can and should be said about their complexities, contexts, and intellectual lineages, as well as about their relationship to contemporary International Relations. Equally, I have not tried to provide a systematic defence or critique of these thinkers, or of the tradition I attempt to reconstruct, though I have inevitably done a little of both. I do not claim that these thinkers adequately resolve the issues they confront; and I most definitely do not claim to do so myself. My concern is to develop a broader view of the 'tradition' of Realism against which current controversies can be read, and to reflect on its significance. In this context, the limitations of a somewhat more cursory approach seem to me both unavoidable, justifiable, and useful despite their inherent drawbacks.

There are a number of obvious objections to the starting points of this study which must be addressed even at this early stage. The first of these concerns the divide between 'classical' and 'neo' Realism. For neorealism, of course, the essence of Realism lies in the adoption of three familiar tenets: states-as-actors, rationality, and international anarchy. States are taken to be materially self-interested rational calculators existing in a condition of anarchy. Without an overarching authority to enforce rules and guarantee security, distrust and self-help are the dominant characteristics of the international system.[13] In Kenneth Waltz's influential

[13] Despite interesting moves away from strictly Waltzian neorealism, by reintroducing domestic politics under the rubric of 'neoclassical' Realism, the underlying positions here remain resolutely rationalist. See, for example, Legro and Moravcsik, 'Is Anybody Still a Realist?'. An overview of some of the issues involved can be found in Stephen G. Brooks, 'Dueling Realisms', *International Organization*, 51:3 (1997), and

formulation,[14] for example, this means that there is a fundamental difference between 'Realist thought' such as that of Hobbes or Morgenthau, that is interested in the individual or the state, and his own 'Realist theory' that takes the international system as its concern.[15] In this view, to reinterpret classical thinkers, and even to challenge the ways in which they have been rather narrowly used in International Relations theory, is largely irrelevant since the most important developments in the field over the past two decades have lain in a renunciation of the importance of traditions, and its establishment on the firmer foundations provided by rationalist social science.

There are three possible responses to this claim. The first, and briefest, is simply to note that despite their declaration of a fundamental divide between 'classical' and 'neo' Realism, these thinkers (including Waltz) continue to claim the 'Realist tradition' as their own with remarkable consistency. A second, more substantive, response is that far from either being ignorant of the claims of social science or modern rationalism, wilful Realism can be understood as posing a direct challenge to those claims. Understanding the role of scepticism, for example, demonstrates how Hobbes is not blind to the wisdom of Enlightenment science. On the contrary, his position emerges from a clear and sophisticated claim about the limits of science and its application to politics. Similarly, it would be difficult to find a thinker more rigorous in the use of principles of rational calculation than Hobbes; but his analysis fits uncomfortably with contemporary rationalism precisely because he questions the epistemic assumptions that it takes for granted. Morgenthau evinces a similar set of concerns in his appraisal of the limits of 'scientific man' in dealing with 'power politics': this is not a simplistic appeal to an *animus*

Gideon Rose, 'Neoclassical Realism and Theories of Foreign Policy', *World Politics*, 51:2 (1998).

[14] Kenneth Waltz, 'Realist Thought and Neorealist Theory', in *The Evolution of Theory in International Relations*, ed. Robert L. Rothstein (Columbia: University of South Carolina Press, 1991).

[15] There is, of course, continuing and often confusing debate between those who accept that there *is* a Realist tradition, but disagree over whether it is an unbroken lineage or marked by a fundamental divide between 'classical' and 'neo' Realism. For the former, see Doyle, *Ways of War and Peace*, part one, who presents Realism as an identifiable tradition running from Thucydides to contemporary neorealism. In addition to Waltz's distinction between the two forms, see Robert Cox's influential formulation of this shift in his 'Social Forces, States, and World Orders: Beyond International Relations Theory', reprinted most recently in R. Cox (with Timothy Sinclair), *Approaches to World Order* (Cambridge University Press, 1996). One version of a 'neoclassical' approach has been suggested by John G. Ruggie in *Constructing the World Polity* (New York: Routledge, 1998), which differs from those classed as such by Rose in 'Neoclassical Realism'.

dominandi[16] emerging from some bizarre reversion to manichean theology in the age of reason; it emerges from a sophisticated engagement with the limits of rationalism. One may or may not agree with the views of the limits of Enlightenment science and rationalism provided by these thinkers. But one thing at least is certain: the consistent tendency to read the 'classical' tradition as concerned with crudely 'theological' understandings of sin, of simplistic visions of human nature as 'evil', or as dominated by 'Darwinian' lusts for power, or even – more sophisticatedly – of a too narrow concern with the foundations of sovereign authority to the detriment of an understanding of the international 'system', overlooks not only the complexity of these thinkers, but the ways in which their views can be seen as fundamentally challenging many of the core assumptions of rationalism, rationalist social science, and a 'structural' theory of international politics.

The third and perhaps most paradoxical rejoinder concerns one of rationalism's core assumptions (in fact, perhaps its most fundamental assumption), that of a self-interested rational actor. The wilful Realist tradition does not assume the existence of rational actors; it does, however, seek to *create* them. What are often taken as *assumptions* of rationalist Realist theory (materialism, empiricism, rational actors), and applauded or opposed as such, are historical, ethical, and political practices and objectives of wilful Realism. For these thinkers, rationalism *is* a social construction – what I call a will to objectivity and a political strategy of objectification. A working out of the possibilities, consequences, and *limits* of this strategy as a basis for politics, at both the domestic level (particularly in questions of obligation and commitment) and at the international level, is one of its most important concerns. For these reasons, and for many others which I hope will become apparent in the chapters that follow, a clear divide between 'classical' and contemporary Realism provides a misleading understanding of wilful Realism and its implications for current debates.

Engaging in a reinterpretive study inevitably also raises difficult issues of interpretation itself. These issues have, of course, long been the source of complex and extended discussion in the history of ideas. In recent years they have also occupied increasing attention in International Relations, and although my interests in this study do not lie primarily with the methodological controversies surrounding textual

[16] See, however, the important tracing of Morgenthau's views on human nature provided in Martti Koskenniemi, *The Gentle Civilizer of Nations: The Rise and Fall of International Law 1870–1960* (Cambridge University Press, 2001), pp. 445–54.

interpretation, a brief discussion is certainly necessary. At one level, this study adopts a contextualist method of interpretation. I argue that prevailing interpretations of classic writers in International Relations are often anachronistic in that they have paid insufficient attention to questions of interpretation and the importance of context. On the other hand, I do not read these thinkers with the conviction that I can uncover their settled meanings or intentions. Contextual reading may help in discerning certain elements of a text, but it cannot provide a definitive interpretation. Like Paul Ricoeur, I adhere to the idea that while a text may be multivocal, it is not omnivocal: the relationship between reader and text requires a degree of respect and indebtedness toward the text itself, however much the reader may be directed by his or her own interests. But this distance and multivocality means that any text is subject to contrary readings.

Such considerations lead to a second set of questions concerning interpretive strategies, those surrounding the notion of a 'tradition' itself. In reconstructing *a* tradition, it is often asked, does not one fall prey to the error of believing or contributing to the idea that there is such a thing as *a* or *the* tradition, or even clearly identifiable traditions at all? In rereading a tradition does one not risk reifying and legitimising an essentially arbitrary historical claim of theoretical unity and continuity? Finally, how is one to account for the role of the interpreter in both choosing the relevant contexts and identifying the connections constituting a tradition? Or, as Gerard Holden has asked, 'who contextualizes the contextualizers?'[17]

These issues, too, have bedevilled the history of ideas for ages, and I will make no attempt to address them fully (not to mention trying to resolve them) here. The best that can be done is to clarify briefly where this treatment stands on some of these questions.[18] Traditions are always

[17] Gerard Holden, 'Who Contextualizes the Contextualizers? Disciplinary History and the Discourse about IR Discourse', *Review of International Studies*, 28:2 (2002). See also the thoughtful position staked out in Duncan S. A. Bell, 'Political Theory and the Functions of Intellectual History: A Response to Emmanuel Navon', *Review of International Studies*, 29:1 (2003).

[18] A few diverse considerations include, in International Relations: Brian Schmidt, *The Political Discourse of Anarchy* (Albany: State University of New York Press, 1998), chapter 1; Ian Clark, 'Traditions of Thought and Classical Theories of International Relations', in *Classical Theories of International Relations*, ed. Ian Clark and Iver B. Neumann (Basingstoke: Macmillan, 1996); Tim Dunne, 'Methodology or Mythology?: Traditions in International Relations', *Review of International Studies*, 19 (1993); more broadly: John G. Gunnell, *Political Theory: Tradition and Interpretation* (Cambridge, Mass.: Winthrop, 1979); Miles Kahler, 'Inventing International Relations: International Relations Theory after 1945', in *New*

constructed, both internally by those who see themselves engaged in a common project, or working through and against a common intellectual background; and externally by those who seek to provide insights via a synthetic representation of individual positions. The central claim of this book is that there is sufficient 'family resemblance'[19] to make plausible the case that a wilful Realist tradition exists, and that coming to terms with it more fully produces insights and challenges to our understanding of the history of International Relations as a discipline, to the nature of its theoretical commitments, and to current trajectories within the field. I am not saying that these thinkers represent a unified tradition of thought, where each is an expression of the tradition as a whole; and I am most certainly not arguing that they represent a linear progression in which each successive thinker incorporates and supersedes preceding ideas, or that they are engaged with precisely the same problems. There are also obviously historical resonances and influences on these thinkers beyond those traced here; other intellectual trajectories within the complex web of ideas identified as 'Realism' have been revealingly addressed, and I am by no means claiming that the analysis here constitutes the 'real' Realism. But this should not obscure the fact that in their individualism, concern with the central question of the relationship between empirical knowledge and politics, and their sense of the human createdness of the political world, the thinkers I examine here stress the problems of a particularly *modern* political order and international politics, however different their views on these issues may be. As a result, it is revealing to view them as engaged in a dialogue structured not by the dictates of anarchy, but by the problematic of politics in liberal modernity.

'Wilful Realism' is obviously my own construction of what a tradition incorporating the insights of the thinkers I deal with here might look like. It is not found fully developed in any of them as individuals; nor

Thinking in International Relations, ed. Michael Doyle and John Ikenberry (Boulder, Colo.: Westview, 1997); Richard Little, 'Historiography and International Relations', *Review of International Studies*, 25:2 (1999), and James Tully (ed.), *Meaning and Context: Quentin Skinner and his Critics* (Cambridge University Press, 1989).

[19] An explication of 'family resemblance' is pursued in Ludwig Wittgenstein, *Philosophical Investigations* (Oxford: Basil Blackwell, 1958), paras. 66–7. For a discussion of reading traditions of political thought in terms of families, see Tzvetan Todorov, *Imperfect Garden: The Legacy of Humanism* (Princeton University Press, 2002), pp. 10–11. I will not enter into the controversies between 'internal' and 'external' views of intellectual history here.

does it map perfectly on to their thinking retrospectively. My goal is to put these thinkers back into context precisely in order to then pull them out again, and to see what implications their ideas have for a different understanding of the Realist 'tradition'. Equally, I seek to bring out more fully those dimensions of their thinking that are of contemporary relevance, and to reconstruct a tradition partly in light of its significance for contemporary thinking.

The nature of these concerns inevitably means that I focus on some elements in the texts (and silence or ignore others) in order to highlight the dimensions that are particularly salient to the argument. There is no denying that this results in a degree of partiality in my approach, and it is inevitable that others could point to counter-readings in rebuttal.[20] Other constructions of this tradition would be (and are) different and illuminating and I have learnt a great deal from many that I have encountered (though I suspect their proponents would say not enough!). But this diversity is illustrative of the nature of interpretation itself; I find it difficult to see how it could be otherwise, and even the briefest examination of work in the history of ideas seems to confirm the suspicion. Differences of interpretation need not be seen as a mark of intellectual incoherence or futility. They can instead be grasped as an opportunity for dialogue and debate, rather than being foreclosed through interpretive fiat.

Finally, to present these figures, as I do, as addressing issues directly pertinent to the claims of contemporary theory in International Relations is at one level clearly anachronistic. It is unlikely to satisfy those who adhere to a more rigidly contextualist position that restricts itself to understanding these thinkers solely in their own time and place, and may seem to commit the sin of 'presentism' against which contextualists have railed for so long. I hope, however, that this approach allows an appreciation of central claims by these thinkers which have been elided or obscured by their subsumption within prevailing constructions of 'the tradition' in International Relations theory. As Quentin Skinner has elegantly put it, one of the purposes of intellectual history is to 'uncover the often neglected riches of our intellectual heritage and display them

[20] As Honig has pointed out: 'There is nothing illicit in any of this. Reading is never innocent or passive; it is an engagement, constructive and productive, a practice of knowledge that is never freed of power.' Bonnie Honig, *Political Theory and the Displacement of Politics* (Ithaca: Cornell University Press, 1993), p. 201. This partiality is most apparent in my reading of Morgenthau.

once more to view'.[21] I hope that in displaying some of this richness, this study demonstrates that a concern with ideas and culture, with legitimacy and modernity, and with the construction of individual and collective action and its political and ethical evaluation, does not stand outside and opposed to the Realist tradition. On the contrary, these issues are of crucial importance to some of the most sophisticated thinkers in the Realist canon. It is, therefore, simply inadequate to view them as pertinent only to other schools of thought (or what in the 1980s were termed different 'paradigms') and thus to insulate Realism from these questions via a strategic intellectual pluralism, or to continue along by declaring that they are 'not part of Realist theory' or the Realist tradition. To claim the 'Realist' legacy requires an engagement with questions that have too long been excluded by reference to Realism itself, and challenges contemporary understandings of Realism and categories of debate in International Relations to move well beyond many current confines. As such, a renewed dialogue with classic figures in political thought can serve as a stimulus to a broader intellectual, analytic, and ethical agenda in the study of world politics.

[21] Quentin Skinner, *Liberty before Liberalism* (Cambridge University Press, 1998), pp. 118–19. Although I suspect that I may go somewhat beyond Skinner's more restrained suggestion, that intellectual history should function primarily as an inspiration for 'rumination'. The 'richness' of political Realism in International Relations has been forcefully asserted in Robert Gilpin, 'The Richness of the Tradition of Political Realism', in *NeoRealism and its Critics*, ed. Robert Keohane (New York: Columbia University Press, 1986).

1 Sceptical states: Hobbes

The name of Thomas Hobbes and the tradition of Realism have become virtually synonymous in discussions within International Relations. Indeed the claim that international politics is best described as an anarchic 'Hobbesian state of nature' continues to be one of the prominent and evocative common rhetorical devices and analytic touchstones in the study of world politics, much as it has in varying forms for generations.[1] As Michael J. Smith puts it, Hobbes' 'analysis of the state of nature remains the defining feature of realist thought. His notion of the international state of nature as a state of war is shared by virtually everyone calling himself a realist';[2] while in the words of Hans Morgenthau, it provides the 'stock in trade' of the discipline of International Relations.[3]

[1] A small sample of what is evident from virtually any examination of the literature might include the following diverse examples: the extended contrast with Rousseau in Stanley Hoffmann, *The State of War* (New York: Praeger, 1965), pp. 57–68 especially; Charles Beitz, *Political Theory and International Relations* (Princeton University Press, 1979), part one; Paul R. Viotti and Mark V. Kauppi, *International Relations Theory: Realism, Pluralism, Globalism* (New York: Macmillan, 1993), p. 41. The continuing influence of 'Hobbesian' themes in more popular treatments of power politics is apparent in works such as Kaplan's *Warrior Politics*, pp. 78–88, and Kagan's *Of Paradise and Power*, p. 38. For substantial analyses in International Relations, see Kurt T. Gaubatz, 'The Hobbesian Problem and the Microfoundations of International Relations Theory', *Security Studies*, 11:2 (2001/2), and Donald Hanson, 'Hobbes's "Highway to Peace"', *International Organization*, 38:2 (1984). Sophisticated reappraisals are provided in Boucher, *Political Theories of International Relations*, and especially Noel Malcolm, 'Hobbes's Theory of International Relations' in his *Aspects of Hobbes* (Oxford: Clarendon Press, 2002), pp. 432–56.
[2] Michael J. Smith, *Realist Thought from Weber to Kissinger* (Baton Rouge: Louisiana State University Press, 1986), p. 13. Smith does note, however, that few contemporary realists would share the 'picture of human nature' upon which this view of the state of nature is based. This all-too-easy manoeuvre, I will argue later, has been the source of considerable confusion.
[3] Hans Morgenthau, *Scientific Man versus Power Politics* (University of Chicago Press, 1946), p. 113.

The attractions of Hobbes' thinking for a Realist theory of International Relations are easy enough to see. His stress on the human capacity for mendacity, treachery, and violence seems to accord nicely with long-standing Realist concerns with the 'darker' side of human nature. Alternatively, for contemporary theorists more suspicious of appeals to evil or human nature, Hobbes can also seem to have captured in a particularly graphic form the dynamics of rational action under a condition of anarchy, and to provide a classic account of the difficulties of cooperation and coordination in the absence of an overarching authority with an ability to enforce rules and ensure compliance. Whatever form it has taken, however, the generally accepted vision of Hobbes' conception of International Relations amongst both its proponents and critics centres around his famous depiction of the state of nature as a realm in which 'it is manifest that during the time that men live without a common power to keep them in awe, they are in that condition which is called war, and such is a war of every man against every man'.[4] Transposed from the level of individuals to that of states, the state of nature has long been seen as a compelling image of an international system lacking precisely such a 'common power', thus condemning states to live inevitably in war of each against all.

This chapter will suggest that for all their popularity, prevailing claims about the relationship between Hobbes, the state of nature, and Realism have done far too little justice to Hobbes and his significance for the Realist tradition. Hobbes, I will argue, is not a foundational figure in a tradition that stresses the structural determinations of an international anarchy created by rational actors existing in a global state of nature. Contrary to commonly held views, he is neither a scientific 'positivist', nor a theorist of 'rational action' in the sense that rational choice theory and much of modern social science understand the term.[5] Nor is his a philosophy based upon the assumption of an intrinsically evil 'human nature'. Rather, Hobbes' state of nature is designed to illustrate the relationship between knowledge, belief, and the social construction of action. He seeks to lay bare the foundations of political order, and to reconstruct the practices of knowledge in order to re-establish principles of political obligation and authority – and thus of sovereignty – in an era of endemic conflict. Hobbes' thinking represents a cultural and political strategy: an active, wilful attempt to construct political order.

[4] Thomas Hobbes, *Leviathan* (Indianapolis: Hackett, 1993), p. 76.
[5] David Gauthier, *The Logic of Leviathan* (Oxford: Clarendon Press, 1969).

At the heart of this strategy is an attempt to construct a self-conscious politics of material power, calculation, and interest *not* as theoretical assumptions or assertions, but as concrete social practices facilitating the creation and management of a stable political order.

Seen in this light, Hobbes' 'realism' is very different from that usually ascribed to him in International Relations. Far from yielding an international order directly analogous to his state of nature, Hobbes seeks to construct a practice of sovereignty that supports a politics of limits – and to construct an international order on the basis of the reconstruction of sovereignty. Indeed he stands as one of the most powerful exponents of a Realism that stresses the importance of the relationship between knowledge and action, judgement and responsibility. In short, he is one of the most sophisticated proponents of a wilful Realism.

Scepticism and the state of nature

To unravel Hobbes' vision of international politics, it makes sense to begin where he himself begins: with the problem of knowledge. As numerous philosophic treatments have argued at length, the central intellectual context in which Hobbes' thought must be located is the 'crise pyrrhonienne' of the sixteenth and seventeenth centuries.[6] Led by figures such as Montaigne, this sceptical movement was complex, but its essence lay in the claim that sense-perception was always potentially misleading as a basis for knowledge. That a straight stick appeared bent when placed in water was a classic illustration of how the senses could easily mislead, as were the differences in perception that resulted from the use of magnifying lenses, or the shifts in perceptual capacities due to changes in health or age. The truth of the various and competing perceptions could not, therefore, be settled by the evidence of the senses alone, but rather required a set of rational criteria for their evaluation. But where were these criteria to come from? If they were held to emerge from reason itself, the problem of self-referentiality emerged. Reason, in effect, would be declaring what was reasonable and true on the basis of

[6] See Richard Tuck, 'Optics and Sceptics: The Philosophical Foundations of Hobbes's Political Thought', in *Conscience and Casuistry in Early Modern Europe*, ed. Edmund Leites (Cambridge University Press, 1988); Richard Tuck, *Hobbes* (Oxford University Press, 1989); Flathman, *Thomas Hobbes*, and also Popkin, *The History of Skepticism*. However, as Quentin Skinner has argued, it is important not to overstate the sceptical dimension of Hobbes' thinking, since Hobbes retains a strong commitment to the role of reason, however powerful scepticism and rhetoric may be. Quentin Skinner, *Visions of Politics*, vol. III: *Hobbes and Civil Science* (Cambridge University Press, 2002), pp. 79 and 88.

its *own* definition of what reason was. Yet if, as the sceptics argued, there were many different forms of life and forms of reason, then what would be required would be a Reason to judge all Reasons; and therefore the self-referentiality problem emerges yet again and the sceptical challenge to any definitive claim to know is again in place. Quoting Montaigne, Richard Popkin has summarised the 'problem of the criterion' at the heart of the sceptical challenge in the following terms: 'If our sense experiences vary so much, by what standards are we to judge which are veridical? We need some basis for judging, but how shall we determine objectivity? "To judge the appearances that we receive of objects, we would need a judicatory instrument; to verify this instrument, we need a demonstration; to verify the demonstration, an instrument: there we are in a circle" . . . "Since the senses cannot decide our dispute, being themselves full of uncertainty, it must be reason that does so. No reason can be established without another reason: there we go back to infinity again."'[7]

This sceptical background is crucial in understanding Hobbes' thinking. Knowledge of the truth about empirical and moral questions, he argued, is purely knowledge of things as they *appear* to us as conditioned by our individual appetites and aversions. As Richard Tuck has noted, in this regard Hobbes' 'crucial idea . . . was simply to treat what is perceived by man – the images and so on which are immediately apparent to an internal observer – as bearing no relationship of *verisimilitude* to the external world. Man is effectively a prisoner within the cell of his own mind, and has no idea what in reality lies outside his prison walls.'[8] Empirical knowledge is always hypothetical and conjectural; there is no way to get behind the appearances to the thing itself. *Rational* knowledge, by contrast, is like a language: it consists of a set of formal definitions and relational rules. Tuck's portrayal of Hobbes' position is again exemplary on this point; he argues that for Hobbes 'the actual existence of anything which is the object of our thinking is irrelevant. A language is simply a formal system whose relationship to reality is puzzling and contentious; but it is the only tool we have to *reason* with. Hobbes consistently used the analogy of counting to explain what he meant by reasoning. Just as effective counting consists in understanding the rules of a formal system (the natural numbers) which may not have any relation to reality, so effective reasoning consists in understanding the meanings of words within the system of language without having

[7] Popkin, *The History of Skepticism*, p. 51. [8] Tuck, *Hobbes*, p. 40.

any clear belief about what they refer to.'[9] The connection of this framework to empirical reality is always problematic. For Hobbes, truth is not an objective characteristic of things, but rather resides in a set of accepted and logically related frameworks of definitions and referents. Or, to put this another way, in Hobbes' philosophical nominalism truth is a function of logic and language, not of the relation between language and some extra-linguistic 'reality.'[10]

Seen in this context, Hobbes' view of the world is not objective and 'scientific' in the positivist sense of the term. And this view is not limited to the problem of empirical knowledge; crucially, it extends to the question of moral knowledge as well.[11] That which we view as good, or beneficial, is not so in itself, but is so only because it appears to us as such. And since these perceptions are inescapably conditioned by the different appetites and aversions of each individual, there is no natural harmony or order amongst them. This helps explain the extraordinary stress which Hobbes places on the definitions and relations of words throughout his political philosophy, a stress clearly linked to his thinking on the question of moral and practical judgement and action. Words and concepts are not pale reflections of an 'objective' reality – they are fundamental constituents of the reality of the agents that use them to make sense of their worlds. In this sense, the social world is fundamentally constructed out of the beliefs that individuals have about themselves and their world. As Andrzej Rapaczynski has insightfully noted, for Hobbes: 'Acting on those beliefs that they actually have about themselves, men, being authors of their own actions, *create* the truth of their own beliefs . . . Political science is, more than any other, concerned with postulates and definitions, because what men postulate with respect to the relations of power among themselves they very often *ipso facto* bring about.'[12] Or, as Hobbes tersely expressed it: 'the Actions of men proceed from their Opinions'.[13]

Here we have a basis for understanding Hobbes' state of nature that differs considerably from those who portray it as the outcome of

[9] Tuck, *Hobbes*, p. 42.
[10] I am thankful to Ross Rudolph for stressing the importance of this point to me.
[11] See particularly, Quentin Skinner, 'Hobbes on Rhetoric and the Construction of Morality', *Visions of Politics*, vol. III: *Hobbes and Civil Science*, pp. 87–141.
[12] Andrzej Rapaczynski, *Nature and Politics: Liberalism in the Philosophy of Hobbes, Locke, and Rousseau* (Ithaca: Cornell University Press, 1987), p. 109.
[13] Hobbes, *Leviathan*, p. 233. See also the excellent discussion of 'Hobbes's Irrational Man' that is chapter 3 of Stephen Holmes' *Passions and Constraint: On the Theory of Liberal Democracy* (University of Chicago Press, 1995).

materially self-interested rational actors competing for the same scarce goods within a condition of epistemic agreement. In the view that emerges from an engagement with Hobbes' philosophical nominalism, by contrast, the state of nature derives from precisely the *lack* of any such commonality. In the state of nature, individuals construct their own realities, their own understandings of what is good and bad, desirable and undesirable, threatening and unthreatening, and act on the basis of these beliefs. In *Leviathan*, for example, he puts the point this way: 'whatsoever is the object of any man's appetite or desire that is it which he for his part calleth *good*; and the object of his hate and aversion, *evil*; and of his contempt, *vile* and *inconsiderable*. For these words of good, evil, and contemptibel are ever used with relation to the person that useth them, there being nothing simply and absolutely so, nor any common rule of good and evil to be taken from the nature of the objects themselves.'[14] In *De Cive*, he phrases the issue more simply still, holding that: 'Wherever *good* and *evil* are measured by the mere diversity of present desires, and hence by a corresponding diversity of yardsticks, those who act in this way will find themselves still in a state of war.'[15]

Lacking agreement on what the world *is*, as well as over what it ought to be, the state of nature is anarchic in a sense far deeper than that captured by the 'security dilemmas', or 'coordination problems', or logics of 'relative gains' so beloved by rationalist thinkers. As Jan Blits has argued, the generalised fear that Hobbes sees as the prime motivation for action is not reducible solely to a fear of the potential actions of others. It is constituted by a more fundamental fear of the unknown – and in some basic ways unknowable – nature of reality as a whole. This fear is a spur to knowledge: humans seek to know the causes of things in an attempt to overcome it. But this search for knowledge can ironically also become a source of conflict as the desire to know the final causes of things leads humans to believe in causes – and thus in the power of agents – beyond any material examination. In this way, fundamentally irrational and irreconcilable *beliefs* can arise from the very attempt to counter fear through knowledge, and these beliefs can come to dominate action. As Blits puts it:

> Fear is a pain, and men naturally avoid pain. Men therefore seek to avoid not only the object of fear, but fear itself. But an objectless fear is an unresolvable fear. No one can fight or flee what he cannot identify

[14] Hobbes, *Leviathan*, p. 28.
[15] Quoted in Skinner, *Visions of Politics*, vol. III: *Hobbes and Civil Science*, p. 120.

or know. To be resolvable, fear must attach to something; it must have an object. Thus when an object is lacking, men will find an imaginary one. They will invent an identifiable object they can fear. 'And therefore when there is nothing to be seen, there is nothing to accuse, either of their good, or evil fortune, but some *power*, or agent *invisible*: in which sense perhaps it was, that some of the old poets said, that the gods were at first created by human fear.'[16]

In the state of nature, even the fear of death, which Hobbes considers universal, is unable to create order. For even if all agreed on the desirability of physical self-preservation above all else (which, as will be discussed in a moment, Hobbes doubts), this would not mean that all could agree on what the threats to that preservation were, on how to react to them, or how best to secure themselves against them. Conflict is not simply intrinsic to humanity's potential for aggression, nor can it be attributed to (or resolved by) straightforward utilitarian calculations of competing and conflicting interests. The state of nature is defined not just by a lack of trust, but much more fundamentally by a condition of epistemological indeterminacy which renders even the universal fear of death at best a partial remedy, and the existence of conflict and mistrust endemic.

The conflictual potential of this tendency toward irreconcilable beliefs is exacerbated by a further paradoxical dimension of causal logic. For while Hobbes sees the combination of fear and logic as essential elements in the construction of a stable political order, he is far too astute to believe that this synthesis is straightforward. In fact, he holds that logic itself can be implicated in the distrustful and destructive dynamics of the state of nature. His point here is not that action is governed by a logic of strategic rationality and calculation which makes cooperation under anarchy difficult. As the previous discussions of epistemic indeterminacy and subjective irrationality have illustrated, to view Hobbes and his conception of the state of nature in these 'rational actor' terms is clearly limited. Rather, his argument is that the capacity of individuals to use logic and language to create beliefs about the future leads them to fears and actions in the present that *create* the very conditions they seek to avoid. Logic allows for causal reasoning, for the linking of cause to effect through time (if this, then this . . .).[17] While this process of causal reasoning is crucial to wellbeing and effective action, it also

[16] Jan J. Blits, 'Hobbesian Fear', *Political Theory*, 17:3 (1989), p. 425.
[17] As I will discuss in the next chapter, there are interesting parallels here with Rousseau.

allows speculations about possible futures to govern present actions. Imagined futures can generate current fears, whether these fears are 'realistic' or not. As Rapaczynski points out, this fear is central to the operation of the state of nature because human beings know 'that familiarity is deceptive: the abstractness of his reasoning makes him always capable of picturing some possible consequences of any familiar event that will make it look ominous and threatening to the highest degree. And since his self-preservation mechanism, involving an obsessive fear of violent death, always makes him expect the worst and prepare for it, he is incapable of tranquil enjoyment of anything he now has and constantly strives to *anticipate* any future deprivations.'[18] Or, as Hobbes himself put it, 'For being assured that there be causes of all things that have arrived hitherto, or shall arrive hereafter; it is impossible for a man, who continually endeavoureth to secure himselfe against the evill he fears, and procure the good he desireth, not to be in a perpetuall solicitude of the time to come. So that every man . . . like . . . *Prometheus* . . . in the care of future time, hath his heart all the day long gnawed on by feare of death, poverty, or other calamity; and has no repose, nor pause of his anxiety, but in sleep.'[19]

From this perspective, perceptions of reality (and thus actions) are determined not by current material circumstances alone, but by projections of future developments which – precisely because they are 'imagined' – give rise to fears and actions that bear little necessary relation to current realities or developments, and which may be out of all proportion to the 'real' situation facing actors. Acting within the logic of worst case scenarios, Hobbesian individuals create an anarchic state of nature in part out of their fear of future harm rather than the calm appraisal of current realities. In so acting, they create the very conditions of distrust that they fear. Logic, so necessary for prediction and preservation, becomes the source of a destructive self-fulfilling prophecy: an illogical war of each against all.

[18] Rapaczynski, *Nature and Politics*, pp. 45–6. Or as Holmes has put it, 'Despite his physicalism, Hobbes is committed to the idea that, in some circumstances, the unreal controls the real. Equipped with imagination and language, human beings respond to the possible as well as the actual, to the dreaded or anticipated future as well as to the experienced present.' *Passions and Constraint*, p. 74. The links to 'worst-case' forecasting in International Relations scarcely need pointing out here.

[19] Hobbes, *Leviathan*, p. 52, quoted in Rapaczynski, *Nature and Politics*, p. 46. Note also Hobbes' pithy comment in *De Homine*, that 'man is famished even by future hunger'; cited by Rapaczynski, *Nature and Politics*, p. 44, n. 32.

Finally, Hobbes argues that the capacity of language to create and communicate abstract ideas and beliefs that have meaning for individuals can lead to conflict as these beliefs themselves become objects of desire and contestation. This is an essential aspect of the pride and 'vainglory' that loom so large in Hobbes' thinking. Insult, for example, is not a threat to an individual's material wellbeing, but is an assault upon a person's idea of 'honour'; and insults may well provoke a reaction in which the dread of dishonour outweighs fears of death or physical harm. These dynamics are even more strikingly and destructively at work in the realm of religion. Not only does religious belief (and authority) depend upon a conviction that a transcendent realm conceived only as an idea (heaven or hell, for example) actually exists, but a commitment to the values of the religious realm can easily become the determining belief governing action. Precisely because they are *beliefs* these commitments are not susceptible to rational discussion or determination, and they may have little or no relation to material interests. Indeed they frequently overwhelm material interests, and are at the heart of the dynamics of fear, distrust, and animosity. As Steven Holmes has nicely captured Hobbes' point:

> Man may be a pleasure/pain machine, but whether he is vexed by a flung insult or gladdened by the burning down of a rival church depends on his beliefs, not his nerve endings. The opinions that guide and misguide people's lives are not themselves the products of rational pursuit of private advantage. Few opinions are picked up and dropped as strategic rationality decrees. An individual does not ordinarily adopt opinions because they promote his self-preservation or material advantage. Beliefs are seldom so rational.[20]

This relationship between belief and action is intensified by the peculiarly mobilising force of language and rhetoric. Names, words, and definitions are particularly important to Hobbes not only because of his philosophical nominalism, but also because as Holmes has noted, 'it is a little-explored dimension of Hobbes' nominalism' that 'people react more emotionally to names than to facts'.[21] Correctly formulated and delivered, words have a capacity for affective mobilisation, for stirring individuals to action, in ways that simple appeals to material self-interest are incapable of achieving. The modern jibe that it is difficult to

[20] Holmes, *Passions and Constraint*, p. 84.
[21] Holmes, *Passions and Constraint*, p. 81. For a contemporary exploration of this theme, see Judith Butler, *Excitable Speech* (London: Routledge, 1996).

convince people to go to war to protect a market is one that Hobbes was more than familiar with. His worry, by contrast, was that rhetoric made it much easier to convince people to kill and to die for considerably less tangible goals – be they creed, religion, or honour; in short, for beliefs.

The state of nature reconsidered

I am not claiming that Hobbes rejects any notion of 'truth', and I am certainly not claiming that his scepticism yields a relativistic nihilism. So crude a contrast would do little justice to the complex epistemological and political conclusions that Hobbes draws from his vision of the human condition. However, a focus on the role of scepticism and belief in the construction of action helps explain a number of puzzling issues concerning his political theory and its relationship to international politics. Nowhere is this more evident than in his conception of the state of nature.

For Hobbes, the state of nature is not an actual condition – it is an intellectual construct, a hypothetical condition seeking to explicate the basic elements of human action. Moreover, focusing on the role of belief in action helps explain one of the central apparent paradoxes of Hobbes' thinking (and particularly of rational actor accounts of the state of nature): to wit, how could human beings ever have left the state of nature? This question is central for debates surrounding the 'logic of anarchy' in International Relations, since it raises the inevitable question of why, if individuals were able to leave the state of nature, states in an international state of nature could not do likewise? If the claim is that the international system is directly analogous to the Hobbesian state of nature, and thereby incapable of transcendence, then the creation of the Hobbesian state – upon which their entire analysis is built – itself seems a logical impossibility.[22] And if this is the case, then relying on the Hobbesian contract as the initial condition which *creates* the international anarchy is fallacious. It is based upon a logic of action which undermines its very premises. Conversely, if it is argued that states could be created, then why does not the move to an international Leviathan

[22] For an application of this argument as part of a critique of the supposedly 'Hobbesian' premises of neorealist international political economy see Naeem Inayatullah and Mark Rupert, 'Hobbes, Smith, and the Problem of Mixed Ontologies in Neorealist IPE', in *The Global Economy as Political Space*, ed. Steven Rostow, *et al.* (Boulder, Colo.: Lynne Rienner, 1994), pp. 62–4. Yet even this 'critical' reading misses the essence of Hobbes' position and simply replicates the familiar terrain of international political theory.

also follow directly? If we adopt the rational-choice reading, Hobbes thus appears hopelessly confused. Either his theory of the creation of the Leviathan is flawed, or his failure to extend the logic of his argument to a global scale is contradictory.

To put this question is to expose one of the most obvious weaknesses of treating Hobbes as a Realist theorist of rational action.[23] Yet is it likely that Hobbes, so renowned for his logical rigour, simply failed to recognise (the fairly obvious point) that his theory seemed necessarily either to require an extension of the contract to the relations between Sovereigns or that, barring this, it was logically contradictory? Taking this question seriously points to the need to examine Hobbes' thinking on this issue more closely. In fact, the question of how cooperation could be 'rational' in anarchy is not Hobbes' question, since his argument is based upon a much broader vision of the relationship between knowledge, order, and authority. As we have seen, for Hobbes individuals act on the basis of opinions and beliefs, and it is precisely this link between belief and action – and, paradoxically, the capacity for *error* – that first yielded authority. Once again, Rapaczynski has provided an incisive analysis of this argument which is worth quoting at length. In his words:

> if for some reason I come to believe that another person possesses sufficient power to enforce his control over some object in dispute between us (be it his control over some resource, an aspect of his personal security, or some behavior of mine) – that is, if I come to believe that he can overpower and kill me if I attempt to interfere with his wishes in some respect – then, according to Hobbes, my fear of death will make it impossible for me to resist that person in that respect and that person will indeed have the power in question. Again, given Hobbes's account of human action, the very fact of believing something makes the belief come true. Finally, if sufficiently many people (though not necessarily all) were to be persuaded that we were all obliged to obey some particular person because of that particular person's superior power to enforce his commands, then by this very fact this person would acquire superior power (since he could now dispose of the power of all those who are not prepared to disobey him) and *all* (not just some) people within the reach of the sovereign's power would be obliged to obey him, since he could now back up his commands with

[23] This point has been most fully explored in the English School reading of Hobbes. As Vincent put it in a criticism of 'Realist' appropriations, 'it is even reasonable to ask why, if Hobbes' view of international politics was really as the Realists take it to be, he did not seek to bring the international anarchy to an end in the same way as *Leviathan* ordered relations among individuals?' John Vincent, 'The Hobbesian Tradition in Twentieth-Century International Thought', *Millennium: Journal of International Studies*, 10:2 (1981), p. 95.

> enforceable threats. This particular version of the phenomenon of self-fulfilling prophecy is what lies at the basis of Hobbes's contractarian argument.[24]

This helps explain how political authority could emerge out of the sceptical and indeterminate human condition that Hobbes conveys via his concept of the state of nature. For Hobbes, society may well have emerged not out of rational calculation, but as a result of the capacity of reason and language for error. False beliefs in the nature of order, the power of others, and indeed of the nature of power itself (as in a belief in supernatural powers) led to obedience on the basis of these beliefs. Authority was established through the mistaken attribution of qualities or powers to others, and once established in authority particular figures were able to use their newly acquired collective capacity to create obedience through a combination of fear, coercion, and the propagation of belief. The prevalence of *error* that is central in the war of each against all is, paradoxically, a source of authority and an explanation of the escape from the state of nature.

Yet if political authority came into being on the basis of mistaken beliefs, it was precisely the limitations of these foundations that were of most pressing concern to Hobbes. The foundations of ecclesiastical or monarchical polities, and of medieval Christendom as a whole, had been fundamentally shaken by the Reformation and the Thirty Years War. Far from being sources of order, previous understandings of knowledge and authority had become irreconcilable sources of conflict – the English Civil War being Hobbes' most pressing concern. In this situation, it was necessary to reconsider and reconfigure the foundations of knowledge and authority, and a central goal of Hobbes' state of nature is to demonstrate to individuals the importance of the relationship between knowledge claims, political authority, and social peace. A return to the state of nature is a metaphor illuminating the dynamics of social conflict arising from the absence of both cultural consensus and a sovereign authority to fix meanings, determine contested facts, and the like. By demonstrating the foundations of the state of war that is the state of nature, Hobbes seeks to convince individuals of the need for a sovereign authority, and of their need to obey it. Moreover, he seeks to provide a rational foundation for political authority that would supplant the now unstable and unsustainable beliefs of traditional political authorities. In the escape from the state of nature that Hobbes proposes, the individual does not

[24] Rapaczynski, *Nature and Politics*, pp. 69–70.

simply alienate the 'right to all things' to a political authority. More fundamentally, what is granted to that authority is the right to decide upon irresolvably contested truths: to provide the authoritative criteria of what is, and thus to remove people from the state of epistemic and ethical indeterminacy that is the basis of the state of nature.

Hobbes uses his scepticism both to show the necessity of his solution and to destroy (what he views as dogmatic) counter-claims to political authority based upon unsupportable (individual) claims to truth. In arguing against (what he views as seditious) individual claims against the authority of the Sovereign in *De Cive*, Hobbes puts it in the following way: '*the knowledge of good and evil belongs to each single man*. In the state of nature indeed, where every man lives by equal right, and has not by any mutual pacts submitted to the command of others, we have granted this to be true; nay, [proved it] . . . [But in the civil state it is false. For it was shown] that the civil laws were the rules of *good* and *evil*, *just* and *unjust*, *honest* and *dishonest*; that therefore what the legislator commands, must be held for *good*, and what he forbids for *evil*.'[25] Earlier in the same work he had phrased the argument even more unequivocally, noting that since 'the opinions of men differ concerning *meum* and *tuum*, *just* and *unjust*, *profitable* and *unprofitable*, *good* and *evil*, *honest* and *dishonest*, and the like; which every man esteems according to his own judgment: it belongs to the same chief power to make some common rules for all men, and to declare them publicly, by which every man may know what may be called his, what another's, what just, what unjust, what honest, what dishonest, what good, what evel [sic]; that is summarily, what is to be done, what to be avoided in our common course of life'. It follows that for Hobbes: 'All judgment therefore, in a city, belongs to him who hath the swords; that is, to him who hath the supreme authority.'[26] And finally, consider the conclusion to the passage from *Leviathan* quoted earlier; holding that 'whatsoever is the object of any man's appetite or

[25] Thomas Hobbes, *De Cive* (Indianapolis: Hackett, 1993), p. 244. This element of this argument was noted by Hans Morgenthau, who wrote that 'There is a profound and neglected truth hidden in Hobbes' extreme dictum that the state creates morality as well as law and that there is neither morality nor law outside the state'. Hans Morgenthau, *In Defense of the National Interest* (New York: Knopf, 1951), p. 34. As Malcolm has importantly pointed out, however, it is essential not to overstate this case. Hobbes does not deny the existence of rational moral principles (the Laws of Nature) arising from the goal of self-preservation; it is the indeterminacy of the concrete application of these principles that is central to his thinking. See Malcolm, 'Hobbes's Theory of International Relations', pp. 437–8. I will return to the links between Hobbes' thinking and that of Morgenthau in chapter three.

[26] Hobbes, *De Cive*, p. 178. See also the rendition in Tuck, *Hobbes*, p. 65.

desire that is it which he for his part calleth *good*; and the object of his hate and aversion, *evil*; and of his contempt, *vile* and *inconsiderable*. For these words of good, evil, and contemptibel are ever used with relation to the person that useth them, there being nothing simply and absolutely so, nor any common rule of good and evil to be taken from the nature of the objects themselves'; he completes the passage by noting that the only sources of judgement in these matters arise either 'from the person of the man (where there is no commonwealth), or (in a commonwealth) from the person that representeth it, or from an arbitrator or judge whom men disagreeing shall by consent set up, and make his sentence the rule thereof'.[27]

For Hobbes, epistemic claims and political claims are clearly connected. A fundamental reason why the Sovereign must be unchallengeable in definitional matters is that to rebel against this authority is to return to the subjectively relative claim to know and the conflict which, for Hobbes, this inevitably entails. This is why the Sovereign ultimately must control language (definitions of what is), and explains his repeated stress on the importance of education (and sovereign control over its institutions) rather than straightforward coercion as the essential element in a successful Sovereign's rule.[28] For Hobbes, mistaken claims about the foundations of knowledge were a source of mistaken political beliefs and were thus at the heart of the conflict he saw around him. Interpretive dissent leads potentially to political dissension and to conflict. In the words of Hobbes' patron, the Earl of Newcastle, 'controversy Is a Civill Warr with the Pen which pulls out the sorde soon afterwards'.[29]

In his endeavour to avert this situation, Hobbes does not rely primarily upon the coercive capacities of the Sovereign. More fundamentally, he undertakes what David Johnston has described as a 'politics of cultural transformation': an attempt to reconfigure political order by demonstrating to individuals the nature and limits of their knowledge, and convincing them of the political consequences of these limits.[30] At

[27] Hobbes, *Leviathan*, p. 28. As Skinner has noted, for Hobbes if we wish to fix 'our moral language unambiguously onto the world, we can only hope to do so by fiat. His conclusion is sceptical, and does little to uphold the dignity of moral philosophy. For all that, however, he may be right.' *Visions of Politics*, vol. III: *Hobbes and Civil Science*, p. 141.

[28] Hobbes, *De Cive*, pp. 262–3.

[29] Quoted in Steven Shapin and Simon Shaeffer, *Leviathan and the Air Pump: Hobbes, Boyle and the Experimental Life* (Princeton University Press, 1985), p. 290.

[30] David Johnston, *The Rhetoric of Leviathan: Thomas Hobbes and the Politics of Cultural Transformation* (Princeton University Press, 1986). See also the insightful treatment in Malcolm, 'Hobbes's Theory of International Relations', pp. 454–5.

the heart of this project lies his attempt to limit the claims of knowledge through the promulgation of an ontological materialism, and the assertion of a materialist understanding of the self and self-interest. While Hobbes has often been portrayed as basing his political vision on the *assumption* of materially self-interested actors, and while this has often been taken as one of the core defining assumptions of Realist thinking, the reality is quite different: Hobbes actually seeks the *creation* of such actors, hoping to limit the basic irrationality of human action through the adoption of practices of material self-interest. His goal is to reconfigure understandings of the world – and, vitally, the *self-understanding* of individuals – in order to reconstruct social order and political authority in a context where previous practices had become unviable and destructive. Similarly, a material definition of power is not a simple assumption of Hobbes' thinking: it is an essential element in his attempt to marginalise the destructive influence of beliefs in 'some *power*, or agent *invisible*', a key element of his politics of cultural transformation.

The epistemic materialism that Hobbes advocates is thus not an abstract methodological assumption, as 'ontological materialism' has come to be understood in International Relations: it is a political commitment, a central element in his attempt to establish new intellectual and practical foundations for authority in a culture racked by violence and conflict. This materialist–empiricist synthesis sought to confront and marginalise issues of 'conscience' and 'enthusiasm'[31] at the heart of seventeenth-century intellectual and political conflict. By limiting discourse to the positive, phenomenal world, politics and society could be freed from the conflict which emerged from non-empirical claims of individual conviction and conscience beyond public demonstration and discussion. Claims of faith were separated from claims of

[31] For a fascinating treatment see Steven Shapin, *A Social History of Truth: Civility and Science in Seventeenth-Century England* (University of Chicago Press, 1994). Clearly, the materialist-empiricist synthesis was neither a simple, nor the only, avenue pursued. As Steven Toulmin's emphasis on Descartes in *Cosmopolis: The Hidden Agenda of Modernity* (New York: Free Press, 1990), and Gerhard Oesriech's *Neostoicism and the Early Modern State* (Cambridge University Press, 1982) demonstrate, the search for solutions was wide-ranging and often interrelated. Generally, however, as Tully has noted, 'enthusiasm', the assertion of the absolute authority of the individual conscience (characteristic, for example, of radical Protestantism), was 'used in a pejorative sense, and a massive attack was waged on all its forms, especially after 1660'. James Tully, *An Approach to Political Philosophy: Locke in Contexts* (Cambridge University Press, 1993), p. 187. As Holmes has insightfully argued, successfully banishing religious strife from politics was also an important means of strengthening the state, and this contribution to state power was part of its attraction. See also Cornelia Navari, 'Knowledge, the State and the State of Nature', in *The Reason of State*, ed. Michael Donelan (London: George Allen and Unwin, 1978).

knowledge and the latter were located in the phenomenal world, not in the realm of 'essence', the enthusiastic consciousness of the believer, or the faith-derived authority of rulers. Hobbes' materialism is driven – in part – by the concern that a belief in non-material entities is the high road to irrationalism and conflict.

Reducing claims about reality, including claims concerning individuals, to material terms – to 'matter in motion' – was part of an attempt to liberate those selves from the violence which had come to attend a non-materialist politics. For example, by rendering the soul either a material substance, a nonsensical conceit, or an unknowable (and thus purely individual and private) matter of faith, Hobbes sought to marginalise the political conflict which he saw as inevitable if action was guided by a concern with salvation.[32] By limiting knowledge claims (as opposed to private belief or faith) to the material realm, a *public* arena of discussion concerning truth could be secured. Even more importantly, in this way a degree of liberty and security from the 'enthusiasm' of others could be achieved. Hobbes' limitation of the grounds of knowledge is spurred by, if not reducible to, a concern with religious toleration and a desire to remove the destructive conflict engendered by irresolvable questions of religious truth from the political realm.[33] Moreover, a purely 'material' understanding of the self (and self-understanding) would make possible a new set of political practices based on the (now rationally, *not* naturally) universal fear of pain and death, which provided a basis for a legitimate theory of sovereignty (the social contract) and obedience to the Sovereign and the laws of nature. The transformation of theory was intimately linked to an attempt to transform practices.

Jettisoning straightforward visions of truth, and devaluing teleological or naturalistic claims that individuals (or certain individuals) have access to absolute truth, became a foundation for tolerance and the platform for an attack upon innatist visions of social hierarchy and authority. These sceptical and voluntarist notions became key planks in a recognisably 'liberal' platform against justifications of social identity and political privilege as simply given, and in the articulation of a liberal

[32] In Blits' formulation: 'In order to establish and maintain civil society, men's common fear of a sovereign must be made to overpower their mutual fear of one another . . . yet even if men fear the sovereign more than they fear one another, they will not enjoy lasting peace unless in the first place they fear "powers visible", that is, death at the hands of other men, more than they fear "powers invisible", that is, hellfire or damnation.' Blits, 'Hobbesian Fear', p. 427.

[33] The role of the 'Independency crisis' concerning the relations between church and state in Hobbes' thought has been highlighted by Tuck, *Hobbes*.

vision of equality and political right. They constitute, in short, a *negative ontology*, a reduction of individuals to purely atomistic individuality, in the name of opposing claims of natural privilege and traditional authority. This universality emerges not from a lack of understanding of the importance of identity but from a conscious *limitation and reformation* of its significance in the political realm in light of the conflict it was seen to entail.[34] Rather than being an implacable opponent of liberalism, Hobbes attempts to construct a politics of wilful limitation: a political culture and set of institutions that will provide a maximum degree of autonomy and diversity within a stable social structure. His absolutist conception of sovereignty has as its goal, paradoxically, the construction of a recognisably liberal politics of toleration and self-creation.

This agenda is central to Hobbes' ontological materialism and his attempt to limit the grounds of disputation in knowledge claims. Through it he sought to rule out of court – to render either meaningless or wholly subjective or private – the key areas of political disputation and violence in his time: 'spiritual' and religious conflict and 'natural' (monarchical) authority. Moreover, as Malcolm importantly notes, this was not a purely 'domestic' agenda; it had an important international dimension since it provided a counter to the supranational claims of the Catholic church (that *'Confederacy of Deceivers'*) to the temporal authority of Sovereigns that Hobbes viewed as a key source of 'rebellions within states, and wars between them'.[35] The reduction of knowledge of the world – including the self – to materiality does not reflect an unexamined epistemic commitment, a naïve vision of scientific practice,[36] or

[34] Perhaps most significantly, new understandings of 'property' and the market, and their role in the construction of new political relations, were advanced. As numerous studies on the emergence of 'possessive individualism' in the seventeenth and eighteenth century have argued, the centrality of property had less to do with the ideological justification of an emerging market society than with an attempt to discern and construct principles of political order and obligation, rights and practices, in response to turmoil and change. Property, as a 'juridical concept of self-ownership', was 'moral, political and military, not economic. It is not concerned with the alienation of labour power but with political power (the power of self-defence). The individual as well as the state are concerned with preservation not consumption'; Tully, *An Approach to Political Philosophy*, p. 82. On this theme see also J. G. A. Pocock, *The Machiavellian Moment: Florentine Political Thought and the Atlantic Republican Tradition* (Princeton University Press, 1975), chapters 3, 6, and 11, especially; and Albert O. Hirschman, *The Passions and the Interests: Political argument for Capitalism before its Triumph* (Princeton University Press, 1977); and in International Relations, Kurt Burch, *'Property' and the Making of the International System* (Boulder, Colo.: Lynne Rienner, 1999).

[35] Malcolm, 'Hobbes's Theory of International Relations', p. 453.

[36] Indeed even Hobbes' specifically scientific claims – such as his (materialist) denial of the possibility of a total vacuum which marked his long controversy with Robert Boyle – were

the influence of nascent forms of capitalist ideology. It is underlain by a desire to delimit the realm of political disputation and conflict, to make room for a politics in principle uninfected by religion, and to allow for religion largely unconstrained by politics. In this way, it would provide the foundation for a stable sovereign authority, and a relatively stable system of Sovereigns, based upon the rational self-interest that Hobbes identifies as the 'Laws of Nature'.[37]

Yet Hobbes recognised that this commitment to materialism and logic was not enough, nor was the existence of a forceful powerful Sovereign authority alone sufficient to ensure the social and political outcomes that he desired. Accordingly, his purpose is not only to demonstrate the nature of, and solution to, the problem of political order; it is also to convince people of his as the only final solution to the dilemma. Crucially, Hobbes comes clearly to see that these two enterprises are not identical. As Johnston notes, the argument of *Leviathan* is not substantively different from that which Hobbes had earlier produced in *De Homine* and *De Cive*. What is strikingly different is the language which Hobbes adopts in *Leviathan*, a shift which reflects his long-standing concern with the role of rhetoric and affect in political action.[38] What Hobbes recognised was that the language of logic (with which he felt he had indubitably demonstrated his position) was not sufficient to effect the *political*

informed by his concerns with the politics of knowledge. See the fascinating treatment in Shapin and Schaeffer, *Leviathan and the Air Pump*.

[37] As Bull noted, the Hobbesian 'Laws of Nature' provide a common, if imperfect, foundation for the coordination of inter-state relations. Rational self-interest provides a common foundation for the coordination of action, the conduct of behaviour, and the creation of relatively stable international orders. In Bull's view, 'imperfect though they are, these laws of nature, "the articles of peace" as Hobbes calls them, are the lifeline to which sovereign states in the international anarchy must cling if they are to survive', and 'contain within them most of the basic rules of co-existence on which states have relied in the international anarchy from Hobbes' time and before it to our own'. And as he correctly concludes, this shows 'how deeply pacific Hobbes' approach to international relations was, at least in the values from which it sprang. There is no sense in Hobbes of the glorification of war, nor of relish for the game of power politics as an end in itself, nor of willingness to abdicate judgement in favour of the doctrine that anything in the international anarchy is permissible'. Hedley Bull, 'Hobbes and the International Anarchy', *Social Research*, 48:4 (1977), pp. 728, 729. As Malcolm has argued, the English School certainly provides the best appraisal of Hobbes' ideas within International Relations: however, it has traditionally paid little attention to the key questions of the construction of subjectivity and action that are essential dimensions of Hobbes' thinking. For a move in the latter direction, see Tim Dunne, *Inventing International Society: A History of the English School* (London: Macmillan, 1998).

[38] Evidenced as far back as Hobbes' translation of Thucydides' *History of the Peloponnesian War*. On this see again Johnston, *The Rhetoric of Leviathan*, and Quentin Skinner, *Reason and Rhetoric in the Philosophy of Hobbes* (Cambridge University Press,1996), and *Visions of Politics*, vol. III: *Hobbes and Civil Science*, pp. 1–141 especially.

understanding and action which it sanctioned. The turmoil of the English Civil War, however, provided not only an illustration of the limits of logic, it also provided, as Johnston has persuasively argued, a political opportunity in which Hobbes' ideas – suitably rephrased – could have political impact.

The extraordinarily powerful, evocative, and metaphorical language of *Leviathan* reflects Hobbes' recognition that the construction of his rational political order required an *affective* element if it was to be effective. Logic alone was insufficient to this task. Nor were the coercive powers of the Sovereign alone sufficient to construct and maintain such a political order. Hobbes does not believe that the simple existence and power of the Sovereign is adequate to ensure a stable political order.[39] No government is powerful enough to regulate totally the lives of recalcitrant citizens, or continually to compel them to obey.[40] Only if the people understand why the polity must be ordered as it must, and only if they continue to view the Sovereign as a legitimate authority and trust in its judgement, can a political order be secure. *Leviathan* is an attempt to create precisely this understanding, acceptance, and support, and through it to legitimise and strengthen the political order of the state.

To this end, Hobbes undertakes the tricky task of mobilising the most basic, powerful, and yet unstable element of his vision of human motivation: fear. Rational (Hobbesian) citizens will accept the rule of the Sovereign in part out of fear of its power. They may also accept it as an outcome of ratiocination. But, finally and significantly, they will accept this rule because of the powerful link which Hobbes draws between the two: because they understand the foundations of the sovereign authority and learn to fear both its power and the disastrous consequences of its dissolution – a return to the warlike state of nature. Fear and reason, logic and affect, are thus linked in Hobbes' attempt to foster an 'enlightened'[41] citizenry and political leadership. However, Hobbes does not seek

[39] This considerably complicates Martin Wight's characterisation of Hobbes as Realist on the grounds that he sees power as an end in itself. See Martin Wight, *International Relations: Three Traditions* (London: Holmes and Meier, 1992), p. 104.

[40] Drawing again on the analysis of religious affiliation in *Behemoth*, Holmes has insightfully noted that 'Hobbes stresses the self-defeating character of attempts to change people's minds by brutal means: "Suppression of doctrine does but unite and exasperate, that is, increase both the malice and power of them that have already believed them". This is a stunning admission from a champion of unlimited sovereign power. Indeed, it sounds more like Locke than Hobbes'. *Passions and Constraint*, p. 93; the quote is from Thomas Hobbes, *Behemoth or the Long Parliament*, ed. F. Tonnies (New York: Barnes and Noble, 1969), p. 62.

[41] Blits, 'Hobbesian Fear', pp. 426–9.

constantly to invoke fear as a means of limitation. Though he recognises the political utility of fear, his political sensibilities are far too subtle to rest with the idea that fear – the most basic and potentially destabilising of passions – provides a simple or straightforward resolution to the difficulties of constructing and maintaining a political order.[42] Rather than valorising fear as the basis of a rigid absolutism, or denying it in the name of a politics of transparency, he seeks to manage a politics of fear in order to construct a political order which can minimise its necessity and to create a recognisably liberal political society in which fear plays a minor but positive role in a politics of self- and sovereign-limitation.

The fear of pain, and particularly of death, on which Hobbes bases so many of his claims and pins so many of his hopes will not operate if individuals believe in an afterlife which transcends and justifies any form of suffering (or the infliction of suffering) in this world. A materialist epistemology and a materialist understanding of the self (and *self-interest*) provide a means of marginalising such destructive beliefs and actions, and of constructing a maximal realm of agreement. This understanding sidelines what Hobbes views as irreconcilably and irresolvably divergent beliefs precisely by casting them *as* beliefs, as matters of private opinion and faith from which a public realm of calculation and prudential order can be safely insulated. The kind of individuals that Hobbes seeks to promote (one might even say create) are those who have literally *learnt* to think of themselves and their worlds in terms of objective material calculation, and who thus provide the foundation upon which a stable politics can be built.

The Hobbesian self is a self of *limits*. It is a disciplined, *wilful* self which confronts its own desires (both physical *and* spiritual) and vanity in order to limit them and thereby create a realm of freedom and

[42] In an insightful reading, David Campbell has stressed this aspect of Hobbes' thinking, using it primarily to stress the negative disciplining role of otherness. I here largely pursue the alternative reading that Campbell notes as possible: discipline is not an end in itself for Hobbes – it is limitation in the name of a strategy of autonomy and pluralism, and an attempt to construct a liberal politics on the basis of the recognition that epistemic pluralism (as embodied in this scepticism) cannot be straightforwardly translated into political pluralism. In this regard, Hobbes can be seen as a profound if somewhat discomfiting exponent of what Judith Shklar called the 'liberalism of fear'. See David Campbell, *Writing Security: United States Foreign Policy and the Politics of Identity*, 2nd edn (Minneapolis: University of Minnesota Press, 1998), pp. 53–60, and n. 19; and Judith Shklar, 'The Liberalism of Fear', in Shklar, *Political Thought and Political Thinkers*, ed. Stanley Hoffmann (University of Chicago Press, 1998). I turn to an assessment of the broader implications of this divergence in chapter five.

order in which a maximum pursuit of individuality becomes possible.[43] Scepticism, for Hobbes, is not nihilism. It is a recognition of the limits of knowledge – a difficult acknowledgement of finitude and limitation in the face of powerful desires for security and the powerful attraction of claims to omniscience.[44] The construction of the Leviathan involves a confrontation, an act of will and self-assertion on behalf of individuals in the name of their own autonomy. The construction of a material self, a recognition of others in similar terms, and the creation of a political culture and sovereign power based upon such principles is not, for Hobbes, an assumption or an objective fact. It is an achievement: a value and a practice to be fostered in the name of individuality, security, and a maximum degree of liberty. That these practices and judgements are difficult, Hobbes fully recognises, but he feels that he has provided as definitive an answer to problems of political order as the limits of human knowledge will allow. And while he may not have been particularly optimistic about the abilities of human beings to live up to these possibilities, he also believes that they are capable of being successfully carried out by rational people who understand (and who are taught to understand) the foundations of politics.

'Hobbesian' international political theory reconsidered

The argument which has been developed thus far can be restated in the following terms: 'natural' human aggressiveness, vanity, and the like are not the sole or fundamental basis for Hobbes' analysis of the state of nature. Nor does that foundation lie in the assumption that utilitarian individuals are equally rational in competitive pursuit of the same things, or that they are objectively determined by the (scientifically discernible) structure within which they find themselves. Rather, the dilemma is that human beings have no *natural* way of agreeing upon what things are – what the reality of the world *is* – in either an empirical or a straightforwardly moral sense. Perceptions of what is good as well as bad, potentially beneficial as well as threatening, are at the most

[43] Flathman provides a detailed and brilliant exposition of this position in his *Thomas Hobbes*. For a treatment of Hobbes as a theorist of individual 'virtue', see David Berkowitz, *Virtue and the Making of Modern Liberalism* (Princeton University Press, 2000), pp. 35–73.
[44] For a subtle and suggestive treatment of a number of analogous themes, see James Der Derian, 'The Value of Security: Hobbes, Marx, and Baudrillard', in *On Security*, ed. R. Lipschutz (New York: Columbia University Press, 1996).

basic level inescapably relative. This is the source of Hobbes' portrayal of the state of nature. It is not simply authority or coordination which is lacking. For Hobbes it is *truth* in the conventional sense which is absent.

Through a combination of shared beliefs and the political power they make possible, particular political orders represent specific resolutions to this situation. The Sovereign is not just a structure for the coordination of individual interests. It is also (and much more fundamentally) the agency which provides stability in conditions of epistemic disagreement, underpins social structures of epistemic concord, provides authoritative (and enforceable) interpretations and decisions in contested cases, and creates conditions of predictability that minimise fear and allow rational cooperation. Seen in this light, the role and capacity of Sovereigns to solve these dilemmas domestically creates – by virtue of their necessarily authoritative role *internally* – a condition in which political orders are necessarily limited and relations between Sovereigns anarchic.

But Hobbes is not content merely to demonstrate these underpinnings of political authority. He does not view all resolutions to this situation as equally viable or desirable. Indeed in the context of the chaotic and conflictual breakdown of previous forms of order – and the understandings of the self, society, and sovereignty upon which they were based – he feels it imperative that the foundations of sovereignty and its requirements be reconstructed. To this end, he articulates a politics of limits: a vision based upon a reasoned understanding of the limits of reason, a materialist ontology and understanding of the self and self-interest, and a finely balanced practice of sovereign authority drawing upon rational understanding, fear of the Sovereign, and fear of its dissolution.

A corollary to this individual recognition of limits is that the rational (Hobbesian) Sovereign will recognise the *practical*, if not juridical, limits upon its authority and will moderate its actions accordingly.[45] This puts considerable practical limits upon the Sovereign for Hobbes, and given its implications for state action it is important to understand fully the rather complex argument he makes in this regard. Hobbesian individuals never give up their right to judge situations for themselves

[45] As Hobbes put it in an early and recently authenticated discourse: 'For it is a great misfortune to a people, to come under the government of such a one, as knows not how to govern himself.' 'Discourse upon the Beginnings of Tacitus', in Hobbes, *Three Discourses*, ed. Noel B. Reynolds and Arlene W. Saxonhouse (University of Chicago Press, 1996), p. 57. See also Malcolm's incisive treatment of these issues in 'Hobbes's Theory of International Relations', pp. 446–8.

in the sense that if they believe their self-preservation to be threatened they retain (via the right of nature) the right of rebellion against the Sovereign. If an individual judges her life to be in danger (and in this realm the individual's judgement remains supreme), or has committed an act which is a capital crime, then even if she is juridically wrong she has by nature the right to defend herself. Equally, should a group come to feel that the Sovereign is not protecting their lives adequately, or should they come to judge that the Sovereign constitutes a threat to their lives, they have the right to band together in mutual defence. As Hobbes puts it: 'But in case a great many men together have already resisted the sovereign power unjustly, or committed some capital crime for which every one of them expecteth death, whether have they not the liberty to join together, and assist, and defend one another? Certainly they have; for they but defend their lives, which the guilty man may as well do as the innocent.'[46]

Ultimately, by this logic, if this group should become strong enough that it threatens the ability of the Sovereign to guarantee the security of other subjects, or they feel that to obey the rebels is necessary to their survival (in their judgement), then these individuals are at liberty to do so. In this way, Hobbes tries to show how on the very basis of the principles of its foundation and within its own logic, civil order can break down and (civil) war emerge. The fragility of this order and the disastrous consequences of its breakdown become a lesson to both citizens and the Sovereign to understand the practical/prudential limits upon their claims and activities. Rational beings should not challenge the Sovereign, Hobbes believes, but this does not mean they will not, and the 'Negligent government of Princes', he argues in characteristically dire terms at the conclusion to Part 2 of *Leviathan*, is naturally attended by 'Rebellion; and Rebellion, with Slaughter'.[47]

The Sovereign should assiduously avoid policies which make rebellion likely. It must educate subjects so that they understand and accept the principles of sovereign authority, and it must maintain sufficient coercive power to 'convince' them if they do not. But even in this latter case, Hobbes accentuates the importance of acceptance and legitimacy, for the coercive capacities of the Sovereign themselves depend upon it. If the people rebel, the Sovereign must, Hobbes argues, have recourse to arms to enforce civil order. But the possession of this coercive power and the ability to wield it are dependent upon the prior and continuing

[46] Hobbes, *Leviathan*, p. 143. [47] Hobbes, *Leviathan*, p. 243.

legitimacy of the Sovereign's authority in the eyes of those who will act on its behalf. The problem, as he pointedly asks in *Behemoth*, is that 'if men know not their duty, what is there that can force them to obey the laws? An army you will say. But what shall force the army?'[48]

Without the social legitimacy which makes it possible, the Sovereign's coercive power is likely to prove chimerical. While the Sovereign thus has *in principle* the right to act in any way it chooses, Hobbes argues that a correct understanding of politics will lead not only to obedient citizens, but to prudential self-limitation of activity by a rational Sovereign. Since, as he states clearly, again in *Behemoth*, that 'the power of the mighty hath no foundation but in the opinion and belief of the people',[49] the Sovereign will avoid actions which too obviously threaten the interests of the citizens for fear that it will lose their acceptance of its authority and foment dissension and rebellion.[50] This places considerable limits (again rationally, not juridically) on state action both domestically and internationally.

In Hobbes' view, Sovereigns cannot act toward each other as individuals might because as a corporate body the Sovereign must consider the relationship between its external relations and relations with its own citizens. The Sovereign, recognising the foundations of its authority, must be careful not to lose the trust of the citizens, or to tip the balance of fear to such an extent that the citizens come to see obedience to the state as a greater threat to their survival than disobedience. Even though the Sovereign has the right to treat its citizens in virtually any way it sees fit, Hobbes believes that it should not, and he believes he has given convincing reasons why it should not. These considerations put limitations on the external actions of the Sovereign beyond those of simple caution or restricted material 'capabilities'. Hobbes' analysis is not simply that an adventurous foreign policy is imprudent. Rather the question of knowledge and social consent is once again key here. Since aggression is not innate but arises in part from uncertainty, Hobbes' Leviathans are not necessarily aggressive toward one another. More importantly, since they must ultimately convince the citizens to obey their judgements of threats (and thus convince citizens themselves to go to war or support preparations for it), the prudent Sovereign will be cautious in engaging

[48] Hobbes, *Behemoth*, p. 59. Again, my thanks to Ross Rudolph for alerting me to this passage.
[49] Hobbes, *Behemoth*, p. 16. Holmes makes this revealing quote the centrepiece of his treatment.
[50] On this theme, see especially Flathman, *Thomas Hobbes*, pp. 121–5.

in the practice, for fear of losing the trust of the citizens in its judgement (just as it should not oppress the citizens unnecessarily for the same reason) and by so doing push them to dissension or rebellion.[51]

Since the Sovereign's authority rests not just on coercive power or the ability to manipulate utilities, but also depends upon its ability to retain legitimacy in the eyes of its citizens, the Sovereign should always weigh the implications of its actions on the lives and opinions of its citizens, and keep these issues clearly in mind. In its external relations, the same logic applies. The Sovereign should not unnecessarily do things which would push the citizens too hard, threaten them or their livelihoods too much, or cause them to question their belief and trust in the judgement and actions of the Sovereign. Indeed in external relations this logic may be even more imperative. For since the Sovereign may be asking (and potentially compelling) the citizens to put their lives at risk in war (and thus potentially allowing them to rebel on the grounds of self-preservation, which is their right by nature), it can only do so if the vast majority of the population continues to trust in its adjudication of the situation (threat) and the necessity of risking their lives. It is in war that the continuance of the Sovereign's rule is potentially most in jeopardy, not just from the power of other Sovereigns, but from domestic dissension. Hobbes, of course, believes that the Sovereign is justified in forcing citizens to go to war, but he nonetheless feels it would be unwise and unreasonable to force them to do so too often or in situations where the judgements of threat decided upon by the Sovereign are shaky enough and risky enough potentially to erode its legitimacy in the eyes of the citizens.[52]

Scepticism about the limits of human knowledge leads Hobbes to great caution in human affairs, especially regarding the relationship of theory to practice. He warns that to act as if we can know (predict) and control the future is to court disaster. Knowing the limitations of human knowledge, and the inability to know God's will or other visions of ultimate human fulfilment, Hobbes believes that rational Sovereigns will not act in an unnecessarily aggressive manner. His vision of foreign policy is cautious and essentially pacific, a position which, as Flathman has

[51] This question was of the utmost importance for Hobbes. In his own time the Monarch's demands for 'Ship Money' for the building of a larger navy, which Hobbes helped collect despite the objections of many citizens, was a crucial issue in the onset of the English Civil War. See Johann Somerville, *Thomas Hobbes: Political Ideas in Historical context* (New York: St Martin's Press, 1992), p. 18.

[52] Hobbes' position on the obligation of citizens to go to war is correspondingly complex and cannot be entered into fully here.

illustrated drawing upon a passage from the *Elements of Law*, is conditioned by – or perhaps founded in – his scepticism: 'Hobbes is far from a supporter of bellicose or expansionist policies. Because no preparation can assure victory, "such commonwealths, or such monarchs, as affect war for itself . . . out of ambition, or of vain-glory, or that make account to avenge every little injury, or disgrace done by their neighbours, if they not ruin themselves, their fortune must be better than they have reason to expect".'[53]

The hubris engendered by religious dogma, political fanaticism, pride, vanity, or (social scientific?) claims to political wisdom will most likely lead to disaster. This fits clearly with both Hobbes' strictures on the claims to religious knowledge and his attacks on militaristic or destructive ideologies of honour.[54] Scepticism leads to a suspicion of, and attack against, dogmatism and (in Hobbes' sense) irrationalism. A transformation of epistemic practice was seen as a means of transforming social and political and ethical practices both within Sovereignties.

In principle, Sovereigns exist in the same situation of sceptical indeterminacy toward one another as individuals in the state of nature. But there are crucial differences between states and individuals which render this a much different situation. The first of these concerns the different physical capabilities of states and individuals. In *Leviathan*, Hobbes argues that: 'Nature hath made men so equall, in the faculties of body, and mind; as that though there be found one man sometimes manifestly stronger in body, or of quicker mind than another; yet when all is reckoned together, the difference between man and man is not so considerable, as that one man can thereupon claim to himself any benefit, to which another may not pretend as well as he.'[55] There is no natural hierarchy in the state of nature upon which order can be based. Characteristics advantageous in the struggle are diversely distributed: some are strong, others quick, still others clever. Moreover, this relative equality of capacities is tied to the existence of these individuals *as* solitary individuals. Even the strongest must sometimes sleep, and all are

[53] Flathman, *Thomas Hobbes*, p. 110.
[54] See especially Keith Thomas, 'The Social Origins of Hobbes's Political Thought', in *Hobbes Studies*, ed. K. C. Brown (Cambridge, Mass.: Harvard University Press, 1965), pp. 96–8 especially. In this sense, too, it is interesting to note that Hobbes can be seen as almost postmodern, at least in the reading given by some to that term. Conversely, this conclusion may reflect more about the confusing nature of contemporary political discourse than anything else. I will return to some of these issues in chapter four.
[55] Hobbes, *Leviathan*, p. 74.

subject to disease, age, and ultimately death, circumstances which make any continuing exercise of domination impossible.

Between Hobbesian Sovereigns, however, the most destructive and fearful aspects of the state of nature have been ameliorated, lessening the radical insecurity and conflict which dominates the state of nature. The Leviathan never sleeps and (except in specific circumstances) it never dies. Ever alert and immortal, it transcends the limitations which simple individuals encounter in their attempts to survive in the state of nature. As a corporate body, its strength is the strength of all its members. The result is that the radical equality which defines the state of nature composed of individuals is not present in the relations between states; they are qualitatively different orders. And since states are not subject to the same conditions as individuals – equality, sleep, mortality – they can transcend some of the more anarchic qualities of the state of nature and create, via the Laws of Nature, more stable forms of coexistence among themselves.[56]

Yet it is important to note that, from a Hobbesian perspective, the fact that states are corporate bodies is not in itself enough to secure an acceptable international order. Just as individuals in the state of nature must come to understand themselves and their world in a rational manner in order to live by the cooperative dictates of the 'laws of nature', so states would also need to adopt rational (i.e. Hobbes') maxims of internal organisation and external behaviour for the international realm to be any more than a contingent and fragile form of order or domination. Hobbes' argument is not that such an order is natural, or that its norms would simply evolve through time. On the contrary, he feels that political orders must be willed and constructed in accordance with the dictates of rationality and with a clear view of its limitations. Other forms of international order certainly can exist – medieval Christendom being perhaps the prime example. But in light of his concern with the violence that attended the breakdown of that order, Hobbes would likely have regarded such orders as unacceptably fragile and prone to conflicts as 'irrational' as the principles upon which they were founded.

These considerations point to the ways in which Hobbes' commitment to the absolute nature of sovereignty is by no means incompatible

[56] This theme has been most fully explored by the English School. See, for example, Bull, 'Hobbes and the International Anarchy', p. 726; and Vincent, 'The Hobbesian Tradition'. For a discussion of the relationship between neorealism and the English School see Barry Buzan, 'From International System to International Society: Structural Realism and Regime Theory Meet the English School', *International Organization*, 47:3 (1993).

with international order and with shared understanding between rationally constituted sovereignties.[57] Based upon the same principles, Hobbesian states will share the same understanding of political order, the same commitment to a politics of limits, and the same constraints on their actions. Moreover, the materialist and empiricist practices that are essential in the constitution of a rational Hobbesian order could provide a common framework of understanding between Sovereigns. The materialist and empiricist practices of knowledge that Hobbes advocates would, if adopted, allow for mutual knowledge and calculation and a partial overcoming of the basic sceptical situation within which different sovereignties encounter each other. These mediating practices of material interest lack the order provided by the authoritative decision-making, cultural legitimation, and coercive capacities that characterise the state. But the international realm is not a state of nature. Materialist and rationalist practices allow the shared construction of concepts of interest, power, and action, and provide the basis for common calculation and adjustment even when Sovereigns are at odds with each other. In short, a materialist balance of power could become a mediating structure of practice between Sovereigns: a *willed* form of (Realist) order.

Finally, and admittedly more speculatively, it is possible to conceive how the principles of legitimacy upon which the practice of sovereignty is based – that is, legitimate action in the eyes of *citizens* – might become transnationalised to a point at which juridically absolute Sovereigns would nonetheless be *practically* constrained by their limits. The issues this raises are highly complex, for Hobbes would undoubtedly continue to insist on the absolute necessity of the Sovereign as a locus of decision in an inherently indeterminate world. But be this as it may, absolute sovereignty and cosmopolitan constraints are not necessarily opposed in Hobbes' vision of the *practice* of sovereignty, however much they may seem precluded by his definition of it.

Conclusion

This interpretation of Hobbes' thought considerably complicates the picture of 'Hobbesian anarchy' so often analogously painted in International Relations.[58] Hobbes is frequently portrayed as a theorist who

[57] Again, see the excellent treatment in Malcolm, 'Hobbes's Theory of International Relations', pp. 451–5; and the discussion of Hobbes' views on trade in Boucher, *Political Theories of International Relations*, pp. 160–1.
[58] See also Navari, 'Knowledge, the State and the State of Nature'.

builds an objective science of politics upon the assumption that individuals are instrumental pursuers of material interests. Indeed it is precisely this image that has made his thinking such a popular touchstone within many neorealist declarations about international politics – with the image of individuals simply elevated to the world of states. For all its popularity, however, this image does little justice to Hobbes' thinking or to understanding a 'Hobbesian' vision of international relations, which is characterised not by 'rational action' in a condition of anarchy, but by his fundamental scepticism, and his understanding of the role and limits of logic and language in the construction of action.[59]

A similar set of conclusions applies to the role played by Hobbes in the structural Realism of Kenneth Waltz. Unlike those who use 'Hobbesian anarchy' as a shorthand characterisation of the neorealist vision of International Relations, Waltz is considerably more precise. To him, Hobbes is a classical Realist (like Morgenthau) in that he finds the source of anarchy in the nature of human beings or the state rather than locating it – as Waltz's structural Realism claims to – in a scientific grasp of the nature of the interstate system itself.[60] In Waltz's view, then, Hobbes provides an example of the errors and limitations of 'reductionist' theory, and as we shall see in the next chapter, Waltz draws instead upon Rousseau for inspiration.

However, casting Hobbes as a 'reductionist' obscures the fundamental challenge which Hobbes' thinking poses for Waltzian structuralism. First, Hobbes challenges the *assumption* of the state that Waltz relies upon. For Hobbes, the state is a highly complex and fragile construction: a practical political project whose international actions are circumscribed not just by its capabilities but also by the practical constraints of its domestic construction. The state cannot be reduced to a set of objective capabilities because the continued existence of these capabilities and the ability to exercise the 'power'[61] which they represent is inextricably bound up with the legitimacy of the political order itself. In relation to Waltz's neorealist formulation, the important point here

[59] For an analysis of other shortcomings in attempting to read Hobbes in this way see Don Herzog, *Happy Slaves* (University of Chicago Press, 1989), chapter 3 especially.
[60] As Waltz puts it: 'The preoccupation with the qualities of man is understandable in view of the purposes Hobbes and Morgenthau entertain. Both are interested in understanding the state.' Kenneth Waltz, 'Realist Thought and Neorealist Theory', in *The Evolution of Theory in International Relations*, ed. Robert L. Rothstein (Columbia: University of South Carolina Press, 1991), p. 35.
[61] A concept which, Waltz admits, has despite its centrality been accompanied by criticisms of an 'absence of efforts on the part of neorealists to devise objective measures of power'. Waltz, 'Realist Thought and Neorealist Theory', p. 36.

is that state power is not simply a 'means' or an objective 'capability'. For Hobbes, it is a result of the resolution of fundamental problems and dilemmas in the construction of a potentially fragile and contingent political order. The existence and exercise of state power, therefore, cannot for Hobbes be viewed in isolation from the constraints and considerations surrounding its genesis and continued legitimacy.

Secondly, Hobbes is a 'reductionist' precisely because he regards as inescapably problematic the form of knowledge upon which Waltz builds his theory of International Relations. The distinction between fact and theory, central to modern empiricism and to Waltz's conception of theory, is one which Hobbes vociferously denied. Much like contemporary post-empiricism, Hobbes denied the claim that 'matters of fact' upon which theories could be built were unproblematically given. In fact, his scepticism provides a challenge to Waltz's conception of theory which is remarkably – and ironically – analogous to that which contemporary critics of empiricism have launched against Waltzian neorealism. He regarded experiential knowledge – or what he preferred to call 'natural history' – as at best probabilistic.[62]

Hobbes cannot be marginalised by a rhetorical banishment as a 'reductionist' theorist. He takes this stance not because he is ignorant of science, but because he is sceptical about its foundations and highly concerned with the structure of knowledge and its political implications. And as we have seen, it is Hobbes' scepticism about the status of empirical knowledge which is the basis for his concerns with questions of order, authority, and legitimacy within the state. These concerns, in turn, are directly reflected in both the theoretical foundation and practical content of his understanding of the relations between states.

Far from seeking to develop either a straightforward rational-choice theory of social life and an analogous account of International Relations, or a 'scientific' theory along the lines of Waltz's structural Realism, it is from the problem of objective empirical knowledge that Hobbes begins. His is a political theory based not upon modern political 'science' in either of these forms, but upon a profound scepticism concerning the very kind of knowledge that provides the foundation of these theoretical positions. Hobbes' vision of politics (and the 'science' of it) is,

[62] Unlike some forms of post-positivism, however, he believed fully in the possibility of rational certainty. His rationalist commitments have been consistently misunderstood, and his relationship to positivist conceptions of science often misconstrued. On this theme see: Shapin and Shaeffer, *Leviathan and the Air Pump*; and, more generally, Ian Hacking, *The Emergence of Probability* (Cambridge University Press, 1984) and Barbara Shapiro, *Probability and Certainty in Seventeenth-Century England* (Princeton University Press, 1983).

as Richard Flathman has vigorously argued, a highly 'chastened' one, both in its epistemological claims and its practical recommendations. While some scholars continue to call for a discipline constructed along the lines of positivist science,[63] this is not a stance which Hobbes would have supported, nor can it be sustained by a reference to the 'Hobbesian' analysis of International Relations. Indeed as Flathman notes, to the extent that Hobbes' ideas in this realm were 'in important respects anticipating views now prominent in the philosophy of science, it is not an account that is likely to warm the hearts of the apostles of science – whether natural or the so-called science of politics'.[64]

For Hobbes, materialism and empiricism were intrinsic elements in an assault upon various forms of innatism and essentialism. In fact, it is probably not too much to say that materialism and empiricism can be considered *epistemic ethical practices*, justified not only in terms of knowledge but also in terms of their practical contributions and consequences. Hobbes sought a transformation of knowledgeable practices and political action. His 'methodological' commitments do not simply involve 'theoretical' innovations (a novel atomism, for example[65]) or a naïve vision of a natural evolution toward 'objective' knowledge. They were part and parcel of an attempt to construct a new set of political institutions and practices *within* the state, a set of practices which had the question of 'security' in the broadest sense at their heart. These new knowledgeable practices sought to provide foundations within which political agreement could be obtained and social concord achieved. They sought, above all, to restore a foundation and provide stability to a culture racked by political conflict and slaughter.

Hobbes' concentration on issues of knowledge, consent, and legitimacy in social action make his thought of great – if often uncomfortable and certainly unfamiliar – relevance to current research in the social construction of International Relations. While his thinking clearly challenges rationalist visions of social science, it also poses substantial challenges to too easy a belief that a turn toward 'constructed' norms and subjectivity represents inherently progressive alternatives to the

[63] In security studies, for example, see Steven Walt, 'The Renaissance of Security Studies', *International Studies Quarterly*, 35:2 (1991).
[64] Flathman, *Thomas Hobbes*, p. 29; see also p. 49.
[65] Again, this is a limitation of otherwise insightful criticisms of the atomist and contractual foundations of liberal-rationalist (and rationalist Realist) theories. See, for example, Nicholas G. Onuf, *The Republican Legacy in International Thought* (Cambridge University Press, 1998), p. 13, and Erik Ringmar, *Identity, Interest and Action* (Cambridge University Press, 1997), p. 59.

essentialist visions of human nature, 'anarchy', or the state often found in Realism or the scientific pretensions of structural neorealism. His anti-objectivist epistemological stance highlights the difficulties involved in constructing and securing fragile and inherently contingent political orders, whether they be domestic or international. It is a much different and more sophisticated vision than that which focuses upon timeless natures or supposedly eternal structural determination, but in its stress on the nature of human subjectivity and the limits of human understanding, Hobbes' analysis raises very difficult questions. For those who would like to appeal to concepts such as relativity and intersubjectivity in the construction of a different understanding of international politics, an engagement with Hobbes serves, to borrow a phrase from John Dunn, as a 'tart reminder' of the less salutary implications which such a position can yield and the questions which it must confront.[66]

In many ways, Hobbes stands as the paradigmatic thinker of the wilful Realist tradition. The recognition that the social and political world must be wilfully constructed by human beings is at the heart of what Stephen Holmes has aptly named the 'Hobbesian moment' in political thought. Hobbes does not hold that anarchy in the sense of a perpetual condition of enmity is the consequence for international order, or that international orders lack possible (and existing) mediating practices between sovereignties. Indeed he tries to foster conditions that support these mediating practices, and to remove barriers to their construction. These practices are, however, premised upon a recognition of the limits of both knowledge and authority. The problem of decision – of the authoritative determination and, if necessary, coercive implementation – of principles of political order remains a defining parameter of political life, and the institutional capacities and cultural practices underlying effective sovereignty remain for Hobbes inescapably particular. But he does not see this particularity as necessarily oppositional, and his goal is to construct political orders and understandings that support as non-oppressive, pluralistic, and pacific an order as possible.

The possibility and practice of such a politics of limits is the Hobbesian wager, and stands at the heart of Hobbes' significance for wilful Realism. Yet perhaps the greatest difficulty which Hobbes confronts is whether the politics of limits which he advocates can function within the fine balance that he suggests. For if a Hobbesian politics of limits fails to work at

[66] John Dunn, 'Political Obligation', in *Political Theory Today*, ed. David Held (Stanford: Polity Press, 1991), p. 47.

the level of civil society, if individuals refuse to adopt the epistemological premises, visions of self-identity, and practices of social and political order that Hobbes recommends – then the Sovereign must impose order, however difficult it may be. The authoritarian implications of this position of juridically unlimited sovereignty have long been a source of concern, from Locke's famous disagreements onward. But they also contain their own instabilities. For this very lack of limitation upon the Sovereign can easily be seen as a spur to fear, particularly if the disciplined limitation which Hobbes in practice requires of the Sovereign is not forthcoming. In both cases, the politics of limits depends upon a functioning of fear which is deeply unstable. An international order based on Hobbesian principles must confront the same dilemmas. Indeed the possibilities and perils of a Hobbesian politics of limits stand as one of the most fundamental challenges confronting the wilful Realist tradition.

2 Rousseau, Realism, and realpolitik

Like Hobbes, Jean-Jacques Rousseau has long been an iconic figure in theories of International Relations. And like Hobbes his writings have often come to occupy an important symbolic role as those of an archetypal 'Realist' who – usually in opposition to the 'idealism' of Kant – correctly grasped the eternal verities of power politics and provided an especially clear formulation of the philosophical principles upon which a modern science of international politics might be constructed.[1] Rousseau's writings on international politics, it is conventionally argued, represent the timeless insights of realpolitik, the bases of its critique of utopianism, and the tragic sense of 'despair' which necessarily characterises a Realist analysis of International Relations. Like many prevailing interpretations of Hobbes, however, this interpretation of Rousseau's analysis of international politics is based upon a series of conceptual, methodological, and philosophical stances which result in a seriously misleading account of the significance of Rousseau's writings for thinking about International Relations. By emphasising only particular aspects of Rousseau's thought, or by treating the writings on international politics in almost complete abstraction from his political

[1] The juxtaposition which portrays Kant and Rousseau as representing the dualistically opposed categories of 'idealism' and 'Realism' in International Relations theory has become almost gospel, and is reflected most clearly in Hoffmann's well-known statement that: 'Whoever studies international relations cannot but hear, behind the clash of interests and ideologies, a kind of permanent dialogue between Rousseau and Kant.' Hoffmann, *The State of War* p. 86. This classification is echoed in virtually every major analysis; see, for example, F. H. Hinsley, *Power and the Pursuit of Peace* (Cambridge University Press, 1963); W. B. Gallie, *Philosophers of Peace and War* (Cambridge University Press, 1978), pp. 18–19; Ian Clark, *The Hierarchy of States: Reform and Resistance in the International Order* (Cambridge University Press, 1981); K. J. Holsti, *The State, War, and the State of War* (Cambridge University Press, 1997), pp. 7–9. I will return to the relationship between Rousseau and Kant at the end of the chapter.

theory as a whole, an interpretation has emerged which is little more than a caricature of his actual position.

The analysis pursued in this chapter seeks to redress some of the shortcomings of conventional appropriations of Rousseau within International Relations theory. It also, however, seeks to assess Rousseau's complex and important relationship to the wilful Realist tradition that is the concern of this book as a whole. In a fashion similar to the appropriations of Hobbes discussed in the last chapter, Rousseau has been subsumed within a tradition of rationalism and Realism focusing on anarchy and rationality as the determining elements of the international system. By contrast, I argue that Rousseau actually stands as one of the first and still most profound critics of a rationalist approach to political analysis in general, and to a rationalist Realism in International Relations in particular. Far from being a simple representative of a unified Realist tradition of anarchy, part of Rousseau's greatest significance lies in his critique of rationalism and realpolitik, and his concern with the construction of a politics of right at both the domestic and the international levels.

Rousseau in International Relations theory

Rousseau's writings on international politics have been subject to a variety of interpretations within International Relations theory. The ways in which these interpretations are derived, the evidence upon which they are based, and the position of the interpreter toward both often differ significantly. Yet most often Rousseau has been located firmly within the tradition of realpolitik. In Stanley Hoffmann's complex and sensitive treatment, for example, the central issue in Rousseau's understanding of international politics revolves around the concept of the state of nature. In this view, the state of nature appears as a 'golden age', an original condition of relative bliss, of 'liberty and happiness' amongst largely disconnected, pre-social individuals;[2] an original 'idyll'[3] from which humanity 'fell' into an anarchic condition resembling the state of nature evoked by Hobbes. Rousseau's objective, Hoffmann claims, was in turn 'to rescue man from the fall into which the passing of the state of nature had plunged him'[4] and deliver him from the anarchy of this now 'fallen state of nature' of '*de facto society*'.[5]

[2] Hoffmann, *The State of War*, p. 56.
[3] Hoffmann, *The State of War*, p. 57.
[4] Hoffmann, *The State of War*, p. 55.
[5] Hoffmann, *The State of War*, p. 72.

According to Hoffmann, this very solution becomes the paradigmatic problem of international politics. Escape from the fallen state of nature involves the creation of particularistic states that solve the problem at the internal or domestic level, but displace it into the newly formed realm of external relations between them. As Hoffmann puts it, 'Men finally became aware and convinced of their common interest in establishing civil societies, but their purpose was to protect the "ins" against the "outs". It was not an end to competition, merely a displacement of it.'[6] This theme is echoed in the interpretations of both F. H. Hinsley and Ian Clark. The solution to the problem of a humanity that has fallen from a blissful state of nature into a condition of Hobbesian anarchy is the creation of the sovereign state; but it is a solution which merely recreates the condition of 'Hobbesian anarchy' at the international level. Clark succinctly summarises the argument as follows: 'Why does civil society bring about this change and produce a state of war? For the simple reason that while it solves one problem of order at the domestic level, it immediately creates another at the international: the institution of the state creates domestic order but initiates international anarchy.'[7] The outcome of these interpretations is the declaration of an unbreachable divide between an 'ideal', but irretrievable, state of nature and a 'frightening',[8] but unchangeable, anarchic system of sovereign states; and Rousseau is declared to be firmly within the gloomy tradition of moral 'despair' which characterises many forms of realism.[9]

Textually, these themes have been further developed in a number of ways. For both Hinsley and Clark, they find their clearest and most striking expression in Rousseau's most explicit writing on international politics: the 'Abstract' and 'Judgement' on the Abbé St Pierre's *Project for Perpetual Peace* and the fragment entitled *The State of War*.[10] In the 'Abstract', Rousseau is said sympathetically – though with already visible hints of scepticism[11] – to represent St Pierre's project. For St Pierre, the creation of the modern state delivered man from the individualistic conflict of an essentially 'Hobbesian' state of nature only to foster the creation of an international state of war inestimably more cruel and destructive. Rousseau paraphrases the argument as follows:

[6] Hoffmann, *The State of War*, p. 73.
[7] Clark, *Reform and Resistance*, p. 62.
[8] Hoffmann, *The State of War*, p. 70.
[9] Clark, *Reform and Resistance*, pp. 66–75.
[10] All references to Rousseau's 'Abstract' and 'Judgement' on St Pierre's *Project for Perpetual Peace*, unless otherwise noted, are taken from *The Theory of International Relations*, ed. M. G. Forsyth, H. M. A. Keans-Soper, and P. Savigear (London: Allen and Unwin, 1970).
[11] Hinsley, *Power and the Pursuit of Peace*, p. 47.

> If the social order were really, as is pretended, the work not of passion but of reason, should we have been so slow to see that in shaping it either too much or too little has been done for our happiness? That, each one of us being in the civil state as regards our fellow citizens, but in the state of nature as regards the rest of the world, we have taken precautions against private wars only to kindle national wars a thousand times more terrible? And that, in joining a particular group of men, we have really declared ourselves the enemies of the whole race?[12]

St Pierre's challenge is to find a way of reconciling these dangerous contradictions, and in response he proposes the formation of a Confederacy of European states based on their common ties and heritage.[13] Such a Confederacy, he argues, would provide for the peace and security of all and thus remove the contradictions and conflicts which currently plague them.

Yet for the dominant vision of Rousseau as a theorist of anarchy, it is in the 'Judgement' of St Pierre's project that Rousseau's Realism emerges full-blown. According to Hinsley, the misgivings earlier expressed in the 'Abstract' emerge as 'positive conclusions in the "Judgement"',[14] where Rousseau is said to reach conclusions that contradict any possibility of the success of St Pierre's project, conclusions that confirm the existence of a perpetual state of war at the international level. According to this reading, Rousseau clearly sees that, despite the project's laudable ends, it can never be realised, since the very thing required for the establishment of the Confederacy – the consent of the individual Sovereigns – cannot be achieved. The very existence of self-interested sovereign states which produce the international state of war renders impossible its transcendence. In Clark's view:

> Rousseau was arguing that if there was a solution then such a federation was it. But, of course, he rejects this as a solution on the grounds that there is absolutely no hope of its realisation. As he puts it ironically, 'all that is needed to establish the federation is the consent of the princes, who, unfortunately, would resist with all their might any proposal for its creation'. And so, having claimed that there is only one possible solution to the ills of international disorder, Rousseau then goes on to dismiss it as being utterly unattainable.[15]

[12] Rousseau, 'Abstract', p. 132. Cf. also Clark, *Reform and Resistance*, p. 62.
[13] Rousseau, 'Abstract', pp. 132–5. [14] Hinsley, *Power and the Pursuit of Peace*, p. 48.
[15] Clark, *Reform and Resistance*, p. 63. For a fuller account see chapter 3 of Hinsley, *Power and the Pursuit of Peace*, whose entire analysis stresses this interpretation. Hoffmann's

The clearest and most well-known proponent of a 'structural' reading of Rousseau along these lines is Kenneth Waltz.[16] For Waltz, however, it is not the 'Abstract' and 'Judgement' which provide the key to understanding the value and power of Rousseau's analysis, but rather the parable of the stag-hunt in the *Discourse on the Origin of Inequality*. In the parable, it will be recalled, a cooperative stag-hunt among a group of men fails because one of its members defects in order to catch a nearby hare for himself. Waltz notes that 'The defector obtains the means of satisfying his hunger but in doing so permits the stag to escape. His immediate interest prevails over consideration for his fellows.' Waltz then goes on to claim that: 'The story is simple: the implications are tremendous', because this brief parable illustrates perfectly the logic of the 'systemic', or 'third-image', approach to the analysis of international politics. It is the insecurity of the actors, the inability of each to rely on the cooperative actions of the others, and the possibility of purely self-interested, beggar-thy-neighbour rationality existing among any one of them that force each to act in this manner.[17] Rousseau's genius, for Waltz, is in his understanding that it is the 'system' which is the cause of international conflict, and that it is the very nature of this anarchic system which precludes its transcendence.

Regardless of the way in which it is formulated by these different writers, this theme represents the dominant interpretation and appropriation of Rousseau's work in International Relations theory. It is claimed that it constitutes his fundamental insight, his enduring legacy to the study of international politics, and his affinity with a purported historical tradition of Realism. A return to the state of nature is impossible, and we are left in an essentially 'anarchic' international world. According to these readings, while Rousseau may not like it, he grasps both the logic and the nature of international politics and is realistic enough to understand the world as it is: governed by realpolitik.

position on this issue is more ambiguous. Rather than seeing Rousseau's analysis as outlining the eternal structure of international politics he seems to regard it as exemplifying the *problematic* within which International Relations take place. This is most clearly evident in his *Duties beyond Borders* (Syracuse, NY: Syracuse University Press, 1981).

[16] Kenneth Waltz, *Theory of International Politics* (Reading, Mass.; Addison-Wesley, 1979), p. 47.

[17] Kenneth Waltz, *Man, the State and War* (New York: Columbia University Press, 1959), p. 160. Cf. also, Waltz, *Theory of International Politics*, chapters 5 and 6.

Recasting Rousseau: history, reason, and the state

Developing a different understanding of Rousseau's writings on international politics requires locating these writings within the wider and more complex context of his overall theoretical position, most particularly within the context of his philosophy of history and society. Rousseau's analysis of the Abbé's *Project*, in particular, must be seen in the light of his overall vision of the society of his time, and indeed when so viewed it becomes apparent that his analysis of international politics represents a furtherance of his fundamental critique of that society. My argument here will be divided into two parts, the first being a direct location and analysis of the writings on St Pierre's *Project* within the framework of Rousseau's broader philosophical position, and the second a more general discussion of his relationship to contemporary Realist theories of international politics.

As with the discussion of Hobbes in chapter one, the logical place to begin a reassessment of Rousseau and International Relations is where Rousseau himself begins, with the state of nature. In Rousseau's state of nature, humans exist as largely disconnected individuals. They are adequately equipped to survive the rigours of nature alone. Their contacts with other humans were fleeting, involving brief periods of mating or child rearing, or chance encounters with others over food or shelter where flight to other available resources was generally preferable to the pain and uncertainty of fighting. The relative equality of individual capacities, the solitary nature of individual life, and the relative availability of resources and the ability to move freely in search of them made the dominance of one individual over another either unattractive or fleeting.[18] In this natural condition, human beings were:

> wild rather than wicked, and more intent to guard themselves against the mischief that might be done to them, than to do mischief to others,

[18] Stressing the difficulties of ongoing domination in such an asocial context, Rousseau notes that 'should I happen to meet with a man so much stronger than myself, and at the same time so depraved, so indolent, and so barbarous as to compel me to provide for his sustenance while he himself remains idle; he must take care not to have his eyes off me for a single moment; he must bind me fast before he goes to sleep, or I shall certainly either knock him on the head or make my escape. That is to say, he must in such a case voluntarily expose himself to much greater trouble than he seeks to avoid, or can give me.' Jean-Jacques Rousseau, 'Discourse on the Origin of Inequality', in Rousseau, *The Social Contract and Discourses*, trans. and intro. G. D. H. Cole, rev. J. M. Brumfitt and John C. Hall (London: Dent, 1983), pp. 73–4. In short, the inequality that allows domination is not natural – it requires a social structure to be effective.

> were by no means subject to very perilous dissensions. They maintained no kind of intercourse with one another, and were consequently strangers to vanity, deference, esteem, and contempt; they had not the least idea of 'mine' and 'thine', and no true conception of justice; they looked upon every violence to which they were subjected, rather as an injury that might easily be repaired than as a crime that ought to be punished; and they never thought of taking revenge, unless perhaps mechanically and on the spot, as a dog will sometimes bite the stone which is thrown at him. Their quarrels therefore would seldom have very bloody consequences.[19]

This vision of the state of nature is clearly very different from that painted by Hobbes. But this is not simply a disagreement over whether 'human nature' is good or evil, benign or belligerent, where Rousseau is simply more optimistic. Nor is Rousseau's state of nature an anthropological or archaeological attempt to show how Hobbes' account of this original condition was empirically wrong. Nor, despite the occasional expression of a certain wistful nostalgia for this conjectural original state, is it a call to give up society and return to the woods. For Rousseau makes it clear that in speaking of the state of nature he is not seeking to uncover an ideal condition to which humanity either can or should aspire to return. Instead, the state of nature serves as a philosophical device for determining the essential nature of humanity itself, performing the paradoxical role of a condition which we must try to conceive even though we are beyond it, and yet which our very being beyond allows us to conceive. As he puts it, 'For it is by no means a light undertaking to distinguish properly between what is original and what is artificial in the actual nature of man, or to form a true idea of a state which no longer exists, perhaps never did exist, and probably never will exist; and of which it is nevertheless necessary to have true ideas, in order to form a proper judgement of our present state.'[20]

Here the use of paradox, which is the very foundation of Rousseau's philosophy, is clearly exhibited. It is only from a position outside the state of nature that we can recognise what is important about it, as well as its desirable qualities, which have been almost completely lost. Equally importantly, by grasping the meaning of the state of nature we can grasp the dynamics that have yielded the contemporary situation, and how it might be moved beyond.[21] Contrary to the assertions of many in

[19] Rousseau, 'Discourse on the Origin of Inequality', p. 69.
[20] Rousseau, 'Discourse on the Origin of Inequality', p. 39.
[21] Equally importantly, for Rousseau, to abstract straightforwardly from a given present condition to what human beings are 'by nature' is to commit a basic logical error. First,

International Relations, the idea of the state of nature as an idyll from which we have fallen is not the point of departure for Rousseau. It is only in leaving the state of nature that we become truly human. The development of self-consciousness and the 'human quality of free agency' separates humanity from the 'brutes' and allows the development of morality,[22] and this development is synonymous with departure from the state of nature. It is, moreover, only in the context of the consciousness of self and others – that is, in society – that humanity's full potential may emerge. The state of society is inherently superior to the state of nature for it is only in society that true humanity may develop, whereas in the latter:

> each one of us would have remained isolated among the others, each one of us would have thought only of himself; our understanding would have been unable to develop; we should have lived without feeling anything and we should have died without having lived; all our happiness would have consisted in not being conscious of our wretchedness; there would have been neither kindness in our hearts nor morality in our actions and we should never have enjoyed that most delicious sentiment of the soul which is virtue.[23]

Rousseau makes it clear that such a state of nature – even if it existed – would itself be far from ideal, for in it people were not fully 'human' at all. Humanity, for Rousseau, is constituted in part by self-conscious relationality, and self-consciousness is itself inseparable from a consciousness *of* relationality. As he phrased it in his letter to Christophe de Beaumont: 'The man who has made no comparisons and has seen no relationships has no conscience . . . In such a state as this a man only knows himself, he does not see his own well-being to be identified with or contrary to that of anyone else; he neither hates anything or loves

it assumes that what human beings have become is equivalent to a static notion of what they are. Second, it makes conclusions dependent on what 'facts' are taken as salient, since abstracting from a situation of concord and cooperation would yield conclusions directly opposed to an analysis which began by looking at conflict – each postulate is a contingent fact generalised into a universal, and each is ultimately impossible to prove. Thus Rousseau argues that abstracting directly from historical experience is an inherently unreliable guide to what is essential.

[22] Rousseau, 'Discourse on the Origin of Inequality', p. 54. A useful and more sustained criticism of the conception of the state of nature as Rousseau's ideal condition – although one with which I am not in complete agreement – is A. O. Lovejoy's 'The Supposed Primitivism of Rousseau's Discourse on the Origin of Inequality', in A. O. Lovejoy, *Essays on the History of Ideas* (Baltimore: Johns Hopkins University Press, 1952).

[23] Rousseau, 'The General Society of the Human Race', in *The Social Contract and Discourses*, p. 157.

anything; but limited to no more than physical instinct, he is no one, he is an animal. This is what I have demonstrated in my Discourse on Inequality.'[24]

It is the capacity for separation and abstraction, for distinction, for the discernment of identities, differences, and relational comparisons that, for Rousseau, marks humanity's rational nature, its capacity for scientific and moral knowledge, and its potential for development and progress. The self is a concept only comprehensible to a being able to abstract itself from a purely unified consciousness, and to reflect upon itself as a self. This, for example, leads Rousseau to reject a basic premise of Hobbes' state of nature: the fear of death. The fear of death presumes a conception of the self in time, aware of its own mortality. This fear – Rousseau is very clear – is not the same as instinctual fear of harm or pain. 'Natural' creatures (animals, humanity in the state of nature) exhibit physical fear, but they have no fear of death *per se*: 'the only evils he fears are pain and hunger. I say pain, and not death: for no animal can know what it is to die; the knowledge of death and its terrors being one of the first acquisitions made by man in departing from an animal state.'[25] It is only a self-conscious creature (humanity outside the state of nature) that can conceive of its own mortality, fear its own death, and thus give rise to the dynamics Hobbes explores.

Similarly, scientific knowledge is only possible for beings capable of abstract and relational thought, and who possess language.[26] History is only possible for a creature with a concept of passage and continuity through time – a past, present, and future – rather than an eternal present. Society is only possible for a being capable of identifying itself in relation to (and with) others. Through the hypothesis of a state of nature in which this capacity was absent, Rousseau thus seeks to provide a grasp of the distinctiveness of humanity; and it is only this distinctive humanity that makes the generation of such an hypothesis possible. From the position of humanity, as free self-conscious beings, it is paradoxically possible to grasp the meaning of the state of nature, but from this position we can never return to it:

[24] Rousseau, in *The Indispensable Rousseau*, comp. John Hope Mason (New York: Quartet Books, 1979), p. 33. For a fuller exploration, see Tracy B. Strong, *Jean-Jacques Rousseau: The Politics of the Ordinary* (Thousand Oaks, Calif.: Sage, 1994), pp. 81–5; and especially the very subtle treatment of these themes in Todorov, *Imperfect Garden*, pp. 178–206 especially.
[25] Rousseau, 'Discourse on the Origin of Inequality', p. 55.
[26] Rousseau, 'Discourse on the Origin of Inequality', pp. 59–62, where Rousseau also provides a revealing analysis of how language and conceptual abstraction are implicated in distancing human beings from feeling and conscience.

> So the sweet voice of nature is no longer an infallible guide for us, nor is the independence we have derived from her a desirable state. Peace and innocence escaped us forever, even before we tasted their delights. Beyond the range of thought and feeling of brutish men of the earliest times, and no longer within the grasp of the 'enlightened' men of later periods, the happy life of the Golden Age could never really have existed for the human race. When men could have enjoyed it they were unaware of it; and when they could have understood it they had already lost it.[27]

The state of nature is thus necessary as a relational concept allowing human beings to understand what they are through a comparison to what they are not. It is not a situation wherein essentially unchanging beings existed in a time before society and government: it is a vision which allows us to understand what kind of beings humans must 'naturally' be (i.e., in substantial ways, *non*-natural beings) in order for it to have been possible for them to have become what they are. The development of the self takes place through its engagement with a world of externalities, both natural and human. It is via this interaction, these relations of Otherness, that the Rousseauian self develops.[28] This movement represents a shift away from nature to history or, more correctly, to human nature as historical. Through a relational process of encounter between the self, the material world, other selves, and its own temporal changes, the human subject develops historically.[29]

For Rousseau, the difficulty is that while this capacity and process literally makes humanity possible, and while the emergence from the state of nature into self-consciousness, free agency, and social relations provides the potential for the greatest possible good of mankind, it also provides the possibility for the greatest corruption and degradation. The source of this process paradoxically lies also in the relational structure of the self and self-consciousness. The capacity for reason that defines humanity is also the source of a new and profound *inhumanity* which is destructive in ways far beyond those operative in the state of nature.

The source of this degradation lies not outside the realm of reason, but within it; and reason – an essential aspect of the potential deliverance of humanity – becomes a key part of its degradation.[30] The problem, Rousseau argues, is that the relational process of self-consciousness

[27] Rousseau, 'The General Society of the Human Race', p. 156.
[28] See, for example, Rousseau, 'Discourse on the Origin of Inequality', pp. 76–7.
[29] Rousseau, 'Discourse on the Origin of Inequality', p. 81.
[30] 'It is reason that engenders *amour-propre*, and reflection that confirms it: it is reason which turns man's mind back upon itself, and divides him from everything that could

has taken on an invidious form where such comparisons have become wholly *negative*, a process which is both exemplified and intensified by the evolution of private property. The natural 'care for the self' (*amour de soi*), that all creatures have in terms of a concern with their needs and wellbeing, is overwhelmed in human history by an egoistic self-love (*amour propre*) which rather than providing a basis for mutuality embodies a negative and oppositional relationship between the self and others. Having moved from solitary individuality to collective living,

> Men began now to take the difference between objects into account and to make comparisons; they acquired ideas of beauty and merit, which soon gave rise to preference . . . Each one began to consider the rest, and to wish to be considered in turn; and thus a value came to be attached to public esteem . . . From these first distinctions arose on the one side vanity and contempt and on the other shame and envy . . . Thus, as every man punished the contempt shown him by others, in proportion to his opinion of himself, revenge became terrible, and men bloody and cruel. This is precisely the state reached by most of the savage nations known to us: and it is for want of having made a proper distinction in our ideas, and seen how very far they already are from the state of nature, that so many writers have hastily concluded that man is naturally cruel, and requires civil institutions to make him more mild; whereas nothing is more gentle than man in his primitive state, as he is placed by nature at an equal distance from the stupidity of the brutes and the fatal ingenuity of civilized man.[31]

The development of the self paradoxically means that its own sense of value risks becoming wholly dependent upon its contrast to others. Within this logic of self-consciousness, others become competitors rather than compatriots, objects whose value is determined only in relation to a self which is constantly compared to them, and at risk from them, in both a physical and a psychological sense. The process set in motion by the dynamics of *amour propre* is viciously circular: even the successful can never rest, can never be secure, since their status is always relative to the judgements and achievements of others, and these others never rest in their desire to prevail. The dynamics of self-identity and the conditions of individual life come to be defined by envy and disdain, fear and disgust. Humanity becomes governed by a desire for domination

disturb or afflict him. It is philosophy that isolates him, and bids him say, at the sight of the misfortunes of others: "Perish if you will, I am secure".' Rousseau, 'Discourse on the Origin of Inequality', p. 68.

[31] Rousseau, 'Discourse on the Origin of Inequality', pp. 81–2.

and the result is a perpetual insecurity in which 'Insatiable ambition, the thirst of raising their respective fortunes, not so much from real wants as from the desire to surpass others, inspired all men with a vile propensity to injure one another, and with a secret jealousy, which is the more dangerous, as it puts on the mask of benevolence, to carry its point with greater security.'[32]

Under the sway of *amour propre*, Rousseau argues, reason itself comes to be reduced to instrumentality and calculation. Other human beings, and the world in general, are reduced to the status of objects valued only in terms of their relative use and as comparative markers of the relative superiority or inferiority of the self. Reason becomes simply a process of the calculation and instrumental manipulation of these objects. Divorced from feeling and defined as pure instrumentality, reason becomes driven by egoistic drives beyond reason. Indeed in this development reason becomes doubly irrational: spurred by irrational drives of comparative self-worth and reduced solely to structures of objectivism and instrumentality, reason is reduced to a narrow complicity in the production of these dynamics, and is severely restricted in its capacity to reflect upon its own situation, treating it instead as natural, objective, and inescapable.

The natural sympathy or compassion which Rousseau views as an equally important part of human sensibility is overwhelmed by this process of objectification and calculation in the service of *amour propre*. As he puts it in one of his most striking formulations, a person who only reasons is a 'depraved animal'; that is, such a person is worse than an animal for while having gained self-consciousness and the capacity for sophisticated calculation, they have also taken on the negative characteristics of *amour propre*. In this process, individuals have lost the capacity for *pitié* – for sympathy and fellow-feeling – and have at the same time cast off the natural limits determined by the satisfaction of purely physical and material needs.[33] The relationship between their self-identity and the world of nature and other humans has become overwhelmingly negative, defined by envy and disparagement, and governed by dynamics of appropriation and domination in the service of a sense of self under constant threat from the very externalities through which it defines itself. Such a self is driven inexorably by a need to identify itself positively through superiority to what it is not, and since such

[32] Rousseau, 'Discourse on the Origin of Inequality', p. 87.
[33] For example, Rousseau, 'Discourse on the Origin of Inequality', pp. 68–9.

comparisons are always contingent (and since others are driven by similar dynamics) individuals live in a perpetual insecurity, in a combined condition of fear, avarice, and mendacity.

As a consequence of this evolution, humanity largely lost the potential for moral relationships and virtuous action. Their relations, in short, evolved to resemble the situation so graphically described by Hobbes' state of nature. The crucial difference, however, is that in Rousseau's view Hobbes mistakenly identified this situation with humanity's natural condition,[34] when it was only so in part, representing not a fixed human nature but a condition made possible – but not necessary – by the deeper 'nature' which is humanity's capacity for self-reflection, choice, and freedom. The development of self-consciousness, and with it freedom, has degenerated into pure egoistic individualism, objectification, and instrumentality; the human race became sociable, but on a basis which rendered social relations not the realm of freedom and morality but rather of power, slavery, and domination.[35] This, Rousseau holds, is the course of human history, and it is this logic and its development he seeks to sketch in the *Discourse on the Origin of Inequality*. In this context, human life now did resemble an 'Hobbesian' state of nature, and fleeing from it could appear as a paramount necessity. The state emerged from the miseries of this situation, as part of a process in which natural liberty was exchanged for order. To escape the horrors of a world which now did indeed resemble a war of each against all, individuals turned to government. This government, however, was not founded on a 'true' contract reflecting the natural moral freedom of all. Rather, for the misery of anarchic egoism it merely substituted an institution based on exactly the same principles.[36]

The modern state, Rousseau declares, is not the realm of freedom, security, and morality at all. On the contrary, based as it is on the very principles of *amour propre* which necessitated its creation, it is merely another, even more all-embracing, form of domination. A society built upon principles of *amour propre*, and a state which reduces individual

[34] Rousseau, 'Discourse on the Origin of Inequality', pp. 65–6. It is not at all clear, however, how much Rousseau appreciated the more complex sources of Hobbes' position.
[35] Rousseau, 'Discourse on the Origin of Inequality', pp. 86–7.
[36] 'The state is supposedly the restoration of the equality of nature and the termination of the state of war; but in reality it guarantees the perpetuation of inequality in civil society at the same time that it introduces a new form of inequality, political inequality . . .' Asher Horowitz, *Rousseau, Nature and History* (University of Toronto Press, 1987), p. 118. This theme will later be discussed in greater detail. For an interesting discussion of Rousseau's critique of 'civil society', see Part 3 of Lucio Colletti's *From Rousseau to Lenin*, trans. J. Merrington and J. White (New York: Monthly Review Press, 1972).

relations to bonds of authority and obedience in exchange for a degree of physical security, are for Rousseau two sides of a polity reduced to instrumentality, objectification, and wholly competitive relations. While supposedly instituted for the common good, and masquerading under the guise of right, it remains based on power and illusion:

> Such was, or may well have been, the origin of society and law, which bound new fetters on the poor, and gave new powers to the rich; which irretrievably destroyed natural liberty, eternally fixed the law of property and inequality, converted clever usurpation into inalienable right, and, for the advantage of a few ambitious individuals, subjected all mankind to perpetual labour, slavery and wretchedness.[37]

Rousseau in International Relations reconsidered

Placing Rousseau's understanding in International Relations within the context of his broader political thinking challenges fundamentally many of the uses to which his arguments have traditionally been put in International Relations. In particular, both Kenneth Waltz's influential use of the parable of the stag-hunt as a model for an international 'logic of anarchy', and the tradition of thought that portrays Rousseau's social contract as solving the problem of domestic order only at the cost of creating an insuperable international state of war, significantly distort his thinking and its significance.

Waltz's use of Rousseau's parable of the stag-hunt to convey the 'logic of anarchy' remains one of the most powerful defining metaphors in International Relations theory, and his claim that the logic of the stag-hunt is an important aspect of Rousseau's thinking possesses considerable insight. As Waltz clearly illustrates and documents, Rousseau possessed a sophisticated and detailed understanding of the 'security dilemma' faced by instrumentally rational actors in a condition of anarchy. In numerous passages throughout the *Discourse on the Origin of Inequality*, Rousseau goes to some length to stress the nature of this paradox and to illustrate its importance.[38] However, Waltz fails to grasp the significance of this conception within Rousseau's thought, and in so doing misrepresents its relationship to Rousseau's theory of international politics.

The main flaw in Waltz's position is that the situation which he portrays as representing the eternal determining feature of relations

[37] Rousseau, 'Discourse on the Origin of Inequality', p. 89.

[38] Rousseau, 'Discourse on the Origin of Inequality', pp. 89–90 and 158–59, for example.

between autonomous actors, Rousseau on the contrary portrays as an immature point in the development of humanity. The temporal location of the stag-hunt is in the early stages of the development of humanity where only 'gross ideas of mutual undertakings' based solely on 'present and apparent interests' existed, and where men were still 'perfect strangers to foresight, and were so far from troubling themselves about the distant future, that they hardly thought of the morrow'.[39] The parable which Waltz represents as exemplifying Rousseau's contribution to an understanding of the objective nature of international politics is representative, for Rousseau, of reason in the early stages of the corruption which would culminate in contemporary society. The parable illustrates the emergence of society, but on the bases of caprice and *amour propre* which form the guiding theme of the *Discourse*.

The stag-hunt thus represents a primitive form of rationality which Rousseau acknowledges, but which he argues is disastrously deficient and represents not the eternal form of reason dictated by the logic of the situation, but rather an immature and incomplete understanding requiring supersession. At the time of the stag-hunt, humanity's capacities are both too developed (beyond the relatively cooperative situation of early communal societies[40]) and too limited in terms of the needs of advanced social and economic coordination. The state certainly 'solves' this dilemma for Rousseau, but he does not leave the question at that point. Indeed, his political theory is directed toward an overcoming of this situation. Whether he succeeds in this endeavour is a question to which I shall turn shortly, but what cannot be held is that Rousseau *stops* at the point of the 'logic of anarchy'. To do so is to miss much of what is most important to him and significant in this contribution to political and international thought.

History, reason, and the Abbé's Project

It is in the context of his overarching critique of society that Rousseau's analysis of international politics must be seen. Both the 'Abstract' and the 'Judgement' clearly reflect this position, and when so read present a picture significantly at odds with that traditionally held within the

[39] Rousseau, 'Discourse on the Origin of Inequality', p. 78. Rousseau's analysis here thus points also to long-standing difficulties that rationalist analyses have had with the question of temporal horizons in explaining self-interested cooperation; to wit, just how long is the 'long run' in which cooperation is more beneficial than conflict?
[40] For an argument that these societies represented for Rousseau a form of Golden Age, see Gad Horowitz and Asher Horowitz, *Everywhere They Are in Chains* (Toronto: Macmillan, 1990).

discipline of International Relations. Rousseau's agreement as to the rationality and worthiness of St Pierre's project, and his subsequent complaint that in perceiving the obstacles to it its author 'reasoned like a child', do not reflect (as Hinsley, for example, would have it) a contradiction between Rousseau the 'moralist' and Rousseau the historian and 'Realist',[41] but rather a complex analysis of the politics, domestic and international, which he perceived as characterising his time. It is embedded in a deeper and more sophisticated set of claims about structures of politics and the self, and an understanding of the state of nature not as providing a determining account of human nature and society, but as providing the foundation for an understanding of humanity as 'second nature' – as beyond purely natural determination.

The impact of this broader position finds clear expression in Rousseau's 'Judgement' on St Pierre's proposal for perpetual peace. The first issue here involves Rousseau's assault on what he regards as St Pierre's naïve conception of the modern state. As we have seen, St Pierre viewed the modern state as something which creates 'internal' freedom only at the expense of 'external' conflict. Rousseau explicitly denies this argument. For him the paradox which St Pierre locates between domestic and international politics is insufficient: this paradox also exists at the level of the state itself. Here Rousseau's critique of St Pierre's position almost exactly mirrors that sketched in the *Discourse on the Origin of Inequality*, and which he also levelled in a long and acrimonious dispute against the Encyclopaedists on the nature of modernity.[42] Like the Encyclopaedists, St Pierre failed to grasp the essential nature of both the state and society of his time. As a consequence, Rousseau claims, St Pierre failed to realise that the entity to which he appealed in order to establish his Confederacy would ensure its impossibility. But this was due not to the very division of humanity into citizens of particularistic states, but rather to the nature of that particularistic division itself.

In seeking to base arguments in favour of the Confederation either on the 'glory' (as St Pierre did) or the 'real' interests (as Rousseau himself proposed) of monarchs, it is implicitly assumed that the purpose of the state is the securing of the good life for all its citizens. The extension of this condition to the international level would thus seem the next logical development and desire. The difficulty, as we have seen, is that for Rousseau this is not the nature of the modern state at all. The clearest

[41] Hinsley, *Power and the Pursuit of Peace*, pp. 55–61.

[42] For a summary of this debate see Ernst Cassirer, *The Philosophy of the Enlightenment* (Princeton University Press, 1968), p. 270.

expression of this theme emerges in his analyses of monarchies. Monarchical government, he declares, is merely another form of domination. The interest of the masters is directed solely toward increasing their own power and has little or nothing to do with the interests of the people, the latter being little better than slaves:

> The whole life of Kings, or of those on whom they shuffle off their duties, is devoted solely to two objects: to extend their rule beyond their frontiers and to make it more absolute within them. Any other purpose they may have is either subservient to one of these aims, or merely a pretext for attaining them. Such pretexts are 'the good of the community', 'the happiness of their subjects', or 'the glory of the Nation': phrases forever banished from the council chamber, and employed so clumsily in proclamations that they are always taken as warnings of coming misery and that the people groans with apprehension when its masters speak to it of their 'fatherly solicitude'.[43]

This argument is pursued at greater length in *The Social Contract*. Here Rousseau contends that it is always the first interest of kings 'that the people should be weak, wretched, and unable to resist them',[44] a phenomenon that springs from the very nature of monarchical government; for, as he puts it: 'To see such a government as it is in itself, we must consider it as it is under princes who are incompetent or wicked: for either they will come to the throne wicked or incompetent, or the throne will make them so.'[45] It is instructive to remember in this context, moreover, that Rousseau regarded Machiavelli not as the high priest of realpolitik, but rather as the most profound critic of monarchy,[46] and that Rousseau asks us to remember that it is not he who argues against St Pierre, but rather the 'court sophist, who would rather have a large territory with a few subjects, poor and submissive, than that unshaken rule over the hearts of a happy and prosperous people, which is the reward of a prince who observes justice and obeys the laws'.[47]

The corrupted condition of both the state and society, and the rule of monarchs and sophists which is intimately related to that corruption, are the reasons behind the failure of St Pierre's project, not the nature of the proposal itself. As Rousseau asks with bitter sarcasm: 'And the world still persists in asking why, if such a scheme is practicable, these

43 Rousseau, 'Judgement', p. 158.
44 Rousseau, *Social Contract*, p. 221. This theme is repeated in almost identical form in *The Government of Poland*, ed. W. Kendall (New York: Bobbs-Merrill, 1972), pp. 48 and 52.
45 Rousseau, *Social Contract*, p. 225. 46 Rousseau, *Social Contract*, p. 221.
47 Rousseau, 'Judgement', p. 160.

men have not adopted it. Is it not obvious that there is nothing impracticable about it except its adoption by these men? What will they do to oppose it? They will do what they have always done: they will turn it to ridicule.'[48] The governments of Europe, Rousseau emphatically declares, are based not on right and law but on power and domination. This being the case, he asks, how is it possible to expect agreement between Sovereigns, based on a recognition of mutual rights and interests, when these same Sovereigns would not even accept such principles within their own domains? 'I ask whether there is in the whole world a single sovereign who, finding himself thus bridled for ever in his most cherished designs, would endure without indignation the very thought of seeing himself forced to be just not only with foreigners but even with his own subjects.'[49]

Seen as part of his general critique of monarchical government, Rousseau's objections to the Abbé's plans are fairly obvious. But Rousseau's critique involves considerably more than an assault upon monarchical government: it extends to include all forms of government and society based purely on *amour propre* and instrumental rationality.[50] The Abbé's project, no matter how reasonable, would never be adopted by states in which avarice, *amour propre* and caprice are the motivating principles, and in which the foundation of government is nothing but these principles backed by pure power and domination. Seen within this broader argument, Rousseau's critique of St Pierre emerges not as an analysis of the eternal nature of international politics, but as a philosophically and sociologically informed assessment of the obstacles which he saw to the enactment of the rational argument set forth in the *Project*. In Rousseau's opinion, St Pierre 'judged like a child' *not* in the reasonableness of his plan, but rather in his evaluation of the present reality.

In this light, consider again St Pierre's framing of the problem (or at least Rousseau's formulation of it). In St Pierre's characteristically Enlightenment vision, the problem lies in the foundation of political

[48] Rousseau, 'Judgement', p. 161. Both Waltz (*Man, the State and War*, p. 181) and, especially, Hinsley miss the essential thrust of these arguments and thus transform Rousseau into a type of structuralist in their own image.
[49] Rousseau, 'Judgement', p. 159.
[50] Hinsley, *Power and the Pursuit of Peace*, pp. 49–52, is therefore correct in contending that Rousseau's analysis is not simply a critique of monarchy, but he fails to realise that Rousseau's critique is directed at all forms of government based on such principles. It is also a much broader critique of the corruption which Rousseau sees as characterising modern societies and the governments which preside over them.

orders in passion, not reason. To repeat Rousseau's framing of the issue:

> If the social order were really, as is pretended, the work *not of passion but of reason*, should we have been so slow to see that in shaping it either too much or too little has been done for our happiness? That, each one of us being in the civil state as regards our fellow citizens, but in the state of nature as regards the rest of the world, we have taken precautions against private wars only to kindle national wars a thousand times more terrible? And that, in joining a particular group of men, we have really declared ourselves the enemies of the whole race?[51]

Rousseau's fundamental disagreement with this position lies not in its assessment of the political consequences of this division, but in the assessment of its causes. St Pierre's claim that the state of war reflects the dominance of passion and not of reason is at best partial and at worst badly misleading. To blame the situation on the dominance of passion, and to seek salvation in the rule of Reason is to grievously misunderstand the nature of modern politics and society. For Rousseau, the social order St Pierre criticises is the *outcome* of the evolution and domination of specific forms (and deformations) of reason and passion, forms in which both take on mutually related and destructive logics of *amour propre*. Reason has been reduced almost wholly to instrumentality and objectification, while passion has been reduced mainly to fear, egoism, vanity, envy, and disdain. Reason as pure instrumentality and feeling as pure irrationality are two sides of the same coin, united within *amour propre*. To contrast reason and passion (as does St Pierre) is to misunderstand how in these distorted forms they are actually related to each other within modern knowledge and subjectivity. It is also to operate within a set of choices that can only replicate unsatisfactory and exclusive alternatives which consistently turn in upon each other. Only through a reconstruction of the relationship between reason and passion – an understanding of the conditions under which they have become paradoxically opposed and united, and an effort to bring them back into positive relation – can an adequate understanding of the sources of modern misery and potential alternatives to it be developed. The overarching goal of Rousseau's thinking is to effect such a reconciliation.[52]

[51] Rousseau, 'Abstract', p. 132; emphasis added.

[52] On the complex question of whether Rousseau seeks absolute transparency in human life, see Jean Starobinski, *Jean-Jacques Rousseau: Transparency and Obstruction*, trans, Arthur Goldhammer (University of Chicago Press, 1988).

Just as an emphasis on Rousseau's debates with the Philosophes and the Encyclopaedists over the nature of reason and passion allows a fuller understanding of his criticisms of St Pierre, so a similar emphasis may be used to address interpretations which present Rousseau as a quintessential philosopher of despair. Among the debates which raged in the eighteenth century one of the most important and often vitriolic concerned the validity of the philosophy of optimism in which figures such as Leibniz and Pope declared that the present was 'the best of all possible worlds', and the response, led by Voltaire, that launched a sustained attack upon this complacent view, and which stressed the miseries of the present and the bankruptcy of such an optimistic philosophy.

Rousseau's relationship to this debate was two-sided. On the one hand he adopted, as we have seen, the unflinchingly realistic view of the world which stressed the need to expose the horrors of society for what they were. In this he shared many of the concerns and analyses of his Encyclopaedist contemporaries. But Rousseau refused to accept the despairing conclusions which he viewed as the direct outcome of such a stance. In so doing he again set himself in conflict with the Philosophes, a conflict exemplified in his response to Voltaire's poem on the Lisbon earthquake:

> The optimism you consider so horrible consoles me in the very misery you set forth as unbearable. Pope's poem assuages my pains and fills me with patience; yours increases my agony and forces me to protest against Providence; it takes all comfort from me and drives me to despair. In this strange contrast between what you prove and what I feel, I beg you to relieve my anxiety and to tell me where the deception lies, whether on the side of feeling or of reason.[53]

For Rousseau, as we have seen, the appeal to reason alone – so characteristic of the Philosophes – was inadequate. The abstract reason of the Enlightenment, for all its achievements, possessed the capacity for a denial of humanity in both its imposition of a determinism that precluded free agency, and through its propagation of a formalism, abstraction, and objectification that denied *pitié* and common-feeling. If reason were reduced to an identification with natural science, then as a realm of natural determinism it left little or no room for human agency and even less for optimism. As pure objectivism and instrumentality, moreover,

[53] Quoted in Ernst Cassirer, *Rousseau, Kant, Goethe: Two Essays* (Princeton University Press, 1945), p. 37.

reason was a central part of the problem; it could scarcely be the sole foundation of a solution.

In the midst of the age of reason, Rousseau stands as a theorist of the limits of Enlightenment reason and its rigid contrast with passion. He argues both for an expansion of the realm of reason beyond objectivism and determinism, and for breaking down the strict divide between reason and feeling which had become one of the most important delimiting oppositions of modern politics. His graphic and 'realistic' portrayal of the social and political dynamics which surround him, exemplified in his critical analysis of St Pierre's *Project*, reflects a solid grasp of the issues of power, interest, and domination which many Realists claim characterise international politics. But Rousseau's claim to a more profound form of Realism and his transcendence of realpolitik lie precisely in his refusal to reify or naturalise this condition and thus fall into the trap of despair so often (and too easily) attributed to him. In his attempt to capture the historicity of this situation, Rousseau seeks to demonstrate how an explanation of its emergence and dynamics can be reconciled with the possibility of its overcoming. The ideal and the real are not severed: Rousseau seeks to bring them together in a mutual relationship of comprehension and transformation.

History, reason, progress

Prevailing Realist interpretations of Rousseau effectively construct his thought within a dualism between the 'Golden Age' of the state of nature to which there is no return and the 'frightening' world of the present from which there is no escape, a position exemplified in Hinsley's claim that 'the *Discours sur l'Inégalité*, with its theory of individual rights . . . could only mean the advocacy of a return to the state of nature'.[54] As we have seen, Rousseau most emphatically does not advocate a return to the state of nature, feeling that to be both impossible and undesirable. But this does not mean that he succumbs to a simple dualism which would place him within the fatalistic despair of realpolitik. The clearest expression of his rejection of such an interpretation of his ideas is to be found in the famous 'footnote I' to the second *Discourse* where he writes: 'What then is to be done? Must societies be totally abolished? Must "meum" and "tuum" be annihilated and must we return again to the forest to live among bears? This is a deduction in

[54] Hinsley, *Power and the Pursuit of Peace*, p. 53.

the manner of my adversaries, which I would as soon anticipate as let them have the shame of drawing.'[55]

There is no return to the state of nature, but neither are we abandoned to the horrors of the present. Rather than falling into the fatalism of which he is often accused, Rousseau seeks to understand the development of the present in order to grasp both the source of its errors and the principles of progress. To do this, he returns to the essence of the problematic: freedom must be expressed not in the form of a self-contradictory *amour propre*, but rather on moral principles founded on this freedom itself. Freedom conceived purely upon the principle of egoistic individualism and self-interest is ultimately self-defeating. It results not in freedom and security, but in anarchy, domination, or slavery. True freedom requires the recognition of the absolute moral rights of others as human beings, and the embodiment of these rights through practical action.

This theme is most clearly developed in *The Social Contract*, where Rousseau's emphasis is on the absolute principles of political legitimacy and obligation. The essence of humanity lies in a non-natural realm of self-determination, and in the relational recognition of self and other on this basis. In analysis that bears many important resemblances to that of Kant,[56] Rousseau argues that the recognition of one's own rights and freedom is only non-contradictory when extended to all. Might can never make right.[57] The true expression of freedom is not the capricious egoism of *amour propre*, but the following of laws which all people make for themselves on universal grounds. As he famously put it: 'The problem is to find a form of association which will defend and protect with the whole common force the person and goods of each associate, and in which each, while uniting himself with all, may still obey himself alone and remain as free as before. This is the fundamental problem of which the social contract provides the solution.'[58]

The basis of legitimate political obligation lies in a mutual recognition of the rights of both self and others. For Rousseau, as for Kant, it is humanity's fundamental freedom which provides the ultimate ground

[55] Rousseau, 'Discourse on the Origin of Inequality,' p. 112. Cf. also the statement from *Emile*: 'When I want to train a natural man, I do not want to make him a savage and to send him back to the woods.' Quoted in Asher Horowitz, *Rousseau, Nature and History*, p. 217.

[56] The 'Kantian' reading of Rousseau is most strongly expressed by Cassirer. For an excellent analysis that I will return to and draw upon in a moment, see Rapaczynski, *Nature and Politics*. The tendency in International Relations to oppose Rousseau and Kant is highly misleading, with Kant's thinking bearing the clear marks of Rousseau's ideas.

[57] Rousseau, *Social Contract*, p. 168.

[58] Rousseau, *Social Contract*, p. 174.

of moral and political judgement.[59] The 'contract' which is founded on this principle is particular in form: it is embodied within a specific state. But its principle is universal, and thus applies not only to citizens but to all humanity. This moral right and obligation is not, as both Hoffmann[60] and Waltz[61] argue, a purely 'inner' form of obligation internally exclusive to the particular state. Rather, its form is inner, but its principle is universal.[62]

This concept of political right has profound implications when extended to the interpretation of Rousseau's philosophy of International Relations. Not only can an individual citizen not violate the right of another without contradicting the grounds of his own right, but no true Sovereign – the very embodiment of the general will – may do so either. Thus no state constituted on the principles of the general will can legitimately refuse the recognition of the rights of another Sovereign without in turn becoming self-contradictory: 'the sovereign authority is one and simple and cannot be divided without being destroyed. *In the second place, one town cannot, any more than one nation, legitimately be made subject to another*, because the essence of the body politic lies in the reconciliation of obedience and liberty, and the words subject and Sovereign are identical correlatives the idea of which meets in the single word citizen.'[63]

This link between Rousseau's analysis in *The Social Contract* and his theory of international politics is even more clearly illustrated in *The Government of Poland*. Once again the contradiction inherent in the logic of pure power which underlies realpolitik is incisively exposed as both spurious and ultimately self-defeating; and once again Rousseau argues that it must be transcended: 'The most inviolable of all the laws of nature is the law of the strongest; no legislation, no constitution can exempt anyone from that law. When, therefore, you seek the means of making yourself secure against invasion by a neighbor stronger than you, you are seeking something that does not exist; and were you ever to try your hand at conquests, or at developing offensive power, you would

[59] 'The only legitimate basis of the modern state that Rousseau is discussing in *The Social Contract* is the will, the absolutely free will . . . Society is therefore to be established by convention and does not issue any longer from nature.' Asher Horowitz, *Rousseau, Nature, and History*, p. 170. See also the discussion in Ernst Cassirer, *The Question of Jean-Jacques Rousseau*, trans. and ed. Peter Gay (Bloomington: Indiana University Press, 1963), pp. 63–6.
[60] Hoffmann, *The State of War*, p. 73. [61] Waltz, *Man, the State and War*, pp. 180–2.
[62] An excellent exploration of the importance of this idea, although with only passing reference to Rousseau, can be found in Andrew Linklater, *Men and Citizens in the Theory of International Relations* (London: Macmillan, 1982).
[63] Rousseau, *Social Contract*, p. 237; emphasis added.

be committing an even greater folly. Offensive power is incompatible with your form of government. Those who will freedom must not will conquest as well.'[64]

The same reasoning characterizes Rousseau's attitude toward alliances and the possibilities of confederation. The choice is not between universality and anarchy (world government or the state of war), but confederation is neither an automatic solution nor an *a priori* impossibility. International politics depends upon both the particular historical relationships between states and the nature of these states and citizens themselves. None of these categories can be rendered conceptually distinct or historically static; each is crucial to understanding any specific situation and the political judgements to be made in those situations. In his advice on the government of Poland, for example, Rousseau notes that even a peaceful country must be wary of the states that surround it and, in an extension of the argument developed earlier, warns against the corrupt character of the states of Europe. This does not, however, commit him to a 'third image' of eternal structural anarchy, but rather sets up the particular political and historical problematic within which an international order may and, Rousseau might argue, must be created. The law of nature – the rule of the strongest – must be superseded by the law of reason and the principles of political right. To refuse to do so is to be condemned to perpetual insecurity, strife, and degradation. To remain within the logic of realpolitik, he asserts with bitter sarcasm, is to remain petulant children:

> you will be tied to other peoples by treaties; and you will have the honor of being dragged into every war in Europe. Nor is that all: should fortune damn you with her bounties, you will be able to recover your former possessions, perhaps even to conquer some new ones; and then – like Pyrrhuss, like the Russians, which is to say like little children – you will be able to say: 'When the world is mine, I am going to eat lots and lots of candy'.[65]

Rousseau thus generates a conception of politics which provides the grounds for a critical analysis of both the modern state and the modern

[64] Rousseau, *Government of Poland*, p. 80. Again, this illustrates how a politics built upon humanity's 'second nature' must reflect both an understanding of the laws of nature in a natural scientific sense, and the use of this capacity as a means of limiting the application of such knowledge to the sphere of human and political relations. Natural science is not for Rousseau wholly opposed to a non-deterministic politics – like Kant, he holds that the very possibility of natural science as a capacity of human understanding demonstrates its usefulness in the construction of a politics beyond natural determination.
[65] Rousseau, *Government of Poland*, pp. 67–8.

states-system. History becomes not the story of inevitable despair, but of the development of humanity's capacity for rational freedom. It has amply illustrated (again a theme which Kant was later to make much more explicit) that a truly human existence can only be attained through the rational exercise of freedom, a freedom which has morality as its self-grounding category. In this way history does exhibit a form of 'necessity': it illustrates the contradictory and ultimately self-defeating nature of social and political action based solely on egoistic *amour propre* and the tenets of realpolitik. One aspect of Rousseau's Realism lies not simply in his recognition of the problem, but also in his clear exposition of the consequences of maintaining such a position.

Rousseau identifies realpolitik as being not a timeless part of nature, which is therefore real in the objective sense of a natural science, but rather as being 'second nature' – constructed, self-fulfilling action. Rather than providing an analysis which pre-empts discussion and renders the realm of international politics a set of particular variations on an eternally tragic theme, Rousseau's analysis focuses on the constraining effects of historical structures and relationships well beyond a deterministic 'logic of anarchy'. Rather than offering an eternal structural analysis of the 'international system', he critically focuses attention on the nature of particular states and political communities, and the relationships between them. Rousseau does not deny the problems of power, conflict, and insecurity which are the mainstays of realpolitik. But he sees these as problems of humanity's own creation which, as such, are in principle open to being overcome. Rather than providing the ultimate grounds of the division between 'inside' and 'outside', community and anarchy, which has structured and continues to structure much of the debate in International Relations, Rousseau fundamentally challenges it. By refusing to succumb to the dualisms which traditional interpreters of his writings on international politics have imparted to him, Rousseau also refuses to reify the categories of realpolitik into eternal verities. We are the cause of our own miseries and, as he wryly notes, 'it has cost us not a little trouble to make ourselves as miserable as we are'.[66]

Rousseau and the politics of community

As noted at the beginning of this chapter, the contrast between Rousseau and Kant stands as one of the structuring conceptual distinctions within

[66] 'Discourse on the Origin of Inequality', p. 106.

International Relations theory. It should by now be apparent that the conventional presentation of these issues tends yet again to be profoundly misleading. Far from being diametrically opposed, Rousseau and Kant share fundamental beliefs. Indeed, Rousseau exercised a very significant influence on Kant's thinking and, as Ernst Cassirer has argued at length, Rousseau's formulation of the principles and politics of abstract and universal right can be read as a crucial inspiration for a position later formalised by Kant.[67]

Yet while recognising the relationship between Rousseau and Kant provides a corrective against their standard opposition in International Relations theory, it also offers a means of drawing out significant further aspects of Rousseau's thinking about international politics, particularly his continuing emphasis on the centrality of the state. Kant's liberalism is based upon the principle of individual autonomy and a formal, rational structure of right.[68] Like Kant, Rousseau too rejects the idea that a politics of right, either domestic or international, can be founded solely upon self-interest. However, he also believes that abstract right and abstract reason cannot alone provide foundations for political order, for two important reasons. First, he argues that even if all agreed on the primacy of universal right in politics, this would not in itself solve the problem of determining the content of this right. Second, Rousseau confronts the problem of making a politics of right attractive – of how a commitment to principles of right can prevail over the attractions of self-interest, and how individuals can be mobilised to feel obligation toward those principles.

Like Hobbes, Rousseau recognises that political philosophy requires an affective dimension if it is to be politically effective: the embodiment of principle in practice is essential, and philosophical cogency alone is scarcely likely to carry the day.[69] His resolution to this problem lies in his vision of the role of *institutions* of both politics and culture, and in an

[67] See, particularly, Cassirer, *The Question of Jean-Jacques Rousseau*, and *Rousseau, Kant, Goethe: Two Essays*. This claim has itself, however, been a source of considerable subsequent criticism.

[68] Though it can be argued that Kant's thinking is more complex. I have pursued some of these issues in 'Reason and Realpolitik: Kant's "Critique of International Politics"', *Canadian Journal of Political Science*, 25:1 (1992), and 'The Discipline of the Democratic Peace: Kant, Liberalism and the Social Construction of Security Communities', *European Journal of International Relations*, 7:4 (2001).

[69] For a thoughtful and insightful struggle with a number of analogous questions concerning the politics of identity and affective political power, see the concluding chapter of Iver B. Neumann, *The Uses of the Other: The 'East' in European Identity Formation* (Minneapolis: University of Minnesota Press, 1999).

attempt to reunite reason and feeling in order to provide both substantive content and affective power for a politics of right.[70] For Rousseau, 'civil society' – a realm dominated either by *amour propre* or particularistic affective bonds of family, community, or creed – cannot alone provide these foundations. These bonds, by their very nature, lack the universality required by his principle of political right. Such a bond can, however, be provided through the institutions of political right expressed in the state. This is particularly true of the institutions of law and the principle of the Rule of Law. For Rousseau, law is not simply a set of rules. The coming together of individuals or their representatives for the determination of laws when there are no natural rules is both an expression and affirmation of political community. This aspect of Rousseau's thinking has been captured by Rapaczynski, whose treatment is worth quoting at length. As he puts it:

> In coming together agents will probably differ on most issues concerning the policies that they should follow. But what brings them together is the very moral insufficiency of their individual existence. The community itself is the main value of their moral system, so that as long as the expression of their will takes the form of a law that unites them by providing a common standard of behavior, the exact content of the law is of secondary importance. Clearly, insofar as pragmatic considerations must be taken into consideration, the laws of a given community represent a certain particular set of interests, although they are collective and not individual interests. But when a given standard of behavior is made actually binding on all the citizens without exception, and not (as in the case of individual morality) only potentially applicable to other men, the quality implied in the categorical imperative becomes *more than a purely formal requirement*: it becomes a real political bond and an object of emotional attachment to be preserved for its own sake.[71]

The Social Contract seeks to provide a structure and a principle for the substantive determination of values within a flexible but legitimate and *legitimating* structure. Equally importantly, however, as a participatory realm of collective action and determination of values, the political community and its institutions will be perceived as a *value in itself*, that is, it will be *affectively effective* and will generate a commitment from citizens

[70] It is important to note, however, that for Rousseau this recovery of an affective dimension is not narrowly strategic. It also represents a recovery of conscience, compassion, and feeling that has been diminished in the evolution of society.
[71] Rapaczynski, *Nature and Politics*, pp. 259–60.

toward the institutions of the state and, through these institutions, to each other.[72] Democratic institutions – concretely existing texts, rituals, and participatory structures – practically constitute and symbolically represent the principles of the polity. A legislature, for Rousseau, is not just a building or a decision-making structure; if correctly constituted politically, institutions themselves become the expression of commonality – representations of right capable of competing affectively with the egoism, instrumentality, and objectification of *amour propre*. His commitment to the state is not an assumption; it arises from a sophisticated philosophical and sociological attempt to construct an ethical and political order at both the domestic and international levels.

Rousseau's desire for strong political unity within the state emerges from his incisive appreciation of the limits of abstract principles of right to deliver politically upon their promise. His vision of a small, participatory polity is not driven (certainly not wholly) by a romantic admiration for the Greek polis. It is intimately concerned with the construction of a moral polity, a polity that can provide content and meaning for its citizens, a common sense of being citizens with moral bonds, and which can commit them to defend these bonds against those who threaten the community within and without. This commitment to particularity – to individual, autonomous communities, political institutions, and procedures of the General Will – does not derive from a rejection of universality. It is an attempt to reconcile principles of universal right with political effect, to give abstract right political power.

For Rousseau, the state is not just the locus of authoritative decision. State institutions built on universal principles (the rights of all citizens) can, precisely *because* they represent all citizens, become objects of attachment for those citizens. Democratic sovereignty is necessarily particular in order to solve the problems of concrete content and affective attachment in a politics of right. But it is not wholly exclusionary or oppositional, and its citizens do not, for Rousseau, of necessity

[72] In Rapaczynski's incisive formulation: 'The main thrust of Rousseau's identification of politics and morality lies . . . in his view that the insufficiencies of pure reason, insofar as either its emotional strength or its inability to determine unambiguously a set of substantive moral commands is concerned, are remedied by putting an individual's actions in the context of a community of agents. It is in this light that Rousseau's theory of the general will should be understood . . . '. Rapaczynski, *Nature and Politics*, pp. 250–1. As Asher Horowitz has pointed out, Rousseau's relationship to constitutionalism is complex, since many forms of liberal constitutions presuppose a transcendent foundation which Rousseau rejects. These themes are explored with great insight in his *Rousseau, Nature and History*.

come into conflict with other polities. Although the universal principle of right is always expressed – for both philosophical-political and sociological reasons – through particular institutions, Rousseau's thinking does not sever 'inside' and 'outside' in the name of either a sovereign right of ultimate decision, or a culturally exclusive structure of emotional attachment to a particular community. On the contrary, he seeks to build a theory of political right, legitimacy, institutional structure, and political culture that links the domestic and the international within a politics of right. Indeed, Rousseau has more in common with some recent analyses concerning the international dimensions of modern citizenship,[73] criticisms of the dominance of instrumental rationality in modern politics,[74] assessments of the relational dynamics of identity construction, or with attempts to explain the social construction of the democratic peace,[75] than he does with structural theories of anarchy.

Rousseau's thinking contains numerous tensions, and I am in no way suggesting that he resolves satisfactorily the challenges he raises. His attempt to reconcile the universal and the particular, the abstract and the affective, through his theory of state sovereignty has long been subject to criticism. There is little doubt, as critics as early as Benjamin Constant pointed out, that Rousseau pays far too little attention to the ways that the principle of right could become transformed into a logic of domination domestically and a crusading universalism internationally, and that he fails to address satisfactorily the possibility that the inspiring Legislator who would lead the way to a virtuous polity could be transformed into an anti-democratic (and internationally aggressive) political demagogue.[76] Whatever the truth of these charges – and they raise issues too broad to engage in this context – they emerge in the context of his attempt to construct a viable democratic politics: a state and political culture that can support such a politics domestically and make it a principle of state action and international order. This vision of international politics is considerably different, and raises issues markedly more complex,

[73] See, particularly, Andrew Linklater, *The Transformation of Political Community* (Cambridge: Polity Press, 1998) and David Held, *Democracy and the Global Order* (Cambridge: Polity Press, 1995).
[74] For example, many of the essays in *Critical Theory and World Politics*, edited by Richard Wyn Jones (Boulder, Colo.: Lynne Rienner, 2001).
[75] Thomas Risse-Kappen, 'Democratic Peace, Warlike Democracies?: A Social Constructivist Approach to the Democratic Peace', *European Journal of International Relations*, 1:4 (1995).
[76] For a thoughtful discussion see Todorov, *Imperfect Garden*, pp. 73–4.

than Rousseau's conventional place as a theorist of anarchy allows. He refuses to adopt the rigid distinctions of man, the state, and the system (the logical demarcation of first, second, and third 'images') which allow the construction of a timelessly determining international system and leave a misleadingly narrow vision of political possibilities and challenges of modern politics. A Realism that claims his legacy must also seek to confront these challenges.

3 Hans Morgenthau and the historical construction of Realism

> The experience of the 1960s has dispelled the illusion that truth can show power the way in direct confrontation. But historical experience reassures us that truth can indeed make people 'see a lot of things in a new light'. And when people see things in a new light, they might act in a new way.[1]
>
> Hans Morgenthau

Few figures are as closely associated with Realism as Hans Morgenthau. Indeed no assessment of the development of International Relations can overlook the importance of Morgenthau in the intellectual evolution of the field, and his role in placing Realism at the centre of that evolution. Yet despite this centrality, it is difficult to escape the impression that for several decades Morgenthau was more often cited than read, and that in the process he has been reduced by both his supporters and his critics primarily to an implacable opponent of liberalism and an advocate of power politics.[2] In recent years, however, Morgenthau's thinking has become the source of renewed interest, as a series of analyses have sought to recover the depth and complexity of his thinking by locating it within the complex philosophical and political debates and traditions through which it emerged. Focusing in particular on Morgenthau's relationship to the complex legacy of Max Weber, his location within the politics of Weimar Germany, and particularly on his intellectual engagement with the controversial figure of Carl Schmitt, an understanding of Morgenthau's political Realism is now taking shape

[1] Hans J. Morgenthau, *Truth and Power: Essays of a Decade* (New York; Praeger, 1970), preface.

[2] Notable exceptions include Joel Rosenthal, *Righteous Realists: Political Realism, Responsible Power, and American Culture in the Nuclear Age* (Baton Rouge: Louisiana State University Press, 1991), and Greg Russell, *Hans Morgenthau and the Ethics of American Statecraft* (Baton Rouge: Louisiana State University Press, 1990). See also Robert Jervis, 'Hans Morgenthau, Realism, and the Scientific Study of International Politics', *Social Research*, 61:4 (1994).

that bears little resemblance to the conventional portraits that continue to dominate International Relations.[3]

This chapter seeks to build upon and further contribute to this reappraisal. The argument proceeds in three parts. I begin by locating Morgenthau's critique of liberalism, and his fundamental hostility toward rationalism and a science of politics, within the context of his engagement with the arguments of Schmitt and other Weimar critics of liberalism over the nature of politics in modernity, the fate of liberal democracy in Weimar Germany, and the catastrophic consequences (both domestically and internationally) of the rise of fascism. That Morgenthau was a severe critic of liberalism is certainly true; however, to see him simply as an opponent of liberalism is to underestimate the complexity of his engagement with the liberal tradition. Far from constituting an outright rejection of liberalism, Morgenthau seeks an understanding of politics able to provide adequate support for a liberal political order.[4]

In the second part of the chapter, I argue that these concerns lead him to a deep engagement with the role of ideas in politics, with the social construction of action, and, in particular, with an assessment of the relationship between politics, power, and violence. While Morgenthau is often accused of initiating a tradition that marginalises the role of social constructions and 'ideas' in the study of world politics,[5] and routinely criticised for having an implausibly narrow understanding of power, interest, and politics, the apparent simplicity of these concepts in his

[3] See, for example, Tarak Barkawi, 'Strategy as a Vocation: Weber, Morgenthau and Modern Strategic Studies', *Review of International Studies*, 24:2 (1998); Christophe Frei, *Hans Morgenthau: An Intellectual Biography* (Baton Rouge: Louisiana State University Press, 2001); Jef Huysmans, 'The Question of the Limit: Desecuritization and the Aesthetics of Horror in Political Realism', *Millennium: Journal of International Studies*, 27:3 (1998); Koskenniemi, *The Gentle Civilizer of Nations*, pp. 413–509; John M. McCormick, *Carl Schmitt's Critique of Liberalism: Against Politics as Technology* (Cambridge University Press, 1997); A. J. H. Murray, 'The Moral Politics of Hans Morgenthau', *Review of Politics*, 58:1 (1996); Ulrik Enemark Petersen, 'Breathing Nietzsche's Air: New Reflections on Morgenthau's Concepts of Power and Human Nature', *Alternatives*, 24 (1999); and William Scheuerman, 'Another Hidden Dialogue: Hans Morgenthau and Carl Schmitt', chapter 10 of his *Carl Schmitt: The End of Law* (New York: Rowan and Littlefield, 1999). I have benefited greatly from these diverse re-engagements, though I will not deal with all their positions in detail.

[4] In concentrating on Morgenthau's more positive relationship to liberalism, this treatment largely leaves aside the important critique of liberal universalism that he shares with Schmitt. For an excellent discussion see Koskenniemi, *Gentle Civilizer of Nations*, pp. 426–34 especially.

[5] Daniel Philpott, *Revolutions in Sovereignty: How Ideas Shaped Modern International Relations* (Princeton University Press, 2001), pp. 62–3.

thinking is deeply misleading. Emerging from an engagement with Schmitt's 'concept of the political', Morgenthau in fact develops a subtle and powerfully critical understanding of the relationship between ideas, power, and politics. Indeed, for Morgenthau, a correct understanding of the concept – the very *idea* – of politics was essential if a recognition of the role of power in politics was not to be equated with a simple reduction of politics to nothing but power and violence, and Realism reduced to little more than a crude form of realpolitik.

Finally, I suggest that recognising these concerns provides a very different understanding of Realism's key concept of the balance of power, and the relationship between domestic and international politics. For Morgenthau, the essential nature of politics is the same in both the domestic and international spheres. What differs are the social capacities and forms of power available to manage the dynamics of 'politics', maximising its positive potential while minimising its destructive potential. Seen in this light, Morgenthau's thinking has important connections to the tradition of 'Atlantic republicanism', exhibiting a keen concern with the maintenance of a vital, democratic public sphere as the basis for a politics of responsibility, and seeking to foster and support that construction of a vibrant and yet self-limiting politics in both domestic and foreign policy.[6]

Liberalism and 'the political': the dialogue with Schmitt

As William Scheuerman has insightfully argued, Morgenthau's thinking can illuminatingly be read as constituting a 'hidden dialogue' with the controversial jurist Carl Schmitt.[7] After decades of near obscurity, Schmitt's thinking has recently been the subject of an explosion of interest, an explosion whose ripple effects are increasingly felt in International Relations.[8] I cannot in this setting deal with either the

[6] The connection between Morgenthau and liberalism has also been recently noted by Nicholas Onuf, who declares that Morgenthau was a 'confused liberal and a weak theorist'. Onuf, *The Republican Legacy in International Theory*, p. 5. I hope to show that he was a more substantial figure on both counts.

[7] Scheuerman, 'Another Hidden Dialogue'. Morgenthau's reflections on Schmitt can be found in Hans J. Morgenthau, 'Fragment of an Intellectual Autobiography: 1904–1932', in *Truth and Tragedy: A Tribute to Hans Morgenthau*, ed. Kenneth W. Thompson (Washington, DC: New Republic Books, 1977).

[8] The emerging interest in Schmitt in International Relations has often overlooked the profound influence which Hobbes had upon Schmitt, an influence also apparent in Morgenthau. See, particularly, Carl Schmitt, *The Leviathan in the State Theory of Thomas*

complexities of Schmitt's work as a whole or the heated controversies to which it has given rise. Instead, I will focus briefly on three key themes: his critique of liberalism; his vision of sovereignty as defined by the capacity for decision; and his understanding of the nature of politics itself – what Schmitt terms 'the concept of the political'. It is within and against these positions that many of Morgenthau's central claims develop.[9]

For Schmitt, sovereignty is defined by the act of *decision*, by the capacity to decide definitively contested legal or normative disputes within the state. In his analysis, all rule-bound orders (such as legal systems) depend ultimately upon a capacity for decision that itself stands outside of the given structure of rules. In his criticisms of legal positivism, for example, he argues that the application of any rule requires the existence of a prior rule which determines which particular rules are to apply to which particular instance. This rule structure is inherently indeterminate: no rule can cover definitively all of the different instances to which different rules might apply. At some level, there must simply be a *decision* (a judgement) on this matter. To say that this decision must itself be governed by rules is only to defer the problem, for even if it were itself determined by a prior set of rules, these rules themselves would require adjudication and decision. If the process were not to go on infinitely, a position of final decision, itself undetermined by rules, must exist, and 'therein', Schmitt argues, 'resides the essence of the state's sovereignty, which must be juristically defined correctly, not as the monopoly to coerce or to rule, but as the monopoly to decide'.[10]

The essence of sovereignty as decision is most clearly revealed in conditions of 'emergency', when a threat to the prevailing political order

Hobbes: Meaning and Failure of a Political Symbol trans. and ed. G. Schwab and E. Hilfstein (Westport, Conn.: Greenwood Press, 1996). For broader readings of these links, see John McCormick, 'Fear, Technology and the State: Carl Schmitt, Leo Strauss and the Revival of Hobbes in Weimar and National Socialist Germany', *Political Theory*, 22:4 (1994).

[9] Other appraisals of the relationship between Morgenthau and Schmitt, include H.-K. Pichler, 'The Godfathers of "Truth": Max Weber and Carl Schmitt in Morgenthau's Theory of Power Politics', *Review of International Studies*, 24:2 (1998), and the sharp appraisal of this view in Jef Huysmans, 'Know your Schmitt: A Godfather of Truth and the Spectre of Nazism', *Review of International Studies*, 25:2 (1999). See also, Frei, *Hans Morgenthau*, pp. 118–19, 160–3; McCormick, *Carl Schmitt's Critique of Liberalism*, 303–5; and for an excellent appraisal with affinities to the position developed here, Huysmans, 'The Question of the Limit'. Surveys of the broader context are: Niels Amstrup, 'The "Early" Morgenthau: A Comment on the Intellectual Origins of Realism', *Cooperation and Conflict*, 13 (1978), and more extendedly, Jan Willem Honig, 'Totalitarianism and Realism: Hans Morgenthau's German Years', in *Roots of Realism*, ed. Benjamin Frankel (London: Frank Cass, 1996).

[10] Carl Schmitt, *Political Theology: Four Chapters on the Concept of Sovereignty*, trans. George Schwab (Cambridge, Mass.: MIT Press, 1988), p. 13.

has reached a point requiring the suspension of normal rules and procedures if the political order itself is to be preserved. These are the situations that Schmitt characterises as the 'exception', and as he puts it in a characteristically pithy phrase, 'Sovereign is he who decides upon the exception.'[11] The exception cannot, for Schmitt, be determined by prior rules that would stipulate what constitutes a true emergency. In such cases, once again, a *decision* must be made, and as he puts it: 'The precise details of an emergency cannot be anticipated, nor can one spell out what may take place in such a case, especially when it is truly a matter of an extreme emergency and of how it is to be eliminated.'[12] It is in such a case that the true nature of sovereignty is revealed.[13] The Sovereign 'decides whether there is to be an extreme emergency as well as what must be done to eliminate it. Although he stands outside the normally valid legal system, he nevertheless belongs to it, for it is he who must decide whether the constitution needs to be suspended in its entirety.'[14] By contrast, the everyday situation of 'normal' politics depends upon the reverse: 'For a legal order to make sense, a normal situation must exist, and he is sovereign who definitively decides whether this normal situation actually exists.'[15]

Schmitt's claim that the essence of sovereignty lies in the act of decision merges powerfully with his famous vision of 'the concept of the political'. For Schmitt, the essence of politics – what he terms 'the political' – lies in the relationship between friend and enemy, and in the possibility of mortal conflict. Friendship and enmity provide the foundational structure of allegiance, of solidarity, that underpin the capacity for effective decision. The commonality of friendship – and the limits prescribed by enmity – define the parameters within which values can be decided upon and the decisions of a 'sovereign' actor or institution accepted by the society at large. Such a commonality, ultimately, is inextricable from enmity – from a group which is 'not us' – and from the possibility of life and death struggle with that enemy, and 'This grouping is therefore

[11] Schmitt, *Political Theology*, p. 5. [12] Schmitt, *Political Theology*, pp. 6–7.

[13] This position is clearly echoed in Morgenthau's analysis of sovereignty in *Politics among Nations*, 4th edn (New York: Knopf, 1967), pp. 299–317.

[14] Schmitt, *Political Theology*, p. 7.

[15] Schmitt, *Political Theology*, p. 13. Schmitt develops his arguments with direct and self-conscious echoes of the tradition of absolute sovereignty and the need for authoritative decision which he identifies with Hobbes. Indeed, as McCormick has argued, it was precisely Hobbes' clear formulation of many of these dilemmas that was behind the extraordinary resurgence of his popularity in Weimar; see McCormick, 'Fear, Technology and the State'. Schmitt's most extended reflections on Hobbes are in his *The Leviathan in the State Theory of Thomas Hobbes*.

always the decisive human grouping, the political entity. If such an entity exists at all, it is always the decisive entity, and it is sovereign in the sense that the decision about the critical situation, even if it is the exception, must always necessarily reside there.'[16]

For Schmitt, oppositional logics are at the heart of all concepts: morality is defined by the contrast between good and evil, aesthetics by the delineation of beautiful and ugly. The concept of the political is akin to these distinctions, but is not reducible to them. It is, in a fundamentally important way, independent of all other concepts and contrasts. As he phrases it, the concept of the political:

> is independent, not in the sense of a distinct new domain, but in that it can neither be based on any one antithesis, nor can it be traced to these. If the antithesis of good and evil is not simply identical with that of beautiful and ugly, profitable and unprofitable, and cannot be reduced to the others, then the antithesis of friend and enemy must even less be confused or mistaken for the others. The distinction of friend and enemy denotes the utmost degree of intensity of a union or separation, of an association or dissociation.[17]

Thus the essence of the political for Schmitt lies in the *intense* separation or dissociation (and, of course, the corresponding unity) which individuals perceive and experience in relation to enmity. It is a defining difference, one categorically distinct from other forms of opposition and more fundamental than any other. The fact that enemies frequently *are* portrayed as evil, ugly, or in competition for scarce resources is misleading. It is not these (potentially malleable) characteristics and perceptions that define the political – it is the perception of basic difference. To quote Schmitt once more:

> The political enemy need not be morally evil or aesthetically ugly; he need not appear as an economic competitor, and it may even be advantageous to engage with him in business transactions. But he is, nevertheless, the other, the stranger; and it is sufficient for his nature that he is, in a specifically intense way, existentially something different and alien, so that in extreme cases conflicts with him are possible. These can neither be decided by a previously determined general norm nor by the judgment of a disinterested and therefore neutral third party.[18]

[16] Carl Schmitt, *The Concept of the Political*, trans. George Schwab (University of Chicago Press, 1996), p. 38.
[17] Schmitt, *Concept of the Political*, p. 26. [18] Schmitt, *Concept of the Political*, p. 27.

In this vision, the specificity of politics cannot be inferred from the specific substantive content of any given issue. Whether issues are viewed as 'political' or 'non-political' (treated instead as 'economic' or 'religious', for example) cannot be determined from the nature of the issues themselves – a fact amply demonstrated by the ways in which these issues have moved from being political to non-political, and back again, throughout history.[19] What makes an issue 'political' is the particularly *intense* relationship that actors feel toward it. In its fullest form this intensification yields an absolute divide between friend and enemy in relation to a (any) given issue. 'The political', as he puts it, 'is the most intense and extreme antagonism, and every concrete antagonism becomes that much more political the closer it approaches the most extreme point, that of the friend-enemy grouping.'[20] Or, as he phrases it even more starkly: 'Every religious, moral, economic, ethical, or other antithesis transforms itself into a political one if it is sufficiently strong to group human beings according to friend and enemy.'[21]

The affinity between this understanding of 'the concept of the political' and a decisionist theory of sovereignty is clear. The capacity for decision is underpinned – indeed almost defined – by its ability to be supported and obeyed by a given political grouping. The fundamental division of friend and enemy and the capacity for authoritative decision are mutually supportive. A sovereign order – quite literally sovereignty in itself – is defined by the existence of such a centre of decision and the acceptance of its decisions by the relevant group. For Schmitt, a 'people' only becomes 'properly political' when it is defined by the capacity for decision, and decision is ultimately underlain by the division between friend and enemy, along with the fear and 'real possibility' of conflict and death that this encounter entails. Both the political and the decisionist vision of sovereignty are defined by the existence of enemies and the capability for setting aside existing norms in the name of preserving the normative and social order and the willingness to engage in mortal conflict. This does not mean that social and political life are continuously and inevitably realms of conflict and enmity. But it does mean, for Schmitt, that the capacity to move beyond conflict involves a resolution to the question of the political – of the locus of authority

[19] Schmitt, *Concept of the Political*, pp. 19–27.
[20] Schmitt, *Concept of the Political*, p. 29.
[21] Schmitt, *Concept of the Political*, p. 37.

and decision – and the generation of a social capacity to defend this authority.[22]

For Schmitt, the politics of the enemy is not normative.[23] It represents the essence of politics in itself. In principle, individuals can come together to form a group around any particular interest, but they will only become properly 'political' if they enter into a friend–enemy relationship where the survival of the group and its ultimate willingness to engage in mortal struggle is at stake. Sovereignty *is* this principle and capacity. In the modern world, it happens to have coalesced around *nationalism*. But for Schmitt, nationalism is simply one expression of the concept of the political in itself:

> It is irrelevant here whether one rejects, accepts, or perhaps finds it an atavistic remnant of barbaric times that nations continue to group themselves according to friend and enemy, or whether it is perhaps strong pedagogic reasoning to imagine that enemies no longer exist at all. The concern here is neither with abstractions nor normative ideals, but with inherent reality and the real possibility of making such a distinction. One may or may not share these hopes and pedagogic ideals. But, rationally speaking, it cannot be denied that nations continue to group themselves according to the friend-enemy antithesis, that the distinction still remains actual today, and that this is an ever present possibility for every people existing in the political sphere.[24]

Schmitt's understanding of enmity as the objective essence of the political also leads him to a significant reformulation of the concept of evil. The evil in human nature is not to be understood as the direct outcome of an atavistic desire for domination or an intrinsic brutality. Rather, pessimism concerning 'human nature' arises out of the basic lack of any 'natural' consensus, and the role of violence, enmity, and imposition in

[22] The hotly contested claim of whether Schmitt sought to destroy or (as he later claimed) to save liberal democracy via these criticisms is beyond my scope here, though I tend to support the former view.

[23] It must be noted that there is a key ambiguity here, for while Schmitt often presents the concept of the political as simply 'objective', it has often been argued that his vision of it is actually underpinned by a vitalistic commitment to violence and enmity as essential to the preservation of a 'full' human life in opposition to the neutralisation and depoliticisation of liberal modernity. On Schmitt as an exponent of a conservative vitalism, see Richard Wolin, 'Carl Schmitt: The Conservative Reactionary Habitus and the Aesthetics of Horror', *Political Theory*, 20:3 (1992); for excellent and somewhat contrasting discussion in International Relations, see Huysmans, 'Question of the Limit', and Koskenniemi, *Gentle Civilizer of Nations*, pp. 432–3.

[24] Schmitt, *Concept of the Political*, p. 28.

the delineation and construction of the polity. In the absence of a natural order, all order will require imposition and the exercise of power in some form, since the natural condition of human beings does not tend toward harmony and mutual understandings of the good. Here, Schmitt explicitly draws the link between his thinking and that of another great theorist of human 'evil', the political thinker whom he most admired: Thomas Hobbes. As he puts it:

> For Hobbes, a truly powerful and systematic political thinker, the pessimistic conception of man is the elementary presupposition of a specific system of political thought. He also recognized correctly that the conviction of each side that it possesses the truth, the good, and the just bring about the worst enmities, finally the war of all against all. This fact is not the product of a frightful and disquieting fantasy nor a philosophy based upon free competition by a bourgeois society in its first state (Tonnies), but is the fundamental presupposition of a specific political philosophy.[25]

This is a very different view from that which emerges from a simple opposition between good and evil, truth and error. It is also fundamentally different from positions that see evil as another word for the inescapability of 'Darwinian' drives for competitive advantage, or a simple psychological desire for domination. The nature of politics, the possibility of the good, cannot be separated from evil in the sense of the necessity of degrees of manipulation, opposition, and imposition. The impossibility of absolute consent and consensus mean that all political life – where *decisions* must be made – inevitably involves the predominance of some wills, values, and choices over others. Even a politics of toleration will involve some form of imposition, since the limits of that which is tolerable must ultimately be decided.[26] All politics, in this sense, involves 'evil', and no properly political understanding can avoid the conclusion that forms of violence will be necessary for political order to be possible at all. What is more, all politics is inevitably exclusionary. The questions of the substantive determination of values and the social capacity which underlies them mean that no universal resolution can be found, and that the good in political life will always involve the evils of imposition, exclusion, and forms of domination.

[25] Schmitt, *Concept of the Political*, p. 61. Or as he also phrases it, any 'genuine political theory' must presuppose humanity as 'evil', not as perfectible or angelic.

[26] For an exploration of some of these issues – though from a distinctly non-Schmittian position – see Donald Moon, *Constructing Community: Moral Pluralism and Tragic Conflicts* (Princeton University Press, 1995).

These arguments concerning sovereignty as decision, the significance of the exception, and the concept of the political, are central to Schmitt's critique of liberalism. Liberalism, he argues, emerged in a context of enmity – of a life and death struggle with absolutism. But in its subsequent development liberalism has obscured these origins and presented itself as the natural and consensual political vision of an enlightened humanity. Enmity and conflict are portrayed as belonging to a bygone era now replaced by pluralism, peaceful competition, and an ultimate harmony of interests. In Schmitt's view, liberalism is thus left with a 'depoliticised' conception of politics, and is thoroughly lacking a cogent theory of political decision and the centrality of the state.[27] Historically speaking, once liberalism had vanquished its defining opponents – the rule of the aristocracy and the threat of religious violence – its essentially empty vision of the political realm (or its role as an instrument in pursuit of divisive individual interests or class politics) became increasingly apparent.[28]

At the centre of Schmitt's critique of liberal-democracy (or 'parliamentarism', as he calls it) lies the claim that in its reduction of politics to individualistic calculation and the advancement of purely subjective values, liberalism reduces politics to a process of technical calculation and competition lacking in any larger meaning, any capacity to decide authoritatively upon substantive values, and – crucially – lacking any broader commitment to liberal-democratic structures in themselves.[29] Liberal-democratic structures are thus reduced to purely formal structures of representation and competition, arenas valued only to the degree that they promote the furtherance of particular interests. Parliamentary institutions, likewise, become little more than venues for the pursuit of narrow sectoral interests, valued by those who participate in them only to the degree that they advance their interests. In such conditions, liberal parliamentarism descends into either a mask

[27] Schmitt, *Concept of the Political*, p. 61.

[28] For a powerful rendition of this claim, clearly influenced by Schmitt, see Reinhart Koselleck, *Critique and Crisis: the Enlightenment and the Pathogenesis of Modern Society* (Oxford: Berg, 1988). As Schmitt succinctly put it: 'There exists a liberal policy of trade, church, and education, but absolutely no liberal politics, only a liberal critique of politics. The systematic theory of liberalism concerns almost solely the internal struggle against the power of the state.' Schmitt, *Concept of the Political*, p. 70.

[29] A theme most extensively developed in Carl Schmitt, *The Crisis of Parliamentary Democracy*, trans. Ellen Kennedy (Cambridge, Mass.: MIT Press, 1988). For an examination of Weber's and Schmitt's views on these questions see Rune Slagstad, 'Liberal Constitutionalism and its Critics: Carl Schmitt and Max Weber', in *Constitutionalism and Democracy*, ed. Jon Elster and Rune Slagstad (Cambridge University Press, 1988).

for the rule of a limited number of powerful groups that control the state, or becomes deadlocked in an intractable clash of interests and incapable of effective decision-making. In the resulting conditions of domination, anarchy, entropy, or alienation, people will be tempted to turn to competing non-liberal, or particularly anti-liberal, political alternatives which do promise comprehensive visions, the promotion of specific interests, or both.[30] Those who are disadvantaged or excluded from the process become ever more cynical and alienated. As a result, the commitment of individual citizens, social groups, and political parties to liberal-democratic institutions is both fragile and eroding, providing both the conditions for the emergence of opponents who do not accept tolerant liberal premises and placing barriers in the way of effective societal mobilisation for the support of liberal democracy itself.[31]

All viable polities, Schmitt argues, must have some way of making decisions in contested cases. However, liberalism effectively destroys the basis upon which legitimate decisions could be reached at the communal level, since each individual or group will only recognise the legitimacy of such a decision and obey it if it is in their interest to do so.[32] What is more, a liberal politics of pure self-interest will be incapable of mobilising support for its defence if individuals do not see this defence as being in their own self-interest. And since the preservation of one's own life is the most basic value of liberalism, it is incapable of defending itself as a political collectivity. As Schmitt himself puts it: 'In case of need, the political entity must demand the sacrifice of life. Such a demand is in no way justifiable by the individualism of liberal thought. No consistent individualism can entrust to someone other than to the individual himself the right to dispose of the physical life of the individual.'[33] Yet, in Schmitt's view, all functioning sovereignties are founded on this principle and capacity; those that do not possess them are unlikely to survive.[34]

[30] For Schmitt, the genius and danger of Bolshevism lay in its claim to combine both these elements via the proletariat and the Communist Party, and Weimar was the quintessential example of a liberal society incapable of meeting such a challenge.

[31] A broad sketch of Schmitt's analysis of liberalism's inability to create an effective political vision can be found in his *Political Romanticism*.

[32] Significantly, in Schmitt's view, *all* cases are fundamentally contestable and indeterminate and there is no natural basis for consensual decision. On how this jurisprudential view is linked to Schmitt's authoritarian politics, see particularly Scheuerman, *Carl Schmitt*, chapters 1–4.

[33] Schmitt, *Concept of the Political*, p. 71.

[34] This is one element of his critique of Weimar liberal democracy, explored most fully in Schmitt, *Crisis of Parliamentary Democracy*.

A resolution to the question of the political underlies even the most stable and liberal of polities, and it is a failure to recognise this fact that is conspicuously lacking in liberal societies. This failure is clearly illustrated in times of crisis, when the bases of liberal order are fundamentally challenged and their philosophical and practical weaknesses fatally exposed. It is only under conditions where the fundamental questions of the political have been resolved that the politics of liberal individualism, rationalism, and calculation can safely and stably occur. Liberalism is a politics of limits, but its limits depend upon a deeper process of limitation – a limited questioning of the contested foundations of the political. Liberalism can certainly countenance conflict – as in economic competition and electoral democracy – but this conflict can only safely occur so long as its participants agree not to challenge fundamentally the structures (pre-eminently the legitimacy of the state *in itself* to make authoritative decisions) that allow it to take place. Liberal institutions, in short, can only function when people do not take too seriously the ultimately irreconcilable nature of their perceptions, values, and interests that liberalism takes as its founding principles; or conversely (and perhaps ultimately), when these structures continue to be underlain by a friend–enemy distinction that underpins them in the final instance.

Schmitt's ultimate attitude toward the implications of these arguments for liberalism, and particularly for democracy, is the source of considerable controversy.[35] There can be little doubt, however, that one direction in which they can be developed (that which Schmitt himself certainly appears to have pursued in the 1930s and 1940s) is that of an authoritarian, anti-democratic stress on the inescapability of decision and the need for its ultimate grounding in either a dictatorial structure or (and often at the same time) in a deeply shared cultural unity of the people and the leadership – a mythologised unity of nation and state within a defining context of enmity.[36]

Morgenthau and the liberal tradition

The sophisticated and radical (or perhaps reactionary) critique of liberalism and form of realpolitik articulated by Schmitt was a key element of the context in which Morgenthau's political Realism developed.

[35] For a largely sympathetic rendering of Schmitt's critique of liberalism in the service of 'radical democracy' see Chantal Mouffe, *The Return of the Political* (London: Verso, 1993).
[36] On the evolution of Schmitt's views on dictatorship, see McCormick, *Carl Schmitt's Critique of Liberalism*, chapter 3, passim. Scheuerman's *Carl Schmitt* provides an excellent and sometimes contrasting discussion as well.

Rather than following these concerns down an anti-liberal path, however, Morgenthau attempts to provide a reconstruction of liberal politics which takes account of the profound criticisms to which liberalism had been subjected. This project underlies his vision of political Realism and is essential in understanding his legacy for International Relations theory.

Morgenthau's critique of liberalism – most fully developed in *Scientific Man Versus Power Politics* – unfolds through an examination of three different variants of liberal thought. The first, in which the historical triumph of classical liberalism is intertwined with rationalist philosophy and an objectivist vision of science, Morgenthau finds theoretically unconvincing and politically misleading. However, like its Weimar critics – including Schmitt – he is convinced that it is essential to grasp the historical genesis of this view in order to understand the influence that rationalism and claims concerning scientific knowledge continue to exert on contemporary attempts to comprehend political life. The second view, which he terms 'decadent' liberalism, emerges as a reaction against the inadequacies of classical liberal theory and conceives a relativistic politics of tolerance as the foundation for liberal politics. Interestingly, and importantly, while Morgenthau sees this vision of liberalism as most *intellectually* adequate, he finds it to be the most politically obtuse. Again, Weimar critiques of liberalism loom large in this position. The third, most complex and misunderstood, vision is that of a tragic or agonistic liberalism, deeply indebted to the thinking of Max Weber, that Morgenthau ultimately identifies with political Realism. In this vision, a liberal polity must be self-consciously created in the context of a clear understanding of the relationship between constructions of knowledge and constructions of politics, and the inescapability of power and 'evil' in politics.

The rise of 'rationalist' theories of politics, Morgenthau argues, cannot be understood outside the early modern European context in which they emerged. In his view, this was not a simple case of the rational triumph of science and objective truth over ignorance and darkness. On the contrary, 'History and the sociology of science have shown how this seemingly spontaneous conquest of nature by reason was actually stimulated by the emotional upheaval which followed the collapse of medieval metaphysics and religion and by new economic and social interests.'[37] Two developments are particularly important in understanding this

[37] Morgenthau, *Scientific Man versus Power Politics*, p. 160.

process: the political struggle of the rising (particularly liberal, middle) classes against the aristocracy, and the violent upheavals of the Thirty Years War.

Morgenthau views the rise of rationalism and empiricism characteristic of modern science as elements of a broader attempt by the rising middle classes of Europe to construct a vision of social and political order which could challenge the legitimacy of the authority and political power of the aristocracy. The reduction of the individual to a wholly material (bodily) self, the reduction of the actions of that self to the pursuit of material interests, and the elucidation of a utilitarian ethics in which that private pursuit was rendered the definition of morality, were all part of an attempt to construct a vision of the individual and social worlds which was *separated* from politics in its aristocratic form. The reduction of ethics to the pursuit of private material interest – exemplified by liberal doctrines such as utilitarianism or the 'harmony of interests'[38] – was, he argues, part of a process of reducing understandings of social and political life solely to questions of fact, to calculations of interest on the basis of material facts, and to the destruction of politics as a sphere separate from the autonomously regulating pursuit of self-interest.[39]

Via this reconstruction, 'politics' became defined almost wholly negatively – as the preserve of an aristocracy which illegitimately used its 'political' authority to infringe upon the private, self-regulating realm of society. This transformation was part of the genius of the rising liberal classes in their wresting of power from the nobility, and it was an essential tool – a powerful social construction – in their ability to do so. It was, in short, a form of 'power politics': an attempt to gain political power by delegitimising existing political authority through the construction of a social world which *did not need politics* in any but a managerial or technical sense.

The problem, however, was that classical liberalism mistook its limitation of the realm of the political as part of its struggle with the nobility for its ability to reduce the political to these new individual and social bases alone. In doing so, Morgenthau argues, it had fundamentally mistaken the nature of politics. As he puts it, liberalism 'had come to identify

[38] A view which Morgenthau shares with E. H. Carr; see E. H. Carr, *The Twenty Years Crisis* (London: Macmillan, 1977). For other views on these developments see Hirschman, *The Passions and the Interests* and Karl Polanyi, *The Great Transformation* (Boston: Beacon Press, 1944).
[39] Morgenthau, *Scientific Man versus Power Politics*, p. 15.

the aspiration for power over man, which is the essence of politics, with the particular manifestation of this lust for domination, which was part of its historic experience, that is, the domination of the middle classes by the aristocracy. Consequently, it identified opposition to aristocratic politics with hostility to any kind of politics.'[40]

We will return to Morgenthau's view of the essential nature of politics at a later point. What is important at this juncture is to recognise how he views the emergence of modern, utilitarian constructions of individuals (which he consistently terms 'rationalist'), and of liberal constructions of the nature and realm of politics, as historically specific to shifts in the construction of social and political order and as tied to the preponderant social power – that of the middle classes – in this new order. But, at the same time, this triumph involved the reduction of the realm of the political wholly to the pursuit of self-interest premised upon both a fixed vision of human rationality and the harmony of interests. Very much like Schmitt, Morgenthau believes that in so doing liberal rationalism was left with an impoverished and inadequate understanding of the nature of politics and the specific requirements for the construction of a stable liberal political order. Before turning to these arguments, however, it is necessary to examine a second element explaining the triumph of classical liberalism's construction of reality and its continuing attraction: its links to the politics of security, and the relationship between knowledge and violence in the long legacy of the Thirty Years War.

As Steven Toulmin has compellingly argued, 'The seventeenth century "Quest for Certainty" was no mere proposal to construct abstract and timeless intellectual schemas, dreamed up as objects of pure, detached intellectual study. Instead it was a timely response to a specific historical challenge – the political, social, and theological chaos embodied in the Thirty Years' War.'[41] Rather than comprising a disembodied intellect, or a self-evident method optimistic in its ability to advance objective knowledge for its own sake, the modernist vision emerged in a context of fear, violence, and conflict. As was demonstrated in chapter one, for Hobbes this relationship between conscience and conflict was fundamental. In a setting where claims to religious truth had become sources of conflict, intellectual and practical reconfigurations were intimately related. Hobbes' 'material' understanding of the self (and

[40] Morgenthau, *Scientific Man versus Power Politics*, p. 45; see also pp. 47–50.
[41] Toulmin, *Cosmopolis*, p. 70. See also J. G. A. Pocock, *Virtue, Commerce, History* (Cambridge University Press, 1985) and Theodore Rabb, *The Struggle for Stability in Early Modern Europe* (Oxford University Press, 1975).

self-understanding) sought to construct a new set of political practices based on the (now rationally, *not* naturally) universal fear of pain and death, which could provide a basis for a renewed vision of sovereignty and understanding of obligation. The transformation of theory was intimately linked to an attempt to transform practices, and the search for new foundations was more than a purely intellectual enterprise: it was tightly bound up with questions of politics – with concrete dilemmas concerning the grounds of political belief, assent, and order.

Morgenthau's views on the emergence of empiricism and materialism – so often now identified with the epistemic stance of 'rationalism' (and Realism) in International Relations – are similar. He traces the premises of a science of society to an historical, social, and political project tied to the rise of classical liberal politics, and to the liberal attempt to reconstruct political order at both the national and international levels. Domestically, the liberal construction of the relationship between knowledge and politics provided a foundation for a new social order; internationally, it provided the social conditions (material calculation, instrumental action) for the construction of the classical balance of power.[42] But a clear understanding of this transformation is not only of historical interest to Morgenthau: he views it as essential in grasping the appeal which these epistemic principles continue to hold for contemporary political analysis. The proponents of 'objectivity' defined in empiricist and materialist terms reflect and continue to play upon this historical linkage between empiricism and materialism as theoretical foundations of objective knowledge, and continue to claim that this objectivity and certainty is necessary both for the maintenance of a liberal political order, and for international political stability in general.

For Morgenthau, it is the connection to this historically located desire for *security* that drives rationalism's proponents on their nostalgic quest for a naturalistic science of social life, not a realistic understanding of either science or society.[43] As he puts it, 'What scientistic philosophy and, under its influence, nineteenth-century political thought and the social sciences refer to as their object of emulation is a ghost from which life has long since departed. It is, indeed, a kind of folklore of science

[42] See most clearly Morgenthau, *Politics among Nations*, pp. 225–7; for an analysis, Martin Griffiths, *Realism, Idealism, and International Politics* (London: Routledge, 1992), pp. 72–3, and Guzzini, *Realism in International Relations*. The affinities between Schmitt's and Morgenthau's understandings of the classical system are drawn out very clearly in Koskenniemi, *Gentle Civilizer of Nations*, pp. 415–22 and 437–40.
[43] For a somewhat similar view, see Michael Dillon, *The Politics of Security* (London: Routledge, 1996).

which receives its dignity from tradition and from the longing for intellectual as well as actual security but not from the inherent truthfulness of its propositions.'[44] The apparently purely theoretical commitments of objectivist theories of knowledge derive significant elements of their attraction and power as much from their embodiment of a specific *vision* of politics as from their status as a solid foundation for the *analysis* of politics. Without such commitments, the proponents of objectivism consistently argue, illegitimate coercion and anarchy are the historically demonstrated alternatives. In this way the ghost of the seventeenth century continues to haunt the modern imagination.

Despite his understanding of this connection between epistemic stances and political practices, Morgenthau did not view this project as philosophically sustainable or historically stable. Indeed the constant admonition to seek security through an appeal to empirical reality, material facts, and a 'scientific' approach to politics is not something he equates with a hard-headed realism. On the contrary, he identifies it with both a lack of understanding and a lack of courage in facing up to the realities of the world.

The failings of rationalist liberalism lie not only in its continuing and uncritical allegiance to an insupportable vision of knowledge. If this was all that was at stake, philosophical naïveté might be not only explicable, but forgivable and largely irrelevant. In Morgenthau's view, however, the issue is far more serious because liberal rationalism is not only incapable of providing a secure theoretical foundation for a liberal political order, it has historically become positively destructive of such an order. Morgenthau regards this failure as one of the defining features of modern politics, and his assessment of it focuses on two key dynamics of liberal thought.

The first – which Morgenthau views as characteristic of the social 'sciences' – is that in the face of their continuing failure to develop such a science, the proponents of certainty and objectivity throw themselves back into the task with ever more energy, and with renewed promises that revelation is both possible and just around the corner. Reflecting on the popularity of empiricist social science in the post-war era, he

[44] *Scientific Man versus Power Politics*, p. 132. At his most ironic, Morgenthau argues that the appeal to outmoded conceptions of science can today be understood as a *retreat* from reality in which: 'Forgetful of the inherent uncertainty of social action and searching in its social endeavours for a security of which the natural sciences know nothing, modern man has taken refuge in a bastion of facts; for, after all, "facts do not lie", and they, at least, are "real".' Morgenthau, *Scientific Man versus Power Politics*, p. 214.

notes that 'The new realists are undismayed by the wreckage surrounding them. If they have failed, it was because the quantity of facts available to them was not enough. The answer to political failure is "more facts", and the accumulation of more facts but leads to more political failures.'[45] This is not simply a critique of crude empiricism; rather, his point is that this 'decadence of the political art' results from 'the mistaken belief, rooted in rationalism, that political problems are scientific problems for which the one correct solution must be found . . .'.[46] Understanding political reality, Morgenthau argues, requires leaving behind both liberal-rationalist epistemology and its corresponding desire for certainty.[47] Neither is capable of understanding or sustaining political order. Indeed he argues that it is necessary to understand the inadequacies of these views as the *source*, not the solution, of subsequent constructions of the liberal project and the political dilemmas which they bequeath.

The second element of Morgenthau's critique is that, bound as it is to an epistemic ethic of certainty, liberal rationalism is badly equipped to deal with the crisis brought on by its own failure. For those unable to ignore the apparently insoluble philosophic dilemmas of liberal rationalism and objectivist science were left with an increasing scepticism about social knowledge, and a tendency to retreat from the public, political realm into a supposedly neutral, private one. Classical liberalism, unable to found itself on objective grounds, thus came to generate its opposite: a wholly relativist scepticism. While he regards this form of thought as *epistemically* (one might currently say, methodologically) more sophisticated than classical liberalism, he views it as *politically* even more naïve, dangerous, and destructive of the principles it seeks to support. It is this dialectic that yields the conceptual and political alter ego of objectivist science and liberal rationalism, a position that Morgenthau terms 'decadent liberalism'.

At the level of epistemology, this sceptical or tolerant liberalism did not see the destruction of certainty as ending the quest for knowledge or rendering it senseless. Instead, it provided a basis upon which modern science and knowledge claims could be produced and contested in an

[45] Morgenthau, *Scientific Man versus Power Politics*, p. 215.
[46] Morgenthau, *Scientific Man versus Power Politics*, pp. 213–14.
[47] As Morgenthau put it in a critical comment on the 'policy science' pervading the Kennedy administration: 'advice and information performs for the President the same function the employment of astrologers and soothsayers did for the princes of old: to create the illusion of certainty where there is no certainty', Morgenthau, *Truth and Power*, p. 149.

open social realm formally divorced from political and religious strictures. Probabilistic claims and contingent knowledge are the best that can be achieved; the objective prediction beloved of classical conceptions of knowledge is simply not possible. Truth was not possible as certainty: but this truth – that there was no clear and certain truth about the world – could be made the basis of a tolerant and open society. The defeat of metaphysical (particularly rationalist) dogmatism thus opened a path in which new ways of understanding could be freely disputed.[48] Nor, at the level of politics, was the absence of a secure foundation for knowledge seen as leaving society without solid foundations. On the contrary, this transformation in the practices of knowledge provided the foundation for religious toleration, and sought to create a political realm secure from theological strife and contestation. The idea that knowledge is *constructed* through theories, and that such knowledge is inherently probabilistic, became a basis for a form of political ethics and a foundation for social practices of toleration. Rather than seeing certainty as the touchstone of knowledge and the basis for the construction of social order, this tradition built upon the concept of *doubt* as a foundation for a liberal order in both knowledge and politics. Since no view could support its claims to absolute certainty, none could legitimately enforce its views on others. A commitment to principles of social and political pluralism, just as to open and unconstrained scientific enquiry, was underpinned by this epistemic stance.

Morgenthau's attitude toward this form of liberalism is central in grasping his thought as a whole. At the level of epistemology and method, he finds the epistemic position of sceptical liberalism much more adequate than that of classical liberalism. Twentieth-century science, he avers, has long since given up the goal of certainty to which the social sciences still anachronistically cling. The social and natural sciences have in our time been reunited, not by the movement of the social sciences toward a model of deterministic laws characteristic of rationalist models of knowledge, but by a movement of the natural sciences toward an *indeterminism* characteristic of knowledge of the social world. As he puts it: 'The best the so-called "social laws" can do is exactly the best the so-called "natural laws" can do, namely, to indicate certain trends and to state the possible conditions under which one of those trends is most likely to materialize in the future.'[49]

[48] See, for example, R. Hooykaas, *Religion and the Rise of Modern Science* (Edinburgh: Scottish Academic Press, 1972). More broadly, see Shapin, *A Social History of Truth*.
[49] Morgenthau, *Scientific Man versus Power Politics*, p. 136.

This pluralistic vision of knowledge marks an advance in a realistic assessment of the limits of human reason and knowledge, and their impact on the social world. The vision of science characteristic of classical liberalism is losing its force in both the natural and social realms, and the sooner this fact is acknowledged, the better. As he puts it, people 'will not forever cherish the redeeming powers of science which demonstrates through its results its moral ambiguity in its own sphere and its scientific ambiguity in the social world'.[50] Moreover, if 'scientific' causality is naïve at the level of contemporary philosophies of science, it is doubly so as concerns the social sciences where in the reflexive nature of human agency 'the "science of politics" – finds its final refutation'.[51]

Despite interpretations of him as a quintessential 'positivist', therefore, Morgenthau's views on the philosophy of science and the nature of the social sciences actually seem to accord surprisingly well with elements of post-positivist thinking in contemporary International Relations.[52] But the challenge which Morgenthau presents to current thinking goes well beyond a relocation of his position within the ongoing epistemological controversies within the field. Indeed his assault upon liberal rationalism is designed primarily to attack the claim that questions of political knowledge can be reduced to, or resolved through, debates over method or epistemology. This could not be more clearly illustrated than in his attack upon the politics of liberalism which corresponds to this pluralist conception of knowledge.

For Morgenthau, the belief that scientific knowledge and political knowledge occupy the same realms needs to be challenged not only in order to dismiss the rationalist attempt to reduce the latter to the former, it needs to be challenged in order that the failure of the rationalist project does not lead to theoretical conclusions that are disastrous as a foundation for (liberal) political practice. A more adequate understanding of the indeterminate nature of our knowledge of the natural world, he argues, cannot be directly translated into a more adequate understanding of the political world. In fact, Morgenthau believes, it is precisely this move that underpins a naïve form of toleration which is potentially destructive for a liberal polity. For all its apparent opposition to a politics

[50] Morgenthau, *Scientific Man versus Power Politics*, p. 8.
[51] Morgenthau, *Scientific Man versus Power Politics*, p. 144.
[52] For readings of Morgenthau as a positivist, see Jim George, *Discourses of Global Politics* (Boulder, Colo.: Lynne Rienner Press, 1994) and Mark Neufeld, *The Restructuring of International Relations Theory* (Cambridge University Press, 1995).

of certainty, sceptical liberalism remains indebted to the same view of the relationship between knowledge and politics as classical liberalism: it continues to assume that an adequate understanding of the nature of *empirical* knowledge can be directly equated with the nature of *political* knowledge. Despite its opposition to objectivist conceptions of knowledge, sceptical liberalism shares this belief – it simply reverses its terms. Now a more adequate (sceptical or contingent) philosophy of *knowledge* can underwrite an analogous (tolerant) philosophy of *politics*. The conviction that there is a direct connection between the two realms remains unshaken.

It is precisely this move that Morgenthau rejects most strongly. The core of his thinking rests in the argument that knowledge of objects in general and knowledge of the *political object* are not the same thing, and that it is a mistake shared by both forms of liberalism that they reduce the latter to the former. Sceptical liberalism may be more epistemically realistic in terms of theories of knowledge. To a degree (as I will discuss at a later point), it represents a positive, pluralistic social ethic, and is a foundation of democratic political practice. But to see this epistemic and ethical stance as directly translatable into a viable political practice, Morgenthau argues, is disastrously unrealistic.

The problem with this liberal relativism, he argues in tones which clearly echo both Schmitt and Weber, is that it can only function in a social situation where liberal principles are already institutionalised, and these foundations are consistently undermined by the inadequacies of liberal theory and the implications of these inadequacies in practice. Left to its own devices, liberalism threatens to sow the seeds of its own destruction. The attempt to ground a liberal politics on a rationalist, objectivist epistemology and a politics of technical manipulation, or to retreat from politics into a wholly private world of self-interest or self-absorption, generates the opposite of the liberal freedom it seeks. Indeed Morgenthau views the rise and success of fascism as product of this liberal heritage, representing both its culmination and its bankruptcy. Fascism, he argues, was not a reversion to premodern barbarism, or a wholly irrational eruption divorced from modern liberalism. Fascism was a tragic culmination of trajectories within the liberal-rationalist project: 'it is truly progressive – were not the propaganda machine of Goebbels and the gas chambers of Himmler models of technical rationality? – and in its denial of the ethics of Western civilization it reaps the harvest of a philosophy which clings to the tenets of Western culture without understanding its foundations. In a sense it is, like all revolutions, but the receiver of the bankrupt age that preceded it'.[53] Similarly, he argues, fascism grew out of the inability of liberalism to provide a meaningful framing of social life. The Germans, he holds, rejected a Western philosophy which they saw as irrelevant and 'embraced in fascism a philosophy which promised to reinterpret their experiences, to guide their actions, and to create a new society'.[54]

A sceptical liberal society is a society which will be at best highly limited in its ability to defend its liberal principles from the consequences of its own dynamics, and which will likely fail to meet such challenges when they arise. These concerns operate at both the domestic and the international level. In each case, it is only when a liberal state's *survival* is threatened that it can be mobilised to defend its political institutions, and by then it is often too late – with the pluralism of the state exacerbating its ineffectiveness in responding to such threats. Whether this is a result of the naïveté of classical liberalism's belief in an underlying harmony of interests, leading to a misperception of the structures of power on which it is based and the conflict which they can generate,[55] or is an outcome of a decadent liberal state's incapacity to mobilise around its values, the result is the same. So long as its basic institutions are functioning internally a liberal state will actually disregard them as something to be defended. It is only when the loss of liberalism's institutions becomes compelling, through a *concrete threat*, that liberal states become mobilised around them. But these limitations, as the cases of the Weimar Republic and the Second World War illustrate, seriously threaten their very ability to survive and to uphold the tolerant, pluralistic values which they – and Morgenthau – prize.[56]

[53] Morgenthau, *Scientific Man versus Power Politics*, pp. 6–7.

[54] Morgenthau, *Scientific Man versus Power Politics*, p. 8; see also his analysis in 'Nazism' in *Twentieth-Century Political Thought*, ed. J. Roucek, (New York: Philosophical Library, 1946). Again, the affinities of Morgenthau's thinking to broader intellectual currents in Germany in the 1930s are apparent: compare, for example, the analysis of rationalisation pursued by Max Horkheimer and Theodor Adorno in *Dialectic of Enlightenment* (New York: Continuum, 1972). Realism's general suspicion of – and often downright hostility toward – technology is clearly traced in Rosenthal, *Righteous Realists*, pp. 154–68. On Morgenthau's familiarity with members of the Frankfurt School, see Frei, *Hans Morgenthau*, and on the broader relationship between Critical theory (particularly of the Frankfurt School) and International Relations see Richard Wyn Jones (ed.), *Critical Theory and World Politics* (Boulder, Colo.: Lynne Rienner, 2001).

[55] Again, here there are clear affinities with Carr's analysis of classical liberalism.

[56] As Joel Rosenthal has insightfully argued, the engagement of Realism with 'public philosophy' was intimately bound up with its concern with 'the decline of the West, the fate of liberalism in the modern age, and the question of pluralism. The problem of pluralism was, in fact, at the root of the realists' unease.' *Righteous Realists*, p. 56.

If part of Morgenthau's goal, as outlined above, was to understand the role which the inadequacies of liberal constructions of the political realm played in this disaster, the second aspect of his thought involves an attempt to understand how it might be countered. As is well known, Morgenthau saw it as his mission to educate the United States – the quintessentially liberal society, in his view – about the limits and dangers of an uncritical liberalism. The struggle over the relationship between knowledge and politics in this often naïve political culture, which Morgenthau now viewed as the great global hope as well as the embattled and endangered bastion of a liberal politics, was one of the vital intellectual and political struggles of the time.[57] To this end, he sought to provide an understanding of political life which would provide a realistic vision of the conditions under which a liberal order might be created and maintained. One of the clearest illustrations of this commitment can be found in his concept of 'politics' itself, an attempt to both confront and overcome the consequences of Schmitt's concept of the political.

The 'politics' of Realism

It is clear that Morgenthau's assessment of liberalism was deeply influenced by the critiques of liberal democracy current in Weimar, and particularly by the position of Schmitt. But it is equally clear that he seeks to counter these attacks via a reconstruction of the liberal position. His assault on liberalism emphasised that its opponents embraced a *political* rationality which was extremely powerful, extremely destructive, and toward which the prevailing responses of the liberal tradition – both intellectual and practical – were conspicuously weak. In response, Morgenthau's Realism represents an attempt to provide a reconstructed political liberalism viable for and in the modern world. To indicate how he attempts to do so, I propose to look in some detail at his conception of politics itself.[58]

The concept of politics may seem a particularly unpromising point from which to argue for a reassessment of Morgenthau's Realism, for

[57] As such, he was part of the broader émigré challenge to the easy equation of American liberalism and political science outlined by Gunnell, *Between Philosophy and Politics*, chapter 1; see also Keith L. Shimko, 'Realism, Neorealism, and American Liberalism', *Review of Politics*, 54:1 (1992).
[58] For an excellent explication of Morgenthau's critique of Schmitt's concept of the political with important connections to the argument I pursue here, see Scheuerman, 'Another Hidden Dialogue'.

however diverse the positions in contemporary International Relations may be there is almost universal agreement that one of the greatest weaknesses of his thinking (and that of immediately post-war Realism in general) lies in its remarkably narrow understanding of politics. Indeed, while liberal institutionalists,[59] social constructivists,[60] historical sociologists,[61] political economists,[62] and even 'neoclassical' Realists[63] may diverge widely on the nature of Realism and its place in the future development of International Relations theory, they are largely united in the conviction that a concern with political economy, the impact of domestic structures, or the influence of culture and identity, all appear remarkably marginal (or at best inadequately developed and unsystematically theorised) within 'classical' Realism, and that a broader, more sociologically and institutionally rigorous theory of the structure, dynamics, and multiple determinants of 'politics' at the domestic level is essential for the further development of International Relations theory, whether 'Realist' or not.

Explanations of the narrowness of classical Realism's understanding of politics abound in discussions of International Relations, and form a key element in accounts of the evolution of the field. Most commonly, this narrowness is traced to the historical conditions of Realism's ascendance, particularly to the dominance of 'high politics', diplomacy, and military conflict at the conclusion of the Second World War and the onset of the Cold War.[64] Under these conditions, it is argued, Realism's narrow

[59] Robert Keohane and Joseph Nye, *Power and Interdependence*, 2nd edn (Glenview, Ill.: Scott, Foreman, 1989).
[60] Friedrich Kratochwil and Yosef Lapid, 'Culture's Ship: Returns and Departures in International Relations Theory', in *The Return of Culture and Identity in International Relations*, ed. Yosef Lapid and Friedrich Kratochwil (Boulder, Colo.: Lynne Rienner, 1996).
[61] Steven Hobden, 'Historical Sociology: Back to the Future in International Relations?', in *Historical Sociology and International Relations*, ed. Steven Hobden and John M. Hobson (Cambridge University Press, 2002), pp. 48–9; Christian Reus-Smit, 'The Idea of History and History with Ideas', in *Historical Sociology and International Relations*, ed. Steven Hobden and John M. Hobson (Cambridge University Press, 2002), p. 126.
[62] Kurt Burch, 'Constituting IPE and Modernity', in *Constituting International Political Economy*, ed. Kurt Burch and Robert A. Denemark (Boulder, Colo.: Lynne Rienner, 1997), p. 26; Geoffrey Underhill, 'Conceptualizing the Changing Global Order', in *Political Economy and the Changing Global Order*, ed. Richard Stubbs and Geoffrey Underhill (Oxford University Press, 1999), p. 10.
[63] Gideon Rose, 'Neoclassical Realism and Theories of Foreign Policy'; Randall Schweller, *Deadly Imbalances: Tripolarity and Hitler's Strategy of World Conquest* (New York: Columbia University Press, 1998), p. 20; Fareed Zakaria, *From Wealth to Power: The Unusual Origins of America's World Role* (Princeton University Press, 1998), pp. 32–5.
[64] Ole Holsti, 'Models of International Relations: Realist and Neoliberal Perspectives on Conflict and Cooperation', in *The Global Agenda*, 5th edn, ed. Charles W. Kegley and

vision of political relations is comprehensible, if ultimately unsatisfactory. To still others, classical Realism's concern with human nature – in particular its concern with an elemental lust for power – overwhelmed any sustained concern with social and historical trajectories and the importance of political structures.[65] From yet another perspective, the assumption of the state as a unitary rational actor precluded by analytic fiat the need to enquire more deeply into the complexities of state structure, domestic preferences, and action,[66] while still other accounts locate its origins in Realism's uncritical adoption of the classical liberal divide between politics and economics.[67] Whatever the explanation, however, the narrowness of the classical Realist vision of politics is seen as a symbol of its limited theoretical bases and utility, and the evolution of the field of International Relations is again presented as a process of moving beyond these limits toward a more sophisticated theory of international politics.

There is little doubt that Morgenthau proposes a very constricted vision of politics. In *Politics among Nations*, for example, he argues that 'a nation is not normally engaged in international politics when it concludes an extradition treaty with another nation, when it exchanges goods and services with other nations, when it cooperates with another nation in providing relief from natural catastrophes, and when it promotes the distribution of cultural achievements throughout the world'.[68] Such an unambiguous statement seems only to confirm suspicions concerning the narrowness of the Realist vision and its obvious – and increasing – inadequacy as a basis for thinking about world politics. Yet, when seen in light of Morgenthau's intellectual background, such dismissals begin to look suspiciously easy, and the narrowness of the Realist vision of politics ceases to be an obvious point of criticism and becomes instead an intriguing question: why would a sophisticated thinker like Morgenthau propound such a narrow and (on the surface) obviously

Eugene Wittkopf (New York: McGraw-Hill, 1998), p. 135; Peter J. Katzenstein, Robert O. Keohane, and Stephen D. Krasner, '*International Organization* and the Study of World Politics', *International Organization*, 52:4 (1998), p. 652; Charles Kegley and Eugene Wittkopf, *World Politics: Trend and Transformation*, 7th edn (New York: St Martins, 1999), pp. 28–34; John Vasquez, *The Power of Power Politics: From Classical Realism to Neotraditionalism* (Cambridge University Press, 1998), pp. 45–59.

[65] Donnelly, *Realism in International Relations*, pp. 43–80.

[66] Katzenstein, Keohane, and Krasner, '*International Organization*', p. 658.

[67] Justin Rosenberg, *The Empire of Civil Society: A Critique of the Realist Theory of International Relations* (London: Verso, 1994), p. 24.

[68] Morgenthau, *Politics among Nations*, p. 26.

simplistic understanding of politics as the basis for a Realist theory of politics and International Relations?

I would like to suggest that Morgenthau's narrowing of the political sphere is neither an oversight nor a result of a lack of analytic sophistication. Rather than ignoring the obvious breadth of political life or the complexity of the concept of 'the political',[69] the limited conception of politics is part of a sophisticated intellectual strategy seeking to address the centrality of power in politics without reducing politics to an undifferentiated sphere of violence, to distinguish legitimate forms of political power, to insulate the political sphere from physical violence, and to discern the social structures which such a strategy requires to be successful.

Power, interest, and politics

In unravelling the nature of politics in Morgenthau's Realism, it is useful to begin by noting the very strong emphasis he places on the importance of the concept of 'politics', and on the autonomy of politics as a sphere of action and understanding. In what is perhaps the most oft-quoted phrase in the history of International Relations, Morgenthau's 'Second Principle of Political Realism' holds that its core lies in the definition of politics as 'interest defined in terms of power'. 'This concept', he argues, is crucial if one is to make sense of international politics, for it

> provides the link between reason trying to understand international politics and the facts to be understood. It sets politics as an autonomous sphere of action and understanding apart from other spheres, such as economics (understood in terms of interest defined as wealth), ethics, aesthetics, or religion. Without such a concept a theory of politics, domestic or international, would be altogether impossible, for without it we could not distinguish between political and nonpolitical facts, nor could we bring at least a measure of systematic order to the political sphere.[70]

Yet despite the almost iconic status that 'interest defined as power' has assumed in presentations of Realist theory, a close examination of Morgenthau's discussion quickly reveals that power and interest are actually remarkably flexible and indeterminate concepts. The forms

[69] Michi Ebata and Beverly Neufeld (eds.), *Confronting the Political in International Relations* (London: Palgrave, 2000); Jenny Edkins, *Poststructuralism and International Relations: Bringing the Political Back In* (Boulder, Colo.: Lynne Rienner, 1999), p. xi.
[70] Morgenthau, *Politics among Nations*, p. 5.

taken by interest and power, and the relationship between them, are fluid, and only foundational in the broadest possible sense. In his 'Third Principle of Political Realism', for example, Morgenthau discusses this fluidity in terms worth quoting at length. Realism, he argues,

> does not endow its key concept of interest defined as power with a meaning that is fixed once and for all. The idea of interest is indeed the essence of politics and is unaffected by the circumstances of time and place . . . Yet the kind of interest determining political action in a particular period of history depends upon the political and cultural context within which foreign policy is formulated. *The goals that might be pursued by nations in their foreign policy can run the whole gamut of objectives any nation has ever pursued or might possibly pursue.*[71]

The objects of 'interest', it turns out, are almost limitless. Literally *anything* could in principle be an interest. A similar indeterminacy applies to power. As he puts it:

> The same observations apply to the concept of power. Its content and the manner of its use are determined by the political and cultural environment. Power may comprise anything that establishes and maintains the power of man over man. Thus power covers all social relationships which serve that end, from physical violence to the most subtle psychological ties by which one mind controls another. Power covers the domination of man by man, both when it is disciplined by moral ends and controlled by constitutional safeguards, as in Western democracies, and when it is that untamed and barbaric force which finds its laws in nothing but its own strength and its sole justification in its aggrandizement.[72]

At this point, a degree of confusion might seem appropriate, for these extremely broad visions of power and interest seem logically to lead not to a narrow conception of politics, but to an extremely broad one.[73] If all interests are indeterminate, and all forms of power are multiple and contextual, then surely this implies that all realms of life in and through which interests are formulated and power is exercised are 'political',

[71] Morgenthau, *Politics among Nations*, pp. 8–9, emphasis added.
[72] Morgenthau, *Politics among Nations*, p. 9.
[73] For a criticism of this breadth, see Inis L. Claude, *Power and International Relations* (New York: Random House, 1962), pp. 25–37. For a discussion of how Morgenthau's view of power has been adopted in different ways by different contemporary Realists, see Legro and Moravcsik, 'Is Anybody Still a Realist?', pp. 22–34; and for its significance in the debate over Realism and the end of the Cold War, see William Wohlforth, 'Realism and the End of the Cold War', in *The Perils of Anarchy*, ed. Sean Lynn-Jones (Cambridge, Mass.; MIT Press, 1995), pp. 9–10.

and that what is required is an extremely broad – almost pervasive – vision of politics rather than its opposite. In fact, it might even be argued that Morgenthau's understanding of power and interest has its closest analogues in social theories more commonly associated with the work of Pierre Bourdieu and Michel Foucault, with their very broad understanding of power and the 'political' field, rather than with the narrow understanding of politics that Realism stands accused of adopting.[74] But despite the obviousness of this conclusion, it is not the path that Morgenthau chooses to follow, and his reasons for not doing so are central in understanding the concept of politics in the Realist theory he develops.

Broadly speaking, Morgenthau's definition of politics as 'interest defined as power' has been given two interpretations in International Relations theory, neither of which comes fully to terms with the complex position he stakes out. The first of these interpretations tends to reduce Realism to a form of materialism. Here, both interest and power are defined primarily in material – and particularly military – terms, and international politics becomes characterised as a struggle for material power. As John Mearsheimer succinctly put it in an oft-quoted statement of this theme: 'Realists believe that state behavior is largely shaped by the *material structure* of the international system.'[75]

The adequacy of this materialism as the foundation for the study of International Relations has been a source of continual debate within the field, and is often presented as marking a fundamental divide between Realists and their critics – particularly social constructivists who stress the importance of ideational phenomena. However, as evidenced in the definitions of power and interest cited above, a reduction of 'interest defined as power' to predominantly material forms of each clearly does not do full justice to Morgenthau's Realist understanding of politics. Confirmation of this point is provided by Morgenthau himself, who felt

[74] Pierre Bourdieu, *Language and Symbolic Power* (Cambridge: Polity Press, 1992) and Michel Foucault, *Discipline and Punish*, trans. Alan Sheridan (New York: Vintage Books, 1979) and 'Two Lectures', in M. Foucault, *Power/Knowledge*, ed. Colin Gordon (New York: Pantheon, 1980). A theme suggestively explored by Richard Ashley, 'The Poverty of Neorealism', *International Organization*, 38:2 (1984). A good, critical survey of 'power' in International Relations is Guzzini, *Realism in International Relations*, pp. 218–22; more broadly, see Barry Hindess, *Discourses of Power: Hobbes to Foucault* (Oxford: Basil Blackwell, 1996).

[75] John Mearsheimer, 'The False Promise of International Institutions', *International Security*, 19:3 (Winter 1994/5). For an innovative recasting of materialism see Daniel Deudney, 'Regrounding Realism: Anarchy, Security, and Changing Material Contexts', *Security Studies*, 10:1 (2000). A very useful survey is found in Guzzini, *Realism in International Relations*, pp. 133–5.

the need to stress the role of diverse forms of power precisely because of the tendency to reduce power to its material aspects. As he put it in a discussion of revisions to the fourth edition of *Politics among Nations*: 'Against the misunderstanding of the central element of power, which, after having been underrated to the point of total neglect, now tends to be equated with material strength, especially of a military nature, I have stressed more than before its immaterial aspects, especially in the form of charismatic power, and have elaborated the discussion of political ideologies.'[76] Material power and the pursuit of material interest are indeed central, but neither power nor interest can be reduced to material forms. To do so does little justice to the multiple, fluid, and relational view of power and interest Morgenthau puts forward. Nor, importantly, does it account for the claim that politics is a *specific* sphere that is distinguishable from the pursuit of material interest characteristic of, for example, the economic sphere.

The question of the specificity of 'politics' is also important when considering the second common interpretation of Realism. In this view, the definition of politics as 'interest defined as power' is seen in essentially instrumentalist terms: if power is a necessary means for the pursuit of interests, then power becomes an end in itself. As a necessary instrument to the achievement of any given interest, power itself becomes a universal interest and, therefore, as John Ruggie summarises this view, 'whatever the ends that leaders may seek to achieve, their doing so is mediated and constrained by all states deploying their power to pursue their own ends, so that power itself becomes the proximate end of any state's foreign policy'.[77]

On the surface, an instrumentalist interpretation of Realism seems more satisfactory; and it certainly captures the open-ended and multiple character of interests and power more fully than does a reductionist materialism. However, in reducing Realism to a form of instrumentalism, this view also fails to account for the specificity of 'politics', and to address the question of why politics constitutes the *autonomous* sphere that Morgenthau insists it does. If the definition of politics is 'interest defined as power', and power is just an instrument for the achievement of other interests, then what differentiates the political sphere from any other realm of social life in which power is essential to the successful pursuit of a given interest? In the economic sphere, for example, the pursuit

[76] Morgenthau, *Politics among Nations*, p. ix.
[77] Ruggie, *Constructing the World Polity*, pp. 4–5.

of economic power is essential for the acquisition of wealth. But if this is the case, what is unique about the 'political' sphere as opposed to that of the economic, and why does Morgenthau explicitly differentiate the political from the economic sphere? In short, if the pursuit of any interest requires power, and power becomes an end in itself in any sphere of social life, then 'interest defined as power' applies equally to all social spheres and ceases to be uniquely useful as a concept for distinguishing 'political' phenomena from other forms of social interaction. 'Politics', accordingly, would again become an extremely broad sphere, not a conspicuously narrow one. While an instrumentalist definition may tell us something about the Realist stress on power as a means to the realisation of interests, it fails to specify what is distinctively 'political' about the sphere of politics in Realist theory.

On closer examination, the most prevalent understandings of 'politics' in Morgenthau's Realism fail to come to terms with either its conceptual specificity, or to explain his remarkably limited definition of the sphere of politics. Similarly, neither provides a satisfactory account of the relationship between power and interest that is at the heart of Morgenthau's Realist conception of politics. These considerations seem to leave open two possible options. From one perspective, they might be seen as still further evidence of the inadequacy of Realism, and yet another reason to consign it firmly to the theoretical (pre)history of International Relations. A second position, however, is to take these apparent inconsistencies as inspiration for a deeper investigation of the Realist vision of politics. Taking this path requires a broader engagement with the philosophical roots, intellectual lineage, and political context underlying Morgenthau's Realism and its relationship to liberalism.

The Weberian legacy

At the heart of Morgenthau's conception of politics lies a reworking of Weber's liberalism,[78] and a recognition and attempt to counter the power of Schmitt's transformation of this legacy into his deeply conflictual concept of the political.[79] In the context of Morgenthau's understanding of politics, this Weberian legacy has two related aspects: a methodological

[78] For an excellent tracing of the various trajectories of Weber's legacy, see McCormick, *Carl Schmitt's Critique of Liberalism*, chapter 1 especially.

[79] That Schmitt's understanding of the specificity of politics had a profound influence on Morgenthau can be seen clearly in his 1933 work on the 'concept of politics' which contains an extended critical discussion of Schmitt and his 'concept of the political'. There, in partial agreement with Schmitt, Morgenthau argues that, 'We must conclude that it is impossible to establish any distinction between political and non-political questions based on their

stance and a philosophical vision of the specificity of politics as a sphere of social life. Each – and the less well-recognised relationship between them – is central in understanding the limited and specific vision of politics in his Realism. When placed in these contexts, Morgenthau's Realist concept of 'politics' and the remarkably narrow definition of political phenomena which he develops emerge as sophisticated and self-conscious attempts to deal with the relationship between politics, power, and violence. His goal is to construct an understanding of politics that, while continuing to recognise its Schmittian dimensions, can avoid reducing politics to a relation of enmity, and that can provide a justification of a public sphere of engagement and potential mediation of differences as a core dimension of politics itself.

The most straightforward element of this limitation lies in the influence that Weber's philosophy of social science had upon Morgenthau. Weber's method of ideal-types had sought to provide a means of classifying different social spheres according to their specific logics. By distinguishing these spheres (as ideal-types) the analyst can abstract specific logics of action from the totality of social life, and then examine how they struggle, interpenetrate and fuse in the production of concrete practices, as, for example, in Weber's classic analysis of the role of radical Protestant morals and aesthetics in the rise of the economic logic of capitalism.[80] The influence of this view on Morgenthau is obvious; as he puts it, 'Intellectually, the political realist maintains the autonomy of the political sphere, as the economist, the lawyer, the moralist maintain theirs. He thinks in terms of interest defined as power, as the economist

subject matter, seeing that the notion of politics is not necessarily inherent in a certain particular subject matter, just as it is not necessarily absent from other particular subject matters' ('Nous devons conclure qu'il est impossible d'établir une distinction, d'après leur objet, entre les questions politiques et nonpolitiques, étant donné que la notion du politique n'est pas nécessairement inhérente à certains objets déterminés, comme elle n'est pas nécessairement absente d'autres objets déterminés'). *La Notion du 'Politique' et la théorie des différends internationaux* (Paris: Librairie du Recueil Sirey, 1933), p. 32. My thanks to Thomas Jorgensen for his help with elements of this translation. Both Scheuerman and Koskenniemi have clearly demonstrated that many of Morgenthau's early works bear the clear marks of his extended engagement with Schmitt's ideas. It has been argued that Schmitt's modification of his theory of the friend–enemy relation in the second edition of *The Concept of the Political* to include the concept of 'intensification' was a direct (and, much to Morgenthau's irritation, unattributed) result of his engagement with Morgenthau's initial work on international law. See Scheuerman, *Carl Schmitt*, pp. 229–34, 258; Frei, *Hans Morgenthau*, p. 161; and Koskenniemi, *Gentle Civilizer of Nations*, pp. 440–3. On the broader legal context see David Dyzenhaus, *Legality and Legitimacy: Carl Schmitt, Hans Kelsen and Hermann Heller in Weimar* (Oxford: Clarendon Press, 1997).

[80] Max Weber, *The Protestant Ethic and the Spirit of Capitalism*, trans. Talcott Parsons (New York: Scribner's, 1958).

thinks in terms of interest defined as wealth; the lawyer of the conformity of action with legal rules . . . the political realist asks "How does this policy affect the power of the nation?" (Or of the federal government, of Congress, of the party, of agriculture, as the case may be).'[81]

Part of the narrowness of the concept of politics is, therefore, an analytic device: an attempt to specify politics as an ideal-type as referring particularly to structures of governance. Yet it is clear that this designation alone is not enough to account for the conceptual specificity of politics or its delineation as an autonomous sphere. If the focus of the political Realist is on how a particular policy increases, for example, the 'power of agriculture', there is no exclusive connection between this and *governmental* structures. Nor is it clear why this 'political' sphere should be separated from, for example, cultural spheres that support particular interests: for instance, a belief in the importance of rural agriculture in maintaining national identity. Once again, the defining concept of the political Realist – interest defined in terms of power – seems strangely amorphous and ill-defined. It seemingly applies to almost any actor, any interest, any form of power, in any given sphere. It either depends on a content that is smuggled in after the definition (interest as the 'national' interest, or power as 'governmental' power), or is completely lacking in content.

Coming to terms fully with the specificity of 'politics' requires a further appreciation of how the roots of this concept lie not in Weber's methodology, but in his political philosophy, and the Nietzschean roots of that philosophy.[82] Weber begins from the postulate of value pluralism: there are no transcendental standards that can provide a ground for conduct, and in modernity individuals are left only with the choice between warring 'gods and demons'.[83] In this disenchanted context, all value choices and the actions that follow from them are inescapably 'political' in the sense that they involve claims about values that are irresolvable by appeal to a transcendent authority, and thus inevitably carry with them the possibility of contestation and conflict with competing visions. But

[81] Morgenthau, *Politics among Nations*, p. 11.

[82] The Nietzschean roots of Morgenthau's thinking have been comprehensively documented in Frei, *Hans Morgenthau*. For a revealing analysis of the development of Morgenthau's early ideas on human desires for power, see Koskenniemi, *Gentle Civilizer of Nations*, pp. 442 and 448–52. The links between Nietzsche and Weber have been nicely outlined by David Owen, *Maturity and Modernity: Nietzsche, Weber, Foucault and the Ambiguity of Reason* (London: Routledge, 1994); see also Steven P. Turner and R. A. Factor, *Max Weber and the Dispute over Reason and Value* (London: Routledge, 1984).

[83] Or as Morgenthau phrased the theme in terms of international politics: 'Nations meet under an empty sky from which the Gods have departed.' *Politics among Nations*, p. 249.

as Mark Warren has insightfully argued, this does not mean that Weber collapses into a facile relativism or into a vision of politics as pure violence. As he puts it:

> Viewed negatively, politics is essentially 'struggle' (Weber 1978a, 1414), the 'striving to share power or striving to influence the distribution of power, either among states or among groups within a state' (Weber 1946, 78). Viewed positively, however, politics involves relating individual value rationalities to group choices, implying that recognition of persons together with processes of discussion, argumentation, and consensus lie behind exercises of power. Political actions are a distinctively human kind of social action: they combine instrumental and value rationality, and thus develop and express what Weber conceives as the human potential for teleological action and self-determination.[84]

Politics is thus identified by its specific duality: an indeterminacy that makes it at one and the same time a realm of power and inevitable struggle, *and* a realm of openness and self-determination. For Weber, the maximisation of the positive potential entailed by this value relativity required a differentiation and separation of value spheres at both the conceptual *and* the social levels. To quote Warren once more: 'Weber does not seek one set of value criteria to ground all others because he sees cultural progress in the differentiation of value spheres, none of which are primary and each of which has its own distinctive kind of rationality and criteria or propriety. This is true for economics, aesthetics, erotic life, language, intellectual life, social life, and so on. Each sphere is necessary for a fully human life, and it would be inappropriate to universalize the standards of one sphere to all others. One does not judge art by logical consistency, love by utility, or righteousness by efficiency.'[85] This is, as he nicely summarises it, a 'politicized neo-Kantian liberalism':[86] adopting Kant's differentiation of spheres of knowledge (the empirical, the aesthetic, the moral), but rather than grounding them transcendentally, legitimates these categorical distinctions politically and ethically in terms of the possibilities of human freedom, and consequentially in terms of social differentiation that will allow the maximisation of that freedom.

Seen in light of this Weberian heritage, the specificity of politics in Morgenthau's Realism becomes clearer. Power and struggle are intrinsic

[84] Mark Warren, 'Max Weber's Liberalism for a Nietzschean World', *American Political Science Review*, 82:1 (1988), p. 35.
[85] Warren, 'Max Weber's Liberalism', p. 38.
[86] Warren, 'Max Weber's Liberalism', p. 31.

to human life. Politics is the sphere of contest over the determination of values and wills; an undetermined realm in which the struggle for power and domination is pure (without content) and thus potentially limitless. The specificity of the political sphere thus lies in power as an interest *in itself*. Politics, as an autonomous sphere, has no intrinsic object of interest; it is literally lacking in any concrete 'interest' except the pursuit of power. This indeterminacy stands in contrast to other social spheres that possess concrete interests, forms of power, and limits that politics does not; for example, the economic sphere has a specific logic of interest (material gain) and a dominant form of power (control over material resources) that define its operation and give it a particular set of limits. Paradoxically, it is the unlimited nature of politics that is the basis of its conceptual specificity, and the basis of the distinction between the political sphere and other social spheres.[87]

Politics, in principle, has no limits – it lacks defined objects of interest or resources of power. Its limits lie only in the confrontation between divergent wills, interests, and the forms of power they can wield. To return to Morgenthau's illustration of 'non-political' issues cited earlier, both legal (extradition) and trade relations are not 'political' because they are conducted within largely shared and settled structures of agreement on the appropriate norms, rules, and procedures. The 'political' struggle for power – the struggle over foundational principles, values, etc. – does not prevail in these relations (unless one actor is explicitly using them to these ends). By contrast, since it has no specific object to govern its interests or its potential forms of power, 'politics' is an almost limitless field of struggle and domination. And as Morgenthau repeatedly makes clear, the conceptual specificity of 'politics' applies across all political realms; at this level, there is no fundamental distinction between domestic and international politics. The primary difference between the two lies in the social resources – institutional and ideational – available for the limitation of the negative logic of politics, and the exploitation of its positive capacities. As he puts it, 'The essence of international politics is identical with its domestic counterpart', a symmetry 'modified only by the different conditions under which this struggle takes place in the domestic and the international spheres'.[88]

[87] This point is also stressed by Frei, *Hans Morgenthau*, pp. 126–8 especially, and Koskenniemi, *Gentle Civilizer of Nations*, pp. 453–4; see also John M. Hobson and Leonard Seabrooke, 'Reimagining Weber: Constructing International Society and the Social Balance of Power', *European Journal of International Relations*, 7:2 (2001), p. 269.
[88] Morgenthau, *Politics among Nations*, p. 32.

This recognition allows us to make sense of Morgenthau's claim that as an ideal-type purely 'political' man would be a 'beast': as a sphere without content or limits, politics is potentially a remarkably destructive dimension of human action.[89] Yet at the same time, politics is the protean centre of social life, and Morgenthau views the indeterminacy of politics as a potentially positive phenomenon, representing the possibility of change, and as a core principle of democracy. As he characterised this ethic in direct contrast to that of Nazism: 'The doctrine of democracy starts with the assumption that all citizens are potentially capable of arriving at the right political decision and that, consequently, nobody has a monopoly of political wisdom to which, at least potentially, the others would not have access . . . Philosophic relativism, political pluralism, the protection of minorities of all kinds and with respect to all kinds of activities are therefore the earmarks of democratic theory and practice.'[90]

The limitless nature of politics is thus the source of both its perils and its possibilities.[91] Morgenthau consistently argues for the delineation (though not exclusion) of the realm of politics from other social realms, particularly the economic and the moral. In particular, the idea that the capacity for authoritative decision and the determination of substantive values, and the ability ultimately to uphold that capacity (both internally and externally) in a life and death struggle if necessary, defines his understanding of political differentiation and thus of relations between political orders.[92] But decision does not necessarily entail enmity, and politics is not exclusively defined and determined by a violent and amoral logic of friendship and enmity.[93] The essential

[89] Morgenthau, *Politics among Nations*, p. 13.

[90] Morgenthau, *Scientific Man versus Power Politics*, p. 144; see also Murray, 'Moral Politics', p. 101.

[91] Similarly, history is neither pure continuity, nor pure change. Rather, the enduringly empty nature of politics – its radical indeterminacy that is part of its constant struggle for power – represents both its unchanging nature *and* its capacity for change. The affinities between Morgenthau's views and Nietzsche's conception of history as 'eternal return' are striking here. For an insightful analogous discussion see James Der Derian, 'Post-Theory: The Eternal Return of Ethics in International Relations', in *New Thinking in International Relations*, ed. Michael Doyle and John Ikenberry (Boulder, Colo.: Westview Press, 1998).

[92] It is tempting to use the more conventional International Relations phrasing here and refer to this as the problem of sovereignty. But as a number of contemporary analyses argue and as Morgenthau was well aware, to lump all forms of political delineation under the rubric of sovereignty is to risk reifying political practice through the application of a concept frequently overlain with all kinds of modern assumptions. For an excellent analysis of sovereignty, see Jens Bartelson, *A Genealogy of Sovereignty* (Cambridge University Press, 1995).

[93] This vision of politics also underlies Morgenthau's oft-misunderstood conception of history. Morgenthau is not guilty of the facile charge that he presents a view of history

emptiness of politics also represents its promise and positive potential. The quest for power without a fixed interest leaves those interests open to transformation and revision, and is thus the condition of change and progress. As a realm without a fixed interest, politics becomes the sphere of activity uniquely concerned with the consideration, generation, and transformation of common interests and understandings: the sphere where the fundamental meanings and values of social life are contested and determined. The lack of fixed understandings of the good and the true is the condition of modern politics, and the basis of its distinctiveness as a realm of freedom, creativity, and change.

Politics is an extraordinarily dangerous sphere. By understanding its essence – its narrow conceptual specificity – it is possible to see the logic of political conflict, and the possibilities for its amelioration. 'Political' conflict cannot be reduced to conflicts of material interest and calculation.[94] It is far more fundamental; indeed elemental. Rather than wishing away this conflict, it is necessary to recognise its nature and attempt to exploit its positive potential. And it is here that the importance of limits in Realism becomes clearer. The process of conceptual limitation is linked to political *practices* of limitation. Far from precluding a broad analysis of political life, the narrow definition of politics becomes the foundation of a sophisticated sociological and institutional analysis, in which a limited conception of politics is deployed in an attempt to constrain the destructive capacities of the logic of 'politics', while retaining its possibilities for creativity. This requires discerning the structures and practices that support this goal, identifying those that are lacking, and developing a *strategy* to maximise the promise of politics and limit its perils.[95]

that does not 'change'. He is well aware of the historical variation of social and political orders – and relations between them – over time. For him, it is this essence of the political as decision, and its connection to violence in the last resort, that is historically consistent. This is even more clearly illustrated by taking seriously one of his most overlooked claims: that nuclear weapons have *revolutionised* International Relations. For Morgenthau, nuclear weapons do not simply modify an eternal structure of anarchy: they challenge the political at its most fundamental level because the classic Schmittian vision of the political as residing ultimately in a life and death struggle no longer makes any sense in an age of mutual annihilation. See, in particular, Hans Morgenthau, 'Four Paradoxes of Nuclear Strategy', *American Political Science Review*, 58:1 (1964).

[94] Contrast to the positions surveyed in Rosecrance that lead him to ask, 'Has Realism Become Cost-Benefit Analysis?', *International Security*, 26:2 (2001).

[95] As Scheuerman puts it: 'Morgenthau argues that the "concept of the political" in the proper sense of the term refers exclusively to "the degree of intensity with which an object of interest to a state relates to the individuality of a state". Political conflicts are those exhibiting an especially intense or passionate character; for this reason, they are refractory

A strategy of limits

Morgenthau's Realist strategy of limitation develops along three dimensions. First, he defines politics and political power as *separate* from other forms of power, particularly physical violence. This provides the basis for a limitation on the legitimate use of violence within the sphere of domestic politics. Second, he seeks to foster the development of other social spheres whose forms of interest and power can balance those of politics, minimising the attraction of its violent potential and counteracting its capacities. Third, he attempts to insulate these spheres from each other. The spheres of morality, law, and economics must be insulated against the intrusion of the logic of limitless domination characteristic of politics, while the openness of the political sphere must be defended against its subsumption within these other spheres. In actuality, these structures and strategies of limitation will always be partial, and political practice will always involve the interpenetration of different spheres and the struggle between them. But this interpenetration must always take place against the background of their basic separation, a separation which is essential for the operation of an ethical and balanced political order.

Morgenthau's thinking clearly bears the marks of his engagement with Schmitt: his understanding of politics as an undetermined realm of pure will reflects a similar position (and Nietzschean–Weberian heritage) on the specificity of 'politics', and he shares the view that the essence of sovereignty lies in the capacity for decision.[96] However, the most important element of this relationship lies in the way that Schmitt's concept of the political provides a key position *against* which Morgenthau's own understanding of a limited politics emerges.[97] The limited vision of politics can, in fact, be seen as a direct attempt to counter

to peaceful legal settlement. Within the sphere of interstate relations, "the specifically political quality is to be seen in the particularly close relation that rulers assert from time to time between the state and certain goods or values that they hold indispensable to its security or greatness". Conflicts concerning such goods and values, whose specific characteristics obviously vary enormously, are political dynamite and thus unlikely to be resolved satisfactorily by judicial devices. In this sense of the term, a dispute can be more or less political (just as it can be more or less warm or cold); intensity is always a matter of degree.' *Carl Schmitt*, pp. 231–2.

[96] Morgenthau, *Politics among Nations*, pp. 307–25.

[97] My position here is indebted to Scheuerman, but differs somewhat from his focus on the idea of intensification. Morgenthau's early work was characterised by an extremely broad conception of politics, whereas his 'American' writings advocate an extremely narrow view. On the surface, this seems to mark either a contradiction or a fundamental transformation in his views. Seen in this perspective, however, it is less a shift in his views than evidence of an increasing sophistication and political judgement. The undifferentiated vision

the Schmittian logic of enmity at both the conceptual and the social levels, and to avoid the radical realpolitik that is one potential outcome of the specific concept of politics he adopts.

As noted earlier, Morgenthau views democracy as based on the claim that there is no fixed idea of the right or the good, and that this openness is, paradoxically, itself the principle of democracy. Democracy, he asserts outright, is based on a 'relativistic philosophy' and a 'relativistic ethos' which is paradoxically protected by 'certain absolute objective principles which legitimize majority rule but are not subject to change by it'.[98] While decision may be the essence of sovereignty, the indeterminacy that is the essence of politics is the principle of democratic sovereignty. This indeterminacy itself must be a value to be defended if it is to survive, and this may require the application of violence. But the only legitimate exercise of violence is in support of the principled openness that is the essence of politics.[99] This is the paradoxical role of the state, and the limit of its *legitimate* exercise of violence.[100] The capacity for coercion may be important (indeed essential) in upholding political structures, but it is not their essence. Violence is only legitimate to the extent that it insulates the 'political' sphere from forms of power derived from physical violence: the state's capacity for violence balances all attempts to bring violence into the political sphere, but this violence is limited to the defence of that order, it is not the principle of its operation.

These concerns are clearly expressed in Morgenthau's distinction between political power and military power. 'When we speak of power', he argues, 'we mean man's control over the minds and actions of other men. By political power we refer to the mutual relations of control among the holders of public authority, and between the latter and the people at large.'[101] This is not merely an institutional distinction, it is a practical and ethical one: politics is a relationship of obligation and identification,

of politics as 'intensification' (1933) is transformed into a practical judgement seeking to limit the sphere of politics in full consciousness of its intrinsically unlimited (and, therefore, potentially destructive) nature, and yet to defend a political sphere of (democratic) indeterminacy and limits. Similarly, my view here differs from Koskenniemi's admirable analysis, since I hold that Morgenthau's turn away from law and toward 'politics' involved precisely an engagement with the question of a democratic public sphere that Koskenniemi views Morgenthau as largely foreclosing.

[98] Morgenthau, *Truth and Power*, pp. 40–1.

[99] On at least some readings, this is Schmitt's position as well. However, to enter into the complex debates surrounding Schmitt and liberal democracy is beyond the scope of this treatment.

[100] Morgenthau, *Politics among Nations*, p. 490.

[101] Morgenthau, *Politics among Nations*, p. 26.

and properly *political* domination takes this form and is constrained by these limits. By contrast 'When violence becomes an actuality, it signifies the abdication of political power in favour of military or pseudo-military power.'[102] The narrow conceptual definition of politics is here part of an attempt to distinguish the exercise of legitimate political power and domination, and particularly to insulate this sphere from the intrusion of physical violence and domination.[103]

Seen in this light, the narrow definition of politics and its clear delineation from other social spheres is not only analytically or methodologically driven, it is a part of a comprehensive political philosophy. Equating political power with physical violence would violate the autonomy of the political, reducing its logic solely to coercion and thus destroying the autonomy of politics itself. By defining politics narrowly, Morgenthau seeks to distinguish the forms of power *appropriate* to politics, to limit their legitimate exercise within the political sphere, to insulate the political sphere to the greatest degree possible from other forms of power, interest, and domination, and to ensure that the openness and capacity for change that is the promise of politics is not foreclosed by the domination of the interests and power structures of other spheres. The conceptual specificity – and thus narrowness – of 'politics' is part of an attempt to justify a political practice in which the indeterminacy of the political sphere is understood in both its positive and negative dimensions.

However, the effectiveness of this strategy requires more than just conceptual clarity concerning the specificity of the 'political'. As Morgenthau was well aware, ideas alone are rarely powerful enough to prevail in social life.[104] For the limited understanding of political power itself to have power, it must possess viable social foundations and be supported by competing interests. In pursuit of these foundations for a politics of limits, Morgenthau invokes one of Realism's most basic concepts: the balance of power.

The idea of a balance of power and interest is justifiably recognised as a key theme in Realism. In light of the argument above, however, it takes on a significance much broader than the narrow focus on the interstate balance of power that has so dominated discussions in International Relations. For Morgenthau, the idea of a balance of power and interest

[102] Morgenthau, *Politics among Nations*, p. 27; Frei, *Hans Morgenthau*, pp. 127–8. See also Rosenthal, *Righteous Realists*, pp. 37–65 and pp. 40–1, especially.
[103] The affinities to Arendt's position in particular are very clearly illustrated here.
[104] Morgenthau, *Politics among Nations*, p. 326.

is as complex and vital at the domestic level as it is at the international. Indeed the two are closely linked. A balance of power at the domestic level supports a politics of limits that, in turn, supports a limited foreign policy and provides a more solid basis for a balance of power at the international level.

Here the conceptual distinctions central to Morgenthau's vision of politics have institutional and social implications, as part of a broadly liberal vision of politics. Distinct social spheres (economic, legal, moral, aesthetic) operating within their specific logics and forms of power can act as limits on the logic of politics and on the reach of the political sphere. While actors in these spheres may be tempted to further their interests and power by dominating the political field, they will also resist attempts by the political sphere to encroach upon their autonomy, and vice versa. What results is a *social* balance of power and interests in which the existence of 'non-political' spheres provides limits on an interest in politics, and generates forms of interest and realms of power with an interest in maintaining politics as a limited sphere. In short, the idea of politics as a *distinct* sphere is linked to a strategy of balancing social spheres and interests against one another in order to limit the reach of politics while also limiting the influence of other spheres on the political.[105]

Yet this strategy of balancing contains a crucial paradox, and a vitally important corollary. In conditions of modernity, the processes of social differentiation must be balanced against their anomic and alienating consequences. In broad historical terms, the capacity for the individual exercise of power through a faith in the ultimate power (and judgement) of God that was a key plank in the moral economy of Christendom, and that provided even the most oppressed with a feeling of power, is no longer operative. The breakdown of this moral economy of interest, along with the corresponding decline of cross-cutting and competing aristocratic hierarchies, destroyed the internal balance of power (and source of limitation) characteristic of feudal and early modern states.[106] The loss of belief in the power of the divine, and of an interest in

[105] See also the excellent treatment of this theme in Hobson and Seabrooke, 'Reimagining Weber', pp. 262–4. Indeed Morgenthau even allows that should these other forces become dominant, they can cause a nation to cease to act 'politically', and a nation's engagement in international 'politics' may wane thereby 'under the impact of cultural transformations, which may make a nation prefer other pursuits, for instance commerce, to those of power'. *Politics among Nations*, p. 26.

[106] These (Nietzschean and Tocquevillian, respectively) themes are of considerable importance to Morgenthau's explanation of the classical balance of power and its breakdown.

religion, has left individuals in the anomic condition of modernity, and societal rationalisation has increased this feeling of powerlessness. The progressive disempowerment created by bureaucratic political parties, conformist pressures of modern citizenship, and the alienating impact of large-scale industrial societies and capitalist production has led to a paradoxical rise in the mobilising power of the state and an increase in the collective interest in, and power of, 'political' logic. As Morgenthau puts it: 'The growing insecurity of the individual in Western societies, especially in the lower strata, and the atomization of Western society in general have magnified enormously the frustration of individual power drives. This, in turn, has given rise to an increased desire for compensatory identification with the collective national aspiration for power.'[107]

For Morgenthau, this process was at the core of the rise of fascism. As a philosophy which rejected a politics of limits, which identified the essence of the political with violence, conflict, and the casting of Others as enemies, and which sought to inject this logic as broadly as possible in a process of social mobilisation, fascism represented the ultimate social expression of an unbounded politics. In a passage worth quoting at length, he argues:

> Thus National Socialism was able to identify in a truly totalitarian fashion the aspirations of the individual German with the power objectives of the German nation. Nowhere in modern history has that identification been more complete. Nowhere has that sphere in which the individual pursues his aspirations for power for their own sake been smaller. Nor has the force of the emotional impetus with which that identification transformed itself into aggressiveness on the international scene been equaled in modern civilization.[108]

While the existence of separate spheres and diverse forms of power and interest blunts the possibility of *unified* social expression of the will to power within the political sphere, it can also be the source of an (unlimited) 'political' logic, giving rise to an international system of endemic and almost irreconcilable conflict. The logic of politics becomes merged with patterns of violence and enmity and extended destructively to all aspects of life, becoming the dominant logic of society as a whole and making its foreign policy wholly one of domination and conflict: a reflection of the domination of the logic of politics within the society.

They are most clearly expressed in *Scientific Man versus Power Politics*; the Nietzschean elements are explored in Frei, *Hans Morgenthau*, pp. 112–20.

[107] Morgenthau, *Politics among Nations*, p. 100.

[108] Morgenthau, *Politics among Nations*, p. 104.

Morgenthau's concern with social balances, with playing off competing interests and limiting the political sphere, has clear affinities with liberal theories of the state, and he makes no attempt to conceal his admiration for liberal and republican systems of checks and balances at both the domestic and the international level.[109] But what marks Morgenthau's Realism off from classical liberalism – and represents an underrecognised aspect of his critique of liberalism – is his insistence that a system of checks and balances, and of autonomous spheres, must continue to recognise the centrality of 'politics', and that balancing as a social strategy will only be effective if it is understood as a *principled strategy*, not a mechanistic process.[110] A failure to recognise these issues was at the heart of classical liberalism's inability to understand the nature of political relations, and its inability to cope with the rise of a 'new nationalism' that reflected a shift in the structures of power and interest under conditions of modernity.[111] In reducing the principle of social differentiation to a mechanistic process of material self-interest, and allowing the political sphere to be dominated continuously by the holders of economic power, liberalism not only lost the sense of conflict and power central to politics, it also lost the sense of indeterminacy and reform that is the positive potential of political conflict. Indeed, it even lost the ability to see that change was necessary and possible. As a result, it gave rise to movements (both domestically and internationally) that rebelled against this order.[112] When this occurred, liberalism was incapable of mobilising purely self-interested actors in defence of the liberal system itself.[113] In the reduction of politics to the pursuit of material

[109] Morgenthau, *Politics among Nations*, pp. 164–7.
[110] A point of considerable relevance to contemporary theories of the 'democratic peace' that focus on the importance of institutional checks and balances.
[111] The nation of the 'new nationalism', he argues, has dissolved the tension between morality and power by subsuming both under its own universalising desires: the 'nation, deeming itself intellectually and morally self-sufficient, threatens civilization and the human race with extinction'. Hans J. Morgenthau, *Politics in the Twentieth Century*, vol. I: *The Decline of Democratic Politics* (University of Chicago Press, 1962), p. 60. I return to these issues in chapter five.
[112] A position Morgenthau shared with E. H. Carr.
[113] This is also true of the technologisation of politics that would lead to a loss of belief and commitment in politics in itself. In this, Morgenthau agrees with Schmitt that the economic realm as one of material calculation and technical manipulation is not the same as the unlimited creative realm of the political. But unlike Schmitt, he does not ascribe to a vitalism in which all other spheres are devalued in contrast to this indeterminacy. Morgenthau's views on the technologisation of politics are most clearly found in his first (*Scientific Man versus Power Politics*, 1946) and last (*Science: Servant or Master?*, 1972) books in English. On Schmitt's critique of politics as technology, see especially McCormick, *Carl Schmitt's Critique of Liberalism*.

self-interest, classical liberalism failed to understand that liberal-democratic institutions required a commitment to the defence of the autonomy and value of the political sphere that could not be reduced to, or produced by, pure self-interest. It was thus doubly and disastrously naïve, giving rise to a paradoxical and destructive synthesis of disenchantment and theology embodied in fascism, and consequently to the equation of politics with physical violence and total domination at both the domestic and international levels.

Morgenthau's conception of 'politics' is not, therefore, just an analytic device: it is a moral and political project. Long-standing claims that his Realism eschews morality, reduces freedom to determinacy, ignores domestic politics, and denies the possibility of progress are badly mistaken. This is not to say that his thinking is without difficulties. Taken in purely analytic terms, his theory of distinct social spheres is certainly susceptible to many of the criticisms commonly levelled at Weberian-inspired methodologies. In particular, his presentation of separate social spheres as defined by specific logics – of economics solely with material gain, or eroticism as wholly with romantic love – risks obscuring rather than clarifying concrete practices. The economic and the 'romantic', for instance, were rarely far apart in the dynamics of dynastic marriage, and the play of power across different social spheres continues to be central to the operation of actual practices and forms of domination.[114] To present social reality in such clear-cut terms is to risk both analytic distortion and political naïveté. It is also to court the charge that in their replication of, for example, the distinction between politics and economics underpinning classical liberal economics, these categories are by no means politically innocent.

Yet it is also important to note that Morgenthau does not assume that these categories and social spheres are natural or given. As we saw earlier, he is well aware that they have evolved as separate spheres through a series of historical struggles and conflicts. The autonomy of religion, for example, developed as a consequence of the political–religious conflicts of the Thirty Years War, while the division between politics and economics reflects the class struggle in which the rising bourgeoisie came to supplant the aristocracy. He also well recognises that the political sphere (like all others) is in reality never pure, and that all spheres interpenetrate in ways that reflect the structures of power and interest operating in different manners at different times and places.

[114] My thanks to Vibeke Schou Pedersen for stressing the need to be clear on this point.

Morgenthau's refusal to accept an exclusive delineation of the political allows him to examine the ways in which political reality is structured according to the interpenetration of different social spheres, while still maintaining that politics has a distinctive core that must not be reduced to other spheres.[115] Even more importantly, this emphasis on the multiplicity and interrelationship of different spheres of life in the constitution of political reality, and his idea of the political as linked to processes of 'intensification', allow Morgenthau not simply a broader analytic purview and greater sociological sophistication than Schmitt, but also provide a means by which Morgenthau can think about the practical construction and evaluation of orders in terms of how these spheres are related, and link moral and political practice.[116] For while he feels that 'there is a great and neglected truth in Hobbes' extreme dictum that the state creates morality',[117] he does not feel that this leads to a wholly decisionist resolution. Rather, the core of moral judgement and practical wisdom lies in the capacity of individuals to recognise their condition, to see themselves and others in the context of mutual moral and epistemic diversity and limitation, as well as their desires for power, and to construct social and political relations that – within this difficult and limiting context – maximise the degree of moral recognition and autonomy granted to each individual, while minimising the degree of violence within and between polities.

In this context, it is particularly revealing to note the affinities between Morgenthau and Hobbes. Hobbes, it will be recalled, sought to use a combination of reason and rhetoric to effect a 'politics of cultural

[115] Morgenthau, *Politics among Nations*, p. 12. Or as he put it concerning the relationship between the political and the moral, morality cannot be 'substituted' for politics, for 'In truth, this substitution is possible only as the price of political failure and, hence, is neither possible nor desirable on rational grounds' yet morality must be 'superimposed' upon other spheres, 'limiting the choice of ends and means and delineating the legitimate sphere of a particular branch of action altogether. This latter function is particularly important for the political sphere. For the actor is peculiarly tempted to blind himself to the limits of his power and thereby to overstep the boundaries of both prudence and morality.' Morgenthau, 'The Moral Dilemmas of Political Action', in *Politics in the Twentieth Century*, vol. I., pp. 325–6.

[116] One of Morgenthau's most interesting *analytic* conclusions on this basis is that the pure power politics and supposed 'realism' of fascism were weak and unsuccessful precisely because of their too-narrow understanding of the constitution of political order in precisely these terms; see *Scientific Man versus Power Politics*, pp. 8–9 and pp. 175–8; see also Scheuerman, *Carl Schmitt*, p. 249 for similar observations.

[117] Hans J. Morgenthau, *In Defense of the National Interest* (New York: Knopf, 1951), p. 34. For a sharp criticism of Morgenthau's restricted use of Hobbes here, which ignores the central role of the Laws of Nature, see Malcolm, 'Hobbes's Theory of International Relations', p. 437.

transformation'.[118] Morgenthau attempts a similar feat, building upon two strands in American political culture. The rationalist language of interest common within American social science, and the appeal to material self-interest of American liberalism and capitalism, provide conceptual resources to be mobilised in support of a politics of limits.[119] Yet at the same time, Morgenthau's mobilisation of liberal themes takes place within a clear understanding of their limits. In this sense, the 'Machiavellian' goal he pursues resembles most closely the influence of Machiavelli upon the tradition of 'Atlantic republicanism' famously traced by J. G. Pocock.[120] Morgenthau's unalloyed admiration for the founders of the American republic (and his rhetorical mobilisation of their legacy) is not just a result of their clear-eyed view of the ubiquity of power in politics and the unreliability of human virtue as a basis for political order. It is also a result of their attempt to develop a series of republican institutions – checks and balances, and a political culture of civic virtue – that not only combated these negative characteristics, but that turned them into resources for facilitating the *productive* possibilities of politics. The appeal to interest is an attempt to structure a politics of liberty through an institutional balance of powers. But to function effectively, as Machiavelli well recognised, it was necessary that this structure of institutional balance be grounded within a deeper commitment to the institutions themselves. Morgenthau's consistent appeal to the wisdom of the Founders is more than a search for intellectual legitimation – it is a part of a sophisticated strategy in which the Founders are mobilised as culturally powerful symbols, as rhetorical allies in an attempt to foster reflection upon the values these institutions embodied, and, as I shall argue in chapter five, to support an understanding of the national interest constructed in light of them.

Morgenthau fits few of the roles conventionally scripted for him in International Relations. He resembles neither a straightforward

[118] For a different reading, see Benjamin Wong, 'Hans Morgenthau's Anti-Machiavellian Machiavellianism', *Millennium: Journal of International Studies*, 29:2 (2000).

[119] The liberal element of Morgenthau's 'domestic' politics has been noted, if somewhat confusingly analysed, by George Liska, *In Search of Poetry in the Politics of Power* (Lanham, Md: Lexington Books, 1998), pp. 71–2 especially. For a reading of Morgenthau's rhetoric see G. Thomas Goodnight, 'Hans J. Morgenthau *In Defense of the National Interest*: On Rhetoric, Realism, and the Public Sphere', in *Post-Realism: The Rhetorical Turn in International Relations*, ed. Francis A. Beer and Robert Harriman (East Lansing: Michigan State University Press, 1996).

[120] Pocock, *The Machiavellian Moment*. This argument is developed in greater detail in Vibeke Schou Pedersen and Michael C. Williams, 'Between Europe and America: Hans Morgenthau and the Rhetoric of a Republican Peace' (forthcoming).

proponent of power politics based upon human 'evil', nor a pioneering advocate of an empiricist 'science' of international politics. Nor can he be recognised in the image of an amoral advocate of the national interest, or an unreflective 'positivist' often painted by his critics. For Morgenthau, a focus on certainty, rationality, and objectivity as natural, as the unproblematic theoretical basis for practice, is politically disastrous. It is only a disenchanted liberal reason that has a chance of wilfully constructing a world based upon the liberal principles he ascribes to. To achieve this requires a *discipline* – an unstable synthesis of disenchantment and belief – that is not natural, both in one's actions and in the evaluation of the actions of others. Here lies the central transition from classical liberalism and the politics of certainty to the Weberian–Morgenthauian disenchanted construction of a liberalism of the will. In this combination of sociological analysis and rhetorical virtuosity in the service of a wilful Realist politics of cultural transformation and political limitation, Morgenthau is indeed, as William Scheuerman has suggested, a worthy descendant of Hobbes.

4 The tyranny of false polarities[1]

'All reification is a forgetting' — Theodor Adorno[2]

The preceding chapters have argued that upon closer examination three classic figures of the 'Realist tradition' bear little resemblance to their standard portrayals in International Relations. This chapter seeks to explore some of the contemporary theoretical implications of this argument. I will try to show that an appreciation of this legacy not only challenges the role scripted for 'Realism' within much of International Relations theory, but poses fundamental challenges to some of the major categorical divides which structure its debates and define its alternatives.

To make this case, I look at three such divisions: Realism versus liberalism, rationalism versus constructivism, and modernism versus postmodernism. These divides are not wholly lacking in plausibility, however they are frequently deeply misleading and have led to a reified (and often caricatured) set of oppositions rather than a framework for substantive engagement with the theoretical and political issues involved. In light of recent discussions about the possibilities of, and need for, 'dialogue' across theoretical positions,[3] a re-evaluation of the Realist tradition can help to reopen conceptual contrasts which have themselves become 'traditions' structuring theoretical debates,

[1] The phrase 'tyranny of false polarities' is from Stephen Holmes' description of political theory in his *Passions and Constraint*.

[2] Cited in Martin Jay, *The Dialectical Imagination* (Boston: Little, Brown, 1973) p. 267.

[3] See, for example, the varying perspectives put forward in Gunther Hellmann (ed.), 'Are Dialogue and Synthesis Possible in International Relations?', *International Studies Review*, 5:1 (2003), and Robert M. A. Crawford and Daryl S. L. Jarvis (eds.), *International Relations – Still an American Social Science?* (Albany: State University of New York Press, 2001).

and which tend to act as barriers to discussion and dialogue rather than as facilitating structures for it.

Liberalism versus Realism

One of the primary implications of the argument pursued in the previous three chapters is that one of the oldest and most pervasive contrasts in International Relations theory – the strict division between liberalism and Realism – is fundamentally misleading both in itself, and as a way of thinking about the evolution of Realism. The most basic source of this confusion lies in the reduction of liberalism to a form of rationalism. Once this move is made, two options follow. Either Realism's rejection of rationalism is a repudiation of liberalism, or its acceptance of rationalism signals its subsumption within liberalism. Each of these moves is prominent in International Relations theory today. The first is the basis of the fundamental opposition between Realism and liberalism that has been a starting point for discussions of International Relations theory for decades. The second has, in recent years, become the basis for the claim that Realism has largely ceased to exist as a definable position in contemporary debate. Noting, for example, how a rationalist vision of state action has come to dominate many (indeed most) forms of Realism over the past two or three decades, Legro and Moravcsik have argued that it is now difficult to see how these overtly rationalist forms of Realism differ substantially from liberal-institutionalist analyses. Provocatively, but tellingly, they argue that this raises the question: 'Is Anybody Still a Realist?'[4]

The Realist tradition explored in this study provides a different way of looking at these questions. It is certainly true that naïve forms of liberal empiricism, rationalism, and utilitarianism have been the continual target of wilful Realist criticism. But this relationship is not purely negative and the wilful Realist tradition needs to be understood as having a *dual*

[4] Legro and Moravcsik, 'Is Anybody Still a Realist?'. This article brought a raft of replies from self-declared Realists (Feaver, *et al.*, 'Correspondence: Brother Can You Spare a Paradigm'), but the diversity of these responses was as intriguing as their individual arguments, prompting their collection under the revealing (and perhaps ironic) subtitle: 'Was Anybody Ever a Realist?'. There is no doubt that key elements in the debates between contemporary (neo) liberals and Realists – such as whether states respond 'offensively' or 'defensively' to the conditions of uncertainty in which they find themselves – have resonances with the tradition traced in the first three chapters of this study. Hobbes, for instance, provides a remarkably sophisticated analysis of just such questions. Like other figures in the wilful Realist tradition, however, he does so from theoretical starting points that stand greatly apart from the rationalist assumptions that structure current debates.

relationship to liberalism.[5] Obscured by the identification of liberalism with an amorphous but largely non-existent 'liberal-idealist' tradition against which self-declared Realists consistently define themselves,[6] the complexities of the liberal tradition and its relationship to Realism have frequently been lost in International Relations. Far from being opposed to liberalism, the Realist tradition I trace here *is* a form of liberalism. What is more, the common claim that Realism is characterised by a lack of concern with domestic politics is equally erroneous. Wilful Realism *is* a theory of domestic politics: it is, indeed, a theory of 'the political' at its most basic level, concerned with the philosophical and sociological conditions of a liberal politics in modernity.[7]

The form of liberalism embraced within the Realist tradition focuses on processes involving the social construction of subjects and political orders, and upon the wilful creation of self-limiting agents and polities. A rejection of rationalist liberalism is here taken as the starting point for an attempt to generate more substantial foundations for identifiably liberal political practices. In this tradition, the essence of a liberal politics does not lie in transparent knowledge of the (rational) self, or in objectivist knowledge of the social and natural worlds. Nor does it lie in a denial of scepticism, voluntarism, wilfulness, and power out of a desire to secure either a liberal polity or political understanding from their purportedly destructive effects. In this vision, by contrast, the irreducible plurality which has been a strong element of almost all forms of liberalism is embraced as a political value and a practical imperative. Will and power are not solely conceived as dangerous and irrational forces that must be negated in the construction of a liberal polity which fosters and secures individual autonomy; they are resources and dynamics which must be taken seriously and worked with if one is to create a viable liberal order.

Grasping this wilful Realist tradition thus requires giving up a narrow identification of liberalism with visions of the self (and the state) as naturally endowed with given and fixed rationalist epistemic capacities, or as naturally grasping and pursuing materialist and utilitarian schemata

[5] A somewhat analogous tracing of two contrasting forms of liberalism can be found in Gray, *Two Faces of Liberalism*.

[6] In this context, see the revealing disciplinary history provided by Schmidt in *The Political Discourse of Anarchy*.

[7] This point is widely acknowledged by thinkers such as Richard Ashley and James Der Derian. A similar point is also made in Guzzini, *Realism in International Relations*, p. 216; and Rengger, *International Relations, Political Theory and the Problem of Order*.

of calculation. Seen in this light, the increasing rationalism of much of contemporary Realism is a movement away from this wilful tradition and toward precisely the form of rationalist liberalism that the wilful tradition rejected in the name of both Realism and a different form of broadly liberal politics.

Realism, liberalism, and rationalism

For wilful Realists contestation does not emerge from essentialised individuals competing for the same (scarce) goods within a context of epistemic agreement, a condition often conveyed by reference to Hobbes' state of nature or Rousseau's stag-hunt. On the contrary, the problem of political life is the *lack* of natural agreement on epistemic and moral questions. An engagement with scepticism becomes a limiting condition of political life. Wilful Realism attempts to account for the social and political consequences of this plurality, and to assess the dangers and opportunities which arise from it. Rather than fleeing from this relational indeterminacy into an apparently comforting but false and ultimately destructive appeal to the certainties promised by empiricism or rationalism, wilful Realists seek its 'resolution' in the social and political world: to transform it from an epistemic dilemma into a non-foundationalist political principle and social practice.[8] The conventionality of the human world is taken on as a creative challenge. Politics is not to be overcome by the verities of empirical social science, nor is it to be despaired of in the absence of such knowledge; it is embraced as providing the conditions of creation.

The central concern of wilful Realism thus becomes the moral and practical consequences of this irreducible plurality. What sets it apart from a simple subsumption within pluralistic forms of liberalism, however, is an acute concern with the practical possibilities of constructing such an order and with the centrality of power, the importance of fear, and the possibilities of violence as key elements in the construction of political orders and relations between them. Indeed this concern with practical consequences is foremost in the minds of wilful Realists, since it can hardly escape their attention that the irreducible plurality they value as an expression and bulwark of individuality could easily turn against that very possibility. At the heart of this position is a concern

[8] It is also valued as a defence against dogmatism. The classic liberal principle of openness concerning knowledge claims is affirmed rather than threatened, and the principle of individual determination of values, desires, and the like, is likewise given support.

with what, following Schmitt, has come to be termed 'the political'.[9] Politics is conceived as a distinct realm, irreducible to economics, the accumulation of empirical knowledge, or conventional morality. This is not to deny the obvious connection between any particular political order and these – and many other – social realms; broad analyses of the 'political' structure of any given context are vital. But the core question of the political, of the foundational basis of political orders, stands at the heart of wilful Realist analysis. In the absence of any natural or given foundation – which wilful Realists take as their first premise – the question becomes the construction of such a foundation and the principles, justifications, and limits (both spatial and juridical) of authority and order. The questions are both practical and ethical: what are the foundational principles of a given political order, and what are the social structures which support and erode those foundations? What are the ethical entailments and consequences of a given resolution to the question of the political? Answers to these questions set the basic context for understanding International Relations. Given resolutions of the question of the political provide the defining parameters of given political orders, and set up the question of the relationship between them. And these relationships are structured consequentially by different 'political' structures.

These concerns make wilful Realists more overtly *political* thinkers, rather than solely political philosophers espousing a pluralistic liberalism. Let me try to illustrate this by reference to that great sceptical liberal, Isaiah Berlin.[10] For Berlin, the idea that there must be *a* truth – be it scientific, social, or moral – reflects a deep and long-standing utopianism within Western thought.[11] The key to political wisdom, and to humane, liberal political practice, lies in Berlin's eyes in a renunciation of these utopian goals and the adoption of a pluralistic, non-dogmatic, tolerant politics. As he puts it with typical elegance:

> if one believes this [utopian] doctrine to be an illusion . . . then, perhaps, the best one can do is to try to promote some kind of equilibrium, necessarily unstable, between the different aspirations of different groups

[9] See R. B. J. Walker, 'International Relations and the Concept of the Political', in *International Political Theory Today*, ed. Ken Booth and Steve Smith (Cambridge: Polity Press, 1995).

[10] For a similar reading of Berlin, and a very sharp criticism of the fatuity of a strict liberal–Realist divide, see Rengger, *International Relations, Political Theory and the Problem of Order*, p. 184.

[11] From this perspective, the 'realism' so often claimed by rationalist positions in International Relations is in fact part of a long utopian tradition.

> of human beings – at the very least to prevent them from attempting to exterminate each other, and, so far as possible, to promote the maximum practical degree of sympathy and understanding, never likely to be complete, between them. But this is not, *prima facie*, a wildly exciting programme: a liberal sermon which recommends machinery designed to prevent people from doing too much harm, giving each human group sufficient room to realise its own idiosyncratic, unique, particular ends without too much interference with the ends of others, it is not a passionate battle-cry to inspire men to sacrifice and martyrdom and heroic feats. Yet if it were adopted, it might yet prevent mutual destruction, and, in the end, preserve the world.[12]

It seems to me that one would be hard pressed to find a clearer expression of the principled stance that underlies wilful Realism.[13] Yet what distinguishes wilful Realists is precisely their concern with the 'yet if' at the beginning of Berlin's final sentence. For wilful Realism is concerned above all with the relationship between these goals and political practice. As a result, it is consistently engaged with the question of the intellectual and social contexts in which such constructive, creative possibilities must take place, and with an analysis of the implications of these conditions for their success. A concern with political power is thus inevitably at the heart of these views – for if the world is not objectively given but is socially and politically constructed, then any evaluation of its current structures and possibilities must have an understanding of power relations at its centre. The conception of power at work in this tradition, however, goes well beyond the rather crude focus on material power which has often been attributed to – and legitimised by reference to – its most prominent practitioners.[14] Rather, one of its key concerns lies in the link between social understandings and specific structures of power, and particularly the role which these understandings play in constituting, mobilising, authorising, and legitimising certain forms and uses of power, and in the construction and defence of a liberal polity.

The construction of a liberal order is in this tradition linked to the adoption of a politics of limits. If politics is a world of creation, the wilful Realist does not see it as the road to perfection. Paradoxically, while

[12] Isaiah Berlin, *The Crooked Timber of Humanity* (Princeton University Press, 1998), pp. 47–8.

[13] And, as I shall discuss later, that of many forms of liberal pragmatism and even postmodern ethics. For a reading that explores the pragmatist elements of Realism, see A. J. H. Murray, *Reconstructing Realism* (Edinburgh: Keele University Press, 1997).

[14] As I shall argue below, the attempt to reduce relations to instrumental calculations on the basis of interest and material power was an attempt to construct practices by these thinkers, not a facile assumption on their behalf.

politics is the realm of human creativity, the essence of this creativity lies in the acceptance of *limits*,[15] and this acceptance is essential in order to overcome the potentially nihilistic and illiberal consequences of the sceptical position. A recognition of createdness does not licence a belief in perfectibility, or in a possibility of perfect understanding of nature or each other. Wilful Realism places an extremely high premium upon the knowledge of limits and the limits of knowledge, and upon the need for self-overcoming and self-discipline in both these regards. A recognition of the limited constructability of the world – a limitation that emerges from its very constructedness, and is thus the objective condition of social and political existence – is a requirement of wilful Realism.

Without exception, this recognition of limits is seen by wilful Realists as among the most difficult things for human beings to accept and to live in practice, and thus as an extraordinarily difficult project to achieve in politics. These problems are formulated in diverse ways: pride; a will to escape our own finitude; the aspiration to achieve 'true' understanding and commonality (community); the desire to construct our own world without constraints; the compelling need for objective and universal understanding in the face of obvious dangers; and a host of other such desires and interests militate against human beings' ability to live with the sense of limits. What is more, as Berlin notes, a politics of limits is not 'wildly exciting', and unlikely to inspire heroic action. In this light, the problem of affective, political mobilisation for the creation of a liberal order is at the heart of concern for wilful Realists.

This understanding of Realism clearly challenges the long-standing argument that liberalism (for better or worse, depending on one's stance) is concerned with the domain of domestic politics, whereas Realism either subordinates or denies this focus.[16] The readings of Hobbes, Rousseau, and Morgenthau developed over the past three chapters have tried to show that this claim is deeply suspect. An understanding of Morgenthau's views along the lines suggested in chapter three, for example, clearly challenges claims that Realism is a theory that ignores domestic politics, or that sees a categorical divide between the

[15] For a significant enquiry, see Jean Bethke Elshtain, *Augustine and the Limits of Politics* (Notre Dame, Ind.; Notre Dame University Press, 1995). Again, see also the perceptive and nuanced treatment in Rengger, *International Relations, Political Theory, and the Problem of Order*, pp. 181–4.

[16] For a still revealing survey, see Fareed Zakaria, 'Realism and Domestic Politics: A Review Essay', *International Security*, 17:1 (1992).

nature of politics within states and that between them. And while recent developments within so-called neoclassical or postclassical Realism have certainly gone some way toward a re-engagement of contemporary Realism with the impacts of state structures and domestic politics previously elided by the rigid structuralism of Kenneth Waltz's neorealism,[17] it is important to note how the classical (wilful) tradition goes well beyond a straightforward incorporation of domestic political dynamics into its analyses, demanding instead an examination of the philosophical and ethical issues surrounding political order as a whole. For Morgenthau (as for Hobbes and Rousseau) the realms of the domestic and the international are inextricable, constituting together dimensions of 'the political' in itself. Far from lacking a theory of domestic politics, Morgenthau's critique of liberalism illustrates his desire to provide a 'realistic' appreciation of the political conditions necessary for a liberal polity and reflects a deep concern with questions of *domestic* political order, the impacts of international politics upon them, and vice versa. This does not reduce international politics to an extension of domestic politics, nor does it deny differences between the two realms. But neither does it categorically divide the two. Different resolutions to the constitution of political relations within states yield different structures of relations between them, and the specific structure of these realms is central in grasping a given international order. Far from being unconcerned with questions of domestic politics at either the philosophic or practical levels, wilful Realism places these issues at the heart of its analysis.

The concern of wilful Realism with the relationship between domestic political order and its international consequences can be seen clearly in its understanding of the balance of power. As discussions of the balance of power have often stressed, sophisticated Realism does not view the rational pursuit of the national interest and the operation of the balance of power as naturally occurring phenomena in any simple sense. The conception of the state as a rational actor is the outcome of a process of political construction, and wilful Realist thought is deeply concerned with the intellectual and sociological resources that might be mobilised in order to have this form of state action prevail. As John Hall has pointed out in a particularly astute treatment, the key to sophisticated Realist

[17] See particularly William Wohlforth, *The Elusive Balance: Power and Perceptions during the Cold War* (Ithaca: Cornell University Press, 1993); and Zakaria, *From Wealth to Power*. Useful surveys are: Brooks, 'Dueling Realisms', and Rose, 'Neoclassical Realism and Theories of Foreign Policy'.

practices of rational calculation is the existence of essentially *liberal* intellectual and social structures – what he calls the 'intelligent state' – which will foster practices of rational calculation and mutual restraint, and allow them to prevail. Drawing upon Raymond Aron's similar insight, Hall argues that 'sophisticated realists also stress that states must calculate, especially given that the goals of state behavior vary. This point was made particularly forcefully by Aron when he emphasized the need to *make* states rational calculators. What Aron meant prescriptively should also be taken sociologically.'[18]

Hall's insights are very much akin to the analysis of wilful Realism developed in this study thus far. His goal is to examine how Realist understandings of international order and liberal structures of domestic order can be combined to foster stable processes of rational calculation and international accommodation. As he puts it 'Liberalism and realism traditionally have been antithetical, but they can and should embrace so as to form a new substance. That substance should be called neither realist liberalism or liberal realism, but the realism/liberalism mix.'[19] Yet this very way of framing the question demonstrates how deeply and misleadingly embedded the liberal–Realist divide is, and how limiting it can be at both the theoretical and sociological levels. For even so sophisticated an analyst as Hall underestimates the degree to which the liberal and realist projects have *always* been combined, an oversight with serious consequences for his understanding of both the theoretical and sociological concerns of the wilful Realist tradition. The issue here is not only of historical interest. It is crucial because the pessimism that is so characteristic of wilful Realism emerges from an engagement with the problems of *creating* the 'Realist–liberal mix' which Hall calls for. It is only by seeing the ways in which Realism and liberalism have long been related within this problematic that we can understand the depth of the thinking of Realism's most profound proponents on precisely these questions.[20] Their primary concerns lay in the possibility of constructing such a set of practices, and one of the most compelling reasons for examining the tradition of wilful Realism is to look at whether it is, even in the eyes of its proponents, 'realistic' at

[18] John A. Hall, *International Orders* (Cambridge: Polity Press, 1996), p. 13. See also the discussion in Rengger, *International Relations, Political Theory and the Problem of Order*, chapter 1.
[19] Hall, *International Orders*, p. 32.
[20] Hall's characteristically ambivalent reading of Morgenthau is yet another reflection of how misreading the Realist tradition has deleterious analytic consequences. See *International Orders*, p. 4, n. 10.

precisely these philosophical and sociological levels.[21] The continuing prevalence of the liberal–Realist divide, however, acts as a barrier to both asking and engaging these questions.

Method, responsibility, and the politics of forgetting in rationalism and neorealism

Why is it that the relationship between Realism and liberalism has been so badly misunderstood within International Relations? Two quite straightforward explanations spring quickly to mind. The first emerges from the fairly obvious observation that the Realist–liberal divide has functioned most often not as a serious point of departure for debate, but as a narrow and usually caricatured set of alternatives, often achieved by reducing an already hackneyed 'liberalism' to an even more suspiciously amorphous, ill-defined and – as it turns out – almost wholly mythical 'idealism' against which easy, supposedly Realist points can be scored.[22]

A second aspect of the explanation is to be found in the peculiarly unified and uncritical nature of pre-war American liberalism that provided the intellectual backdrop for Realism's ascendance within the development of the field of International Relations as an 'American social science'. As a number of intellectual historians have argued, American political science for the first half of the twentieth century was dominated by a rather naïve unity of liberal rationalism (in either its utilitarian or neo-Kantian forms), empiricism, and constitutionalism.[23] As a consequence of the peculiarly narrow forms of liberalism operative within American political discourse, the criticisms of liberal rationalism, facile legalism, and naïve pluralism provided by someone like Morgenthau could easily be taken as rejections of liberalism as a whole. Thus while Realism came to be seen (correctly) as counter to naïve liberal rationalism, this critique was erroneously identified with the liberal tradition *per se*, and Realism was accordingly – and erroneously – identified with an implacable hostility to liberalism *tout court*.

[21] These questions have been innovatively explored by James Der Derian in his probing analyses of what Realism means in an era of *late* modernity; see particularly his, 'The Value of Security: Hobbes, Marx, and Baudrillard'.
[22] This is one of the key themes and conclusions of the history of the discipline undertaken by Schmidt in *The Political Discourse of Anarchy*.
[23] See, for example, Dorothy Ross, *The Origins of American Social Science* (Cambridge University Press, 1991) and Gunnell, *Between Philosophy and Politics*, chapter 1 especially. See also, however, the interesting analysis of early twentieth-century American international law in Koskenniemi, *Gentle Civilizer of Nations*, pp. 474–8.

Yet to explain more fully why this 'Realist tradition' has been so badly misunderstood within the field it is also useful to examine how, quite ironically, the dominant contemporary claimants to the Realist mantle – neorealism, and now neoclassical Realism – have played a key role in this systematic miscomprehension. Briefly put, the increasingly rationalist cast of these forms of Realism places them firmly within the tradition of liberal rationalism and liberal empiricism against which the wilful Realist tradition largely defined itself. This means not only that they rest upon theoretical assumptions and methodological postulates steadfastly questioned by the wilful Realist tradition, but also that the adoption of these rationalist principles has led to a general disavowal of wilful Realism's sceptical stance in the name of social scientific legitimacy and political responsibility.[24] Since this dynamic has contributed not only to a skewed and limited appreciation of the Realist tradition by those who claim to be its inheritors, but has also had important effects on the structure of debate in the field more broadly, it is worth pursuing in slightly more detail.

The increasing unity of neorealist and neoliberal theories within the shared structures of rationalist social science has been one of the most notable developments in International Relations theory over recent years.[25] As has often been noted, despite its structuralist language, Waltzian neorealism was actually grounded in rationalist, microeconomic assumptions that place it clearly within the tradition of liberal rationalism, a foundation that has provided a fertile basis for what Ole Wæver usefully dubbed the 'neo-neo synthesis'.[26] At this level, neorealism does not fundamentally diverge from neoliberalism; both share

[24] Conversely, as I shall discuss in a moment, it is exactly this stance that has made an appeal to 'classical' Realism attractive to opponents of rationalism.

[25] A point pursued in Legro and Moravcsik, 'Is Anybody Still a Realist?'. See also David A. Baldwin, *Neorealism and Neoliberalism: The Contemporary Debate* (New York: Columbia University Press, 1993).

[26] Ole Waever, 'The Rise and Fall of the Inter-Paradigm Debate', in *International Theory: Positivism and Beyond*, ed. Steve Smith, Ken Booth, and Marysia Zalewski (Cambridge University Press, 1996). For further analyses of this synthesis, see Ruggie, *Constructing the World Polity*, chapter 1; and the treatment in Katzenstein, Keohane, and Krasner, '*International Organization* and the Study of World Politics'. Powerful early formulations of this insight were provided by Richard Ashley in 'The Poverty of Neorealism' and 'Untying the Sovereign State: A Double Reading of the Anarchy Problematique', *Millennium: Journal of International Studies*, 17:2 (1998). The argument has since been made from a number of different perspectives, particularly Alexander Wendt, in a number of essays, and most recently in his *Social Theory of International Politics* (Cambridge University Press, 1999), pp. 98–109. Indeed rationalist positions now occupy a largely unified quadrant within many presentations of the field's theoretical alternatives.

essentially similar atomistic and rationalistic assumptions, and a common view of what constitutes legitimate epistemic claims. It has less often been acknowledged, however, that this 'rationalist' unity lies not only in shared methodological assumptions and notions of social scientific legitimacy, but also reflects the convergence of these positions within an essentially liberal-empiricist and rationalist lineage concerning the politics of knowledge.

The core assumptions of social atomism and utility-maximising rational actors which unite rationalist positions bear clear marks of their heritage within the broader liberal-rationalist tradition that Nicholas Rengger has perceptively termed 'cognitive liberalism'.[27] At the heart of cognitive liberalism is the conviction that an adequate approach to political practice requires the adoption of a universal approach to knowledge based on the principles of Enlightenment science. This is more than just an epistemic claim about the correct process for knowledge acquisition: in cognitive liberalism a commitment to objective empirical knowledge is viewed as essential because of its implicit links to responsible practice. As Richard Flathman has nicely put it, this form of liberalism presumes a hierarchy 'with epistemology (and sometimes metaphysics) or "first philosophy" governing moral and political theory, which in turn governs moral and political practice. Empiricism correctly determines how we know and what we can and cannot know. Accepting and thinking within these determinations, liberalism as moral and political theory determines how we can know about morals and politics, what we can and cannot, do and do not know about them.'[28]

This specific linkage between claims about knowledge and claims about political practice – about the relationship between analytic responsibility and political responsibility – is at the heart of rationalism's vision of legitimate knowledge claims. Again, Flathman's characterisation is apposite here. As he notes, in this view:

> Theory is relevant to practice not because it is consonant with but an improvement on the understandings and beliefs of practitioners, but because it provides a basis on which to reject and replace the latter.

[27] Rengger, *International Relations, Political Theory and the Problem of Order*, pp. 104–5. They can also be traced to what Peter Manicas has called the 'societus' tradition of liberal thinking. *A History and Philosophy of the Social Sciences* (London: Routledge, 1984). See also Steve Smith, 'Positivism and Beyond', in *International Theory: Positivism and Beyond*, ed. Steve Smith, Ken Booth, and Marysia Zalewski (Cambridge University Press, 1996).

[28] Flathman, *Toward a Liberalism*, p. 18.

> Until such time as scientific theory has supplanted prescientific beliefs and understandings, the contributions of theory will be based on the discrepancies and disjunctions between theory and practice. In political language, empiricist scientists and those who have mastered their theories should rule. They should rule with a due awareness of the limitations of their theories, but equally with awareness of the yet more severe limitations on nonscientific beliefs.[29]

These cognitive commitments yield particular attitudes toward political responsibility. Because potential cognitive agreement is viewed as the condition for rational political agreement, adherence to these essentially empiricist principles of 'scientific objectivity', however flexibly they may be applied in actual analytic practice, becomes the benchmark of scholarly and political rectitude. Importantly, and paradoxically, even the *failure* to achieve such universal knowledge can be transformed into one of the strengths of cognitive liberalism. So long as the commitment to the possibility of universal knowledge remains intact, failures to achieve it can be seen as evidence of the continuing need for liberal principles of open enquiry in its pursuit. Knowledge accumulation is acknowledged to be a human (theory-dependent) endeavour, and its immediate claims are tempered by acknowledging that all knowledge-claims are in principle contingent and thus progressive.[30] However, this contingency is managed by holding on to the idea that there are some transcendental standards, and that knowledge is essentially cumulative and, in principle, can (will) be objective and capable of gaining universal cognitive assent.[31]

This is where critiques that foreground the quest for *certainty* or the attractions of 'positivism' in modernity (and rationalist International Relations theory) risk becoming slightly misleading, for it is this tension between certainty and doubt that is most powerful (and practically productive) in many expressions of cognitive liberalism. As Flathman has insightfully pointed out, part of the appeal of liberal empiricism lies in its attractive mixture of certainty and doubt. In his words, 'The unique advantages of empiricist-based liberalism result from the combination

[29] Flathman, *Toward a Liberalism*, p. 21.
[30] The popularity of peculiarly limited understandings of Lakatosian 'progressive' research programmes in rationalist International Relations is particularly revealing as an illustration of this dynamic.
[31] Flathman, *Toward a Liberalism*, pp. 22–3. For a good illustration of this stance, see Andrew Moravcsik, 'Theory Synthesis in International Relations: Real Not Metaphysical', *International Studies Review*, 5:1 (2003), and the counterpoint provided by Friedrich Kratochwil, 'The Monologue of "Science"', *International Studies Review*, 5:1 (2003).

of the scientifically warranted certitude it yields on some questions and its philosophically grounded doubt on the all others.'[32] Pointing out the failure of rationalist models to mirror adequately the reality they seek to understand, or to achieve the theoretical synthesis which is so often promised, is not sufficient to dislodge their commitment to this form of understanding, because the commitment itself arises as much from a *politics of* knowledge as from a *claim to* knowledge.

In a politics of knowledge framed by cognitive liberalism, the absence of substantive agreement (indeed the absence of even clear theoretical or methodological grounds upon which such agreement might be adduced, as raised briefly in the 'interparadigm debate' of the 1980s) is consistently sidelined.[33] Instead, the most basic question is defined as whether a particular analyst or position is committed to the *principle* of 'objective' enquiry as understood within the terms of cognitive liberalism. This question then becomes the central point of distinction and theoretical legitimacy, a process clearly illustrated in the development of International Relations theory over the past two decades. Thus, for example, while both Robert Keohane and Steven Krasner have substantive disagreements with the position put forward by Alexander Wendt in his *Social Theory of International Politics*, each prominently declares that one of the things they like most about the argument is that it shows how constructivism need not eschew proper social science and lead to the morass that both associate with 'postmodernism'.[34]

The characteristic link between theory and practice underlying cognitive liberalism has exercised a profound impact on the development of political science and the study of international politics. These commitments underlie neo-neo theory's strong commitment to – if rather narrow understanding of – what Stephen Krasner has invoked as the

[32] Flathman, *Toward a Liberalism*, p. 23. The epistemic adequacy of empiricism has, of course, been at the heart of many of the most pointed and vibrant debates in the field over the past decade. The debate has now come often to centre on the adequacy of scientific realism as a response to these dilemmas. For different views on scientific realism and its implications, see Wendt, *Social Theory of International Politics*, part one.

[33] The stance taken by Katzenstein, Keohane, and Krasner in '*International Organization* and the Study of World Politics' is particularly interesting here. For an insightful analysis of the gradual 'banalisation' of the interparadigm debate and the exclusion of its difficult implications for social constructivism, see Guzzini, *Realism in International Relations*.

[34] Robert Keohane, 'Ideas Part-way Down', *Review of International Studies*, 26:1 (2000); Stephen Krasner, 'Wars, Hotel Fires, and Plane Crashes', *Review of International Studies*, 26:1 (2000). Krasner approvingly notes that Wendt 'puts to rest the notion that constructivism is necessarily postmodern, devoid of an objective referent', p. 131.

'Western rationalist tradition'.[35] After all the methodological arguments have been made and remade, and philosophical foundations debated and denounced, the rationalist position continues consistently to trade on the association of cognitive liberalism with rational practices, and specifically upon a fear of the practical, *political* implications of casting aside a liberal-empiricist stance. Beneath the charges that alternative theoretical understandings lack 'clearly testable hypotheses', or fail to meet the test of 'relevance', or irresponsibly engage in 'prolix debate'[36] lies an entire political metaphysics based in a liberal-empiricist heritage which unifies the vast majority of rationalist thinking about International Relations.

From this position, rationalism is able to set itself up as the judge of other views not only, as many have noted, by smuggling in a hidden empiricism as the defining category of the *epistemological* debate, but also by implicitly linking empiricism to a practical-moral stance equated with *political responsibility*. In short, if a commitment to objective knowledge defined in empiricist terms is the essence of a rational politics, then clearly its denial must also be a denial of such a politics. Claims about the purportedly unified nature of the 'Western rationalist tradition' are mobilised in support of this charge. Beneath the methodological debates, if one listens closely enough, there lies an insistent cry: if empiricism and liberal-empiricist-defined objectivity are false, is not everything lost, are we not left with a world dominated only by nihilism, power, and violence? As David Campbell has put it, part of this hostility can be explained as a result of a 'fear . . . that if one pushes to the logical conclusions of their arguments, and avoids the defensive maneuvers whose sole purpose is to ward off "foreign" theoretical traditions, no longer will it be possible to speak of the state, or any other foundation of politics upon which one can secure the good life'.[37]

This association between rationalism and political responsibility has contributed to the paucity of engagement between rationalists and their critics. Indeed one is sometimes tempted to agree with Michael Oakeshott (hardly a trendy critical theorist) and his frustrated lament

[35] Stephen Krasner, 'The Accomplishments of International Political Economy', in *International Theory: Positivism and Beyond*, ed. Steve Smith, Ken Booth, and Marysia Zalewski (Cambridge University Press, 1996), p. 124.

[36] Terms used by Steven Walt in his nearly archetypal presentation of this position; see, 'The Renaissance of Security Studies'.

[37] Campbell, 'Political Prosaics, Transversal Politics, and the Anarchical World' in *Challenging Boundaries: Global Flows, Territorial Identities*, ed. Hayward Alher and Michael Shapiro (Minneapolis: University of Minnesota Press, 1995), pp. 16–17.

that rationalists are 'essentially ineducable',[38] that the link between theory and practice in rationalist thinking – and the deep political (or even ontological) commitment which it involves – prevents it from coming to terms either with the inadequacies of its theoretical foundations or its understandings of practice. While the conceptions of *action* underpinning rationalist theory have been subject to sustained and penetrating criticism in recent years, the influence of cognitive liberalism upon neo-neo theory – and its broader role in structuring theoretical debates – remains. Attacks upon rationalism as a form of 'positivism', for example, while important in opening up key issues of epistemological debate, have been of limited impact not only because of entrenched methodological differences, but also because of the link between knowledge, practice, and responsible and effective *political* knowledge that underlies cognitive liberalism.

This essentially liberal vision has dominated the methodological development of International Relations as an 'American social science', and has contributed to the construction of a rationalist 'Realist tradition' largely in its own image. The wilful Realist tradition has become subsumed within a politics of knowledge whereby neorealism, empiricism, and rationalism have been conflated with claims to political and scholarly responsibility. In the process, these positions have either redefined the 'Realist tradition' in their own rationalist image (as exemplified in neorealist readings of Hobbes or Rousseau), or have excluded it on the grounds that it is irredeemably based in irrationalistic notions of an 'evil' human nature or an atavistic will to power, and is ignorant of verities of rationalist social science. By contrast, a recovery of the wilful Realist tradition as sketched here allows a re-engagement of the relationship between Realism and the 'Western rationalist tradition' in forms beyond the narrowing of Western rationalism to a form of cognitive liberalism. From the perspective of 'wilful liberalism' that I have associated with wilful Realism, the linkage of cognitive liberalism to responsibility and claims about its role as the bulwark of the 'Western rationalist tradition' are simply not convincing. Scepticism toward liberal empiricism does not, in this lineage, come from outside the Western rationalist tradition, or from outside the Realist tradition, but from within it. Far from being a recent product of irresponsible theorists easily seduced by trendy and

[38] Michael Oakeshott, *Rationalism in Politics* (London: Methuen, 1962) p. 32. I owe the citation originally to its use in Benjamin Barber's insightful discussion, 'Foundationalism and Democracy', in *Democracy and Difference*, ed. Seyla Benhabib (Princeton University Press, 1996), p. 352.

fanciful philosophical endeavours or naïve forms of political romanticism, it is at the heart of the position adopted by some of the most profound thinkers within the Realist – and Western rationalist – traditions. It is indeed a sign of the lamentably narrow historical and philosophical foundations of much 'mainstream' International Relations theory that scepticism toward the claims of cognitive liberalism is so easily and narrowly identified solely with a 'postmodern' position, or that the deep engagement of proponents of wilful Realist tradition with complex currents and implications within the Western rationalist tradition is reduced to mere caricatures.

Perhaps even more important, however, is the claim embedded in the wilful Realist tradition that the rejection of cognitive liberalism and its vision of the relationship between theory and practice is a *requirement* of analytic rigour and political responsibility, not a denial of them. As outlined in the last chapter, it is precisely Morgenthau's rejection of the belief that rationalist conceptions of knowledge can provide a basis for political understanding and order that is at the heart of his assault upon rationalist liberalism. Linking rationalism with intellectual and political responsibility narrows analytic horizons. It leads either to an intellectual enterprise increasingly driven by a concern with method (and thus increasingly divorced from political reality), or to facile conflicts between rationalists and 'relativists' as the incapacity of rationalism to deliver upon its epistemological claims generates an equally naïve counter-movement. Most importantly of all, it stands as a positive barrier to political knowledge and judgement.

For Morgenthau, an anti-liberal-empiricist stance is an essential element *of* political responsibility since it is only via such a stance that one can 'ground' a liberal politics, and because it is only through such a stance that one can appraise the real political practices which defenders of a rational (not *rationalist*) liberal politics must understand in order to be successful. To be faithful to the Western rationalist and Enlightenment traditions requires a commitment to critique not only at the level of epistemic rigour, but also in order to establish a cogent and realistic understanding of what is entailed in bringing into practice many of the liberal-political ideals of the Enlightenment itself. The critical appraisal of liberal empiricism is declared a necessary consequence of an ethical and political stance, not the denial or renunciation of one.

The form of liberalism and vision of responsibility which emerge from this critique are certainly different from that linked to cognitive liberalism, but they are identifiably a product of the Enlightenment project nonetheless. The commitment to a rational politics, while conceived more complexly, is held just as strongly. And the commitment to a politics of responsibility is held even more strongly. Indeed, as we have seen, the connection between cognitive liberalism, legitimate knowledge, and political responsibility is not a conclusion that wilful Realists would endorse; in fact, they would reject it as not only epistemically inadequate, but as itself *politically irresponsible*. The focus of the wilful Realist tradition on the relationship between epistemic stances, socio-historical structures, and prevailing political constructions and practices challenges rationalist presentations of these relations at their very foundations.

Rationalism versus constructivism

As the rationalist neo-neo synthesis has proceeded, it has become increasingly common to distinguish between rationalism and various forms of constructivism as the basic theoretical alternatives within the field,[39] and the ongoing engagements between these positions have generated some of the most sophisticated and important debates of the past decade. However, a reappraisal of the Realist tradition casts these debates in a significantly different light. Simply put, the great irony of a basic rationalist–constructivist divide is that while rationalism defines itself in opposition to various forms of reflectivism, constructivism, and historical sociology, what is now termed 'rationalism' in International Relations theory can itself be best understood as an historical social construction – as a practical response of the liberal tradition to a world without stable foundations. Rationalist assumptions are, in fact, sceptical constructions. The core assumption of the rationalist vision – the self-contained, instrumentally calculating actor – is not opposed to constructivism, it *is* a construction – an attempted *resolution* of the wilful Realist (and wilful liberal) tradition to the inadequacies of rationalism (liberal empiricism) as a basis for rational, responsible, political analysis and practice. What is now taken as the stable foundation of the rationalist position and opposed to contingency of reflectivist and constructivist visions can ironically be seen precisely as a construction *of*

[39] For a survey, Ted Hopf, 'The Promise of Constructivism in International Relations Theory', *International Security*, 23:1 (1998). See also Jeff Checkel, 'The Constructivist Turn in International Relations', *World Politics*, 50:2 (1998); Dale Copeland, 'The Constructivist Challenge to Structural Realism', *International Security*, 25:2 (2000); Peter J. Kalzenstein (ed.), *The Culture of National Security* (Columbia University Press, 1996).

the sceptical tradition, and as a response to the instability, contingency, challenges, and dangers of politics in modernity. What is more, far from being a 'fact' upon which a value-free science of international politics might be built, the commitment to rational action is a *value* at its very foundation.

This can be illustrated clearly by returning to Hobbes. Whereas rationalist positions take for granted a world of rational actors calculating in the context of material gains, Hobbes did not *assume* the existence of such actors; to a significant degree he sought to *create* them. As William Connolly has nicely summarised the point made in more detail in chapter one:

> Hobbes is often held to believe that most human beings are self-interested most of the time and that a sovereign power must be devised that is able to contend with these self-interested beings. But this interpretation exaggerates and misleads. It exaggerates by treating human beings who are to become both self-interested and principled as if they were secure agents of self-interest prior to the education they receive in civil society, and it misleads by pretending that the self-interested individual is the problem when it comes closer to being the solution Hobbes offers for the problem he identifies.[40]

The articulation of scepticism and the construction of an instrumental, materially calculating, and self-interested agent was part of a creative process of subject-construction for Hobbes: a self-conscious political practice seeking to provide a foundation for social order. Similarly, for Rousseau, the evolution of civilisation is the story of the coming into being of such actors, not an ahistorical account that assumes their existence. The same holds true in significant ways for Morgenthau. As both Hobbes and Morgenthau clearly recognised, the articulation and adoption of a rationalist conception of subjectivity and social action *is* a process of social construction. Indeed, it might not be too much to argue that one aspect of Hobbes' significance is that he stands at the heart of the historical moment and processes when this construction is powerfully taking place, while, for Morgenthau, it is one of liberal rationalism's great failures that it does not understand *that* this process took place – that the rise of liberalism was a social construction and part of an historically successful political project whose time (perhaps regrettably for Morgenthau) has passed – and which now

[40] William Connolly, *Political Theory and Modernity* (Oxford: Basil Blackwell, 1988), pp. 26–7.

requires urgent reconsideration. In each of these cases, the articulation of what we might today call a rationalist position – a focus on interests and material, instrumental calculation – is the outcome of recognising the socially constructed, contingent, and practically produced nature of political life.

The attempt to construct rationalist structures of political practice does not lead Hobbes and Morgenthau to appeal to epistemic verities characteristic of liberal rationalism. Here, they differ from contemporary rationalism in International Relations, where cognitive liberalism and political responsibility are quite clearly linked and where they are rhetorically deployed to reinforce the belief that there is a fundamental divide between rationalist certainties and constructivist contingencies. To a significant degree, the wilful Realist claim is precisely the opposite: the *rejection* of liberal-rationalist claims to foundations at the levels of either epistemic claims or principles of subjectivity was seen as necessary in order to defend the *social construction* of subjects and social practices that in many ways resemble the analytic postulates and assumptions of contemporary rationalist theory.

The importance of this point is clearly illustrated in debates over whether ideas matter in international politics, and in rationalist attempts to incorporate 'identity' into their analytic frameworks.[41] From a wilful Realist perspective, the entire way in which this issue has been framed in rationalist analyses – with 'identity' conceived as a 'variable' whose causal influence in specific cases can be measured – is misconceived. For wilful Realists, a rationalistic actor *is an identity*. What contemporary rationalists construe as (non-rationalist) identity factors were seen by wilful Realists as identities in competition with the rationalist subjectivity they sought to foster. The separation of identity 'variables' from the underlying foundation of a rational actor is an outcome of this historical process of subject-construction, not a methodological postulate providing a basis for empirical hypotheses. The very separation of a 'rational actor' distinct from its (non-rational) 'identity' is, in short, the outcome of an historical process of identity construction – the result of a politics of identity. Within rationalist theory in the social sciences this fact has been obscured. Through a process of forgetting, what is actually a social construction and historical practice – the liberal self capable of thinking

[41] The key text here remains Judith Goldstein and Robert Keohane (eds.), *Ideas and Foreign Policy: Beliefs, Institutions, and Political Change* (Ithaca: Cornell University Press, 1993), particularly the editors' joint chapter 'Ideas and Foreign Policy: An Analytical Framework'.

of itself in self-interested, rational terms – has been transformed into an unreflective analytic *assumption* of rationalist social science.[42] For wilful Realists, by contrast, the question is not the conditions under which identity causally matters in relation to an underlying rational(ist)-actor's forms of action. What is central are the conditions under which the *rationalist identity* can dominate over other forms of identity and action, and the further practical and ethical challenges which – if successful – such a rational construction would then have to address.

If this is the case, a divide between rationalist and constructivist positions as a theoretically orienting premise in contemporary International Relations theory generates more confusion than clarification. Indeed rather than viewing the two as divided, it is more analytically useful (and practically enlightening) to treat rationalism as a liberal strategy arising from reflectivist premises and a broadly constructivist problematic.[43] What is important is not the analytic divide between the two, but a recognition of their mutual relationship and of the historical dimensions through which a reflective construction of rationalist practices occurs.

Conventional constructivism and the (Critical) question of consequences

At the heart of the constructivist movement has been a reopening of the question of practice through a critique of the empiricist epistemology and materialist ontology that underpin rationalist conceptions of social action. Through this challenge constructivism has sought to undermine claims about the necessary nature (particularly the necessarily 'Hobbesian' nature) of international politics. As part of the same process, constructivism has challenged the empiricist epistemology and materialist ontology assumed by rationalist theory, holding that cogent understandings of science (drawing particularly upon the realist philosophy of science) require legitimising the ontological status and causal efficiency of non-observable phenomena. There can be little doubt that constructivism's critical focus on the limits of empiricist

[42] For a methodological critique of rationalist treatments of 'ideas' within International Relations, see Mark Laffey and Jutta Weldes, 'Beyond Belief: Symbolic Technologies in International Relations', *European Journal of International Relations*, 3:2 (1998). The revealing *political* lineage has been effectively traced by Stephen Holmes in *Passions and Constraint*; see most particularly chapter 2, 'The Hidden History of Self-Interest'. I have tried to trace some of these issues in the context of security studies in 'Identity and the Politics of Security', *European Journal of International Relations*, 4:2 (1998).
[43] For an exploration of 'liberal strategies' in somewhat analogous terms, see Moon, *Constructing Community*, chapters 3 and 5 especially.

epistemology and materialist ontology as methodological foundations and legitimations of 'neo theory' has made a tremendous contribution toward opening up theoretical debate in the field, and the constructivist position has effectively demonstrated many of the shortcomings of the rationalist stance in methodological terms.[44] But the strength of the constructivist position – its casting of the issue as one of *method*[45] and thus taking on rationalism on its own 'scientific' terms – risks obscuring a series of important issues.

By treating rationalism (both in terms of its vision of agents, and its empiricist epistemology and materialist ontology) primarily or even wholly as a set of methodological assumptions (that is, by casting the issue pre-eminently as one of social science) constructivism unwittingly participates in the rationalist forgetting of its origins and status as an historical construction. The ontological materialism and epistemic empiricism underpinning rationalism must be understood not (or at least not only) as the result of a somewhat naïve and anachronistic understanding of science and knowledge (with a correlative set of methodological commitments); they also need to be understood as a set of practical commitments and as the outcome of practical judgements: as just discussed, they can be understood as political constructions – as epistemic practices tied to attempts to reconstruct social life.

A fuller appreciation of the rationalist heritage helps explain its response to the constructivist challenge, and confusions in the debate between rationalism and constructivism on questions of practice. The way in which these issues have both underlain the debate, and have resulted in a degree of confusion within it, can be very well illustrated by looking briefly at the well-known exchange between John Mearsheimer and Alexander Wendt over the adequacy of a constructivist approach to world politics. Attempting to cast more recent theoretical developments within the older categories of Realism and idealism, Mearsheimer argues that 'realism and critical theory have fundamentally different epistemologies and ontologies, which are the most basic levels at which

[44] It is worth noting, however, how the role of both Critical and post-structural positions in leading this opening is being increasingly ignored (literally written out) in many constructivist accounts of the evolution of International Relations theory. In some cases, one might be led to believe that social constructivism was miraculously born in the Ivy League circa 1990, and emerged heroically to take on the entrenched powers of rationalism. This charge is not true of some of constructivism's best practitioners (in particular Alexander Wendt), but it does exemplify an interesting – if disingenuous and worrying – form of academic politics.

[45] See, for example, Wendt, *Social Theory of International Politics*, p. 7, on this complex question.

theories can be compared. Realists maintain that there is an objective and knowable world, which is separate from the observing individual. Critical theorists, on the other hand, "see subject and object in the historical world as a reciprocally interrelated whole," and deny the possibility of objective knowledge.' In sum, 'Where realists see a fixed and knowable world, critical theorists see the possibility of endless interpretations of the world before them.'[46] This leads Mearsheimer to posit two general contrasts between the competing positions: 'Realists believe that state behavior is largely shaped by the *material structure* of the international system', and they believe in the possibility of objective knowledge. By contrast, Critical theorists have an 'idealist' ontology and a 'relativist' epistemology.[47]

In his rejoinder, Wendt holds that Mearsheimer's contrasts reflect and rely upon a particularly anachronistic vision of the philosophy of science. He points out that his constructivism's 'realist' philosophy of science remains committed to objective knowledge, even if it discards an empiricist foundation for such knowledge, and notes further that believing a scientific approach requires a 'clean distinction between subject and object' involves maintaining a positivist position when 'almost all philosophers of science today reject such a naive epistemology'.[48] At the level of method, therefore, the issue seems at a minimum to reflect competing visions in the philosophy of science rather than the opposition between 'science' and idealism that Mearsheimer seeks to impose; at most, constructivism might be said to trump Mearsheimer's neorealism, beating it at its own game by basing itself upon a more cogent and contemporary understanding of science. At the level of method alone, therefore, the constructivist response is capable of meeting Mearsheimer's challenge on its own terms, and perhaps of besting it.

Yet it soon becomes clear that what is at stake in these discussions goes far beyond questions of method *per se,* and Mearsheimer's rejoinder revealingly takes the issue onto another plane. There, he argues that, paradoxically, even if one were to concede the issue of epistemic foundations to Wendt, the neorealist case would actually be strengthened.

[46] Mearsheimer, 'False Promise', p. 41. Mearsheimer's sweeping characterisation and critique of what he lumped together as 'Critical' theories of international relations has itself been subject to numerous rejoinders, but I am here less interested in its substantive claims than in how it embodies the continuing legacy of the liberal tradition.
[47] John Mearsheimer, 'A Realist Reply', *International Security*, 20:1 (1995), p. 91.
[48] Alexander Wendt, 'Constructing International Politics', *International Security*, 20:1 (1995), p. 75.

Without a belief in objectivity and certainty, Mearsheimer holds, Wendt cannot be sure that alternative possibilities will not be worse than Realist practices. As he puts it, 'a fundamental problem with Wendt's argument [is that] because his theory cannot predict the future, he cannot know whether the discourse that ultimately replaces realism will be more benign than realism. He has no way of knowing whether a fascistic discourse more violent than realism will emerge as the hegemonic discourse.'[49]

Two important points are revealed in this move. First, Mearsheimer's response demonstrates how neorealism has taken on the legacy of cognitive liberalism. The epistemic dilemmas of his position are countered by mobilising cognitive liberalism's vision of the relationship between theory and practice, and explicitly linking this to claims about responsible political practice. Second, casting the issue in this way involves Mearsheimer in revealing contradictions. To note only one point: in defending neorealism as a functioning practice which should not be discarded in favour of an uncertain Critical alternative, Mearsheimer effectively contradicts the charge of 'idealism' he levels at Critical theorists: one simply cannot say that it is dangerous to believe in the practical power of theory ('idealism') on the one hand, and then say that a particular theory (neorealism) guides practice and that it is practically dangerous to change it, on the other. If neorealism is a (positivist) *theory of* the objective dynamics of international security, then changing the theory will make no difference to the reality. If, on the other hand, Mearsheimer wants to argue that policy is actually driven by neorealist theory, that neorealist theory *is* practice in this sense, then his earlier claims that Critical theory errs in its focus on the causal role of ideas cannot be sustained.

The epistemic dilemmas of Mearsheimer's position again reflect the deleterious consequences of misunderstanding the historical genesis of the rationalist position. However, his questioning of the relationship between theory and practice does pose fundamental challenges to the constructivist stance, and gestures clearly in the direction of concerns at the heart of wilful Realism. Seen from the perspective of the wilful Realist tradition, it is not enough simply to show how social constructions function, or to view the issue solely within the terms of social scientific method. The principle of social construction brings with it an inescapable ethical and practical imperative: constructions must not just

[49] Mearsheimer, 'A Realist Reply', p. 92.

be understood, they must be appraised and evaluated in terms of their ethical claims and practical consequences. While it is clear, as Wendt argues, that no *necessary assumptions* about the functioning of a given system follow from the adoption of a constructivist position, this view begs the question of responsibility – the concern with the practical and consequential entailments of different constructions – that was crucial to the wilful Realist tradition. In this sense, Wendt's otherwise useful claim that constructivism be viewed solely as a 'method' rather than as a substantive claim about the nature of international politics risks being seriously misleading.

Here, the relationship between the wilful Realist tradition and current distinctions between 'conventional' and 'critical' constructivism is particularly revealing.[50] For conventionality, after all, can mean above all the acceptance of conventions, not only of methodological conventions, but of the idea that the world consists of nothing but competing conventions, and that the sole task of scientific thought is to describe these as best it can. In this way, 'positivism' is an admirably honest (if somewhat mischievous) moniker for the procedure undertaken by this form of conventional constructivism. But like positivism in general, this means that constructions must be treated as conventions, as simply the way things are in all their variety. The question of whether those conventions are good or bad – either in themselves or in relation to others – is by definition unanswerable. This might be taken for a healthy pluralism, but its lack of any critical position is one which wilful Realism finds intensely troubling.

The issues at stake here are nowhere more clearly illustrated than in the relationship between Realism and constructivism over the dynamics and implications of collective identity formation. Constructivists have long argued that collective identity formation needs to be understood as a relational process in which self and other, ego and alter are formed in a process of mutual constitution.[51] It has been argued with increasing frequency, however, that constructivist analyses of collective identity formation provide a potential common ground of engagement between Realism and constructivism, and that rather than providing a critique

[50] See, for example, Hopf, 'Promise of Constructivism'; Richard Price and Christian Reus-Smit, 'Dangerous Liaisons?: Critical International Theory and Constructivism', *European Journal of International Relations*, 4:3 (1998); and Jutta Weldes, *Constructing National Interests* (Minneapolis: University of Minnesota Press, 1999).

[51] Alexander Wendt, 'Collective Identity Formation and the International State', *American Political Science Review*, 88:2 (1994), and *Social Theory of International Politics*.

of Realism they actually support a more sophisticated form of Realism, and allow the extension of Realist insights into relations between non-state groups. Robert Jervis, for example, has argued that 'Realism points to the reciprocal relationship between identities and conflict, arguing that conflict both grows out of and stimulates the perception of group differences,'[52] and that 'Social psychologists have long known that perceptions – and misperceptions – of what people have in common often grow out of conflicts as internal unity is gained by seeing others as the Other.'[53] In a similar vein, Jennifer Sterling-Folker has argued that a Realist 'rereading' of constructivism's understanding of collective identity formation can contribute to a deeper understanding of Realism's core claims about the inherently oppositional, and often conflictual nature of inter-group relations – whether those relations are between state or non-state (e.g. ethnic) groupings. Drawing upon recent work in sociobiology, where classical Realist concerns with sin are replaced with Darwinian concepts of selection,[54] she argues that:

> One obvious implication is that the in-group and out-group distinction should be considered a constitutive element of individual identity formation. This means that members of groups will be primed to see the members of other groups as competitors. It produces the well-documented phenomenon in the social identity theory literature that 'no matter how trivial or ad hoc the groupings, and in the apparent absence of any competing values, the mere perception of another group leads to in-group favoritism and out-group discrimination'. The act of discrimination based on group membership is not learned behavior according to this realist rereading, but rather results from the unowned process of group formation that operates ontologically before both social interaction and the specific practices human beings create.[55]

Perhaps the most extended version of this argument is Johnathan Mercer's attempt to fuse constructivist and Realist theories in his treatment of 'anarchy and identity'.[56] Mercer accepts fully the claim that collective identities are socially constructed in relational contexts, but

[52] Robert Jervis, 'Realism in the Study of World Politics', *International Organization*, 52:4 (1998), p. 988.
[53] Jervis, 'Realism in the Study of World Politics', p. 989.
[54] Bradley A. Thayer, 'Bringing in Darwin: Evolutionary Theory, Realism, and International Politics', *International Security*, 25:2 (2000).
[55] Jennifer Sterling-Folker, 'Realism and the Constructivist Challenge: Rejecting, Reconstructing, or Rereading', *International Studies Review*, 4:1 (2002), p. 84.
[56] Johnathan Mercer, 'Anarchy and Identity', *International Organization*, 49:2 (1995). Both Jervis and Sterling-Folker cite Mercer in support of their claims.

argues that this supports rather than challenges neorealism. Basing his analysis in social psychology, and Social Identity Theory (SIT) in particular, Mercer argues that the individual only finds self-identity in the group, and that 'people seek a positive self-identity that they gain by identifying with a group and by favorable comparison of the in-group with out-groups. These comparisons explain the pronounced tendencies for relative gains.'[57] By placing the formation of individual identity via group identity as prior to the relations between groups, this view adopts the constructivist principle that identity is constructed while denying that anarchy is what states make of it. In fact, he argues, 'the more carefully one examines the question of state identity in anarchy, the stronger the assumption of egoism becomes'.[58]

Yet as Mercer acknowledges, the claim that individual-group identity formation processes are prior itself requires explanation. Indeed if we look carefully at his analysis it turns out that the process of identity formation is underpinned by a set of claims about the nature and role of *concepts* and categorisations in individual identity formation. 'Categorization' or the 'cognitive requirement for simplification', he argues, is a 'necessity' in social life and action. Categorisation in turn involves comparison, and it is this necessary relationship between concepts and categories that ultimately explains the inescapably anarchic nature of intergroup relations. As Mercer puts it:

> Categorization explains comparison. When we categorize, we accentuate similarities within our group and differences between groups. Creating categories demands comparisons. These intergroup comparisons are not evaluatively neutral. Because our social group defines part of our identity, we seek to view our group as different and better than other groups on some relevant dimensions. In short, categorization is a cognitive requirement that demands comparisons; the motivational need for a positive social identity leads to comparisons that favor the in-group.[59]

In this vision we thus have a direct link between the nature and role of concepts and the nature of relationships between social groups. Categorisations are necessarily comparisons, and comparisons are dichotomous: in/out, us/them. Relations between groups necessarily resemble the nature of the concepts which underlie their construction and inevitable opposition.

[57] Mercer, 'Anarchy and Identity', p. 241.
[58] Mercer, 'Anarchy and Identity', p. 230.
[59] Mercer, 'Anarchy and Identity', p. 242.

It is in this context that wilful Realism's concern with the critical evaluation of conceptual constructions and their consequences becomes particularly relevant. Indeed, as we saw in the last chapter, it is precisely these kinds of arguments that motivate Morgenthau's detailed engagement with conceptual analysis and that explain his otherwise seemingly abstruse concerns with the concept of 'politics'. Morgenthau would deny neither the importance of conceptual constructions in action, nor the power of dichotomous or oppositional renditions of them.[60] However, he argues that such understandings are radically and dangerously incomplete. They transform a claim about the nature of concepts into a claim about the nature of politics. It is exactly this move that Morgenthau finds in Schmitt, and it was precisely in an attempt to oppose an oppositional logic of identity formation – of politics as defined by the inescapable opposition of friend and enemy – that he develops his concept of politics. For Morgenthau, conceptual clarity is essential since it makes possible the *political judgement* that this stark form of division is not necessary, and underwrites a responsible political opposition to it.[61] One cannot just observe the fact that groups come into conflict and deduce from this conflict's inevitability. Nor can one uncritically accept a conceptual logic built upon binary oppositions, and deduce that those divisions dictate the necessary parameters of political practice. On the contrary, political Realism requires a recognition of the relational structure of identity formation which retains a vision of politics that does not fall prey to a purely oppositional understanding of this process; it requires a responsible 'political' stance that *opposes* both of these constricted understandings of political knowledge and action.

The importance of this issue can be brought out by looking at the question of judging actual political practices and strategies of identity formation. If, for example, the process of collective identity formation is necessarily oppositional, how is one to evaluate political strategies

[60] Mercer presents the relationship between his ideas and those of Morgenthau as 'I argue that our cognitions and desire for a positive social identity generate competition. Thus for cognitive and motivated (rather than structural or social) reasons, ego and alter will compete against one another. This view of politics fits with Hans Morgenthau's belief that international conflict has its roots in human nature. However, Morgenthau thought people had an insatiable thirst for power. I argue only that groups are inherently competitive . . .' 'Anarchy and Identity', p. 247.

[61] Morgenthau's intellectual debt to the classical Kantian trilogy of understanding, judging, and willing is clearly apparent here. This is unsurprising given not only his intellectual background, but also his very close personal and intellectual relationship with the most influential of post-war Kantian political thinkers: Hannah Arendt.

that seek consciously to manipulate and mobilise in-group/out-group animosities in the pursuit of political power? This poses directly the question of what it means to be a Realist: if Realism is the theory of power politics *par excellence*, does this mean that the height of political Realism lies in the mobilisation of social capacities and political power by casting Others – whether they be states or other collectivities – as enemies? Recent treatments have tended to shy away from these considerations in favour of an analytic neutrality. Thus, in Mercer's formulation: 'The application of SIT to international politics suggests that we are stuck in a self-help system. It does not show, however, that war, conflict, and misery are natural and inevitable products of international politics. National leaders can pursue policies that increase their neighbours' and their own security . . . They can do what they want; their competition can be either cooperative or coercive.'[62] Similarly, in Sterling-Folker's view: 'This does not mean that negative comparisons or intergroup competition must necessarily involve violence, since variance in access to natural resources and intergroup exposure also affect how much violence is a necessary component of group competition. Nor does it exclude the possibility that particular types of social practices might act as mitigating circumstances for intergroup violence. Yet neither possibility obviates the selection-by-competition logic operating across groups.'[63]

This neutrality is not without attractions, and recognising that the relational construction of collective identities is a process with no necessary outcomes clearly resonates with elements of Morgenthau's Realism. Politically, however, it is less satisfactory, for it begs the question of how (indeed if) such conceptions of Realism are able to make judgements about – and take political stances toward – xenophobic political strategies. Morgenthau, by contrast, did not shy from a consideration of these issues. As we have seen, it is scarcely surprising that he did not do so, for his thinking was formed against an historical background where such issues were of the greatest political and personal importance. In a political context where extreme formulations of in-group/out-group relations were linked to extremely violent political strategies at both the domestic and international levels, the ability to make judgements about those strategies was an essential element of political responsibility.

[62] Mercer, 'Anarchy and Identity', p. 252.
[63] Sterling-Folker, 'Realism and the Constructivist Challenge', p. 85.

There is no doubt that Realism asserts the need for a clear understanding of the difference between domestic structures that effectively support what I previously called 'positive' political relations and an international sphere that is largely defined by their absence: the realm of international politics is defined by different centres of decision, and by the social processes – including relational constructions of collective identity – that underpin them.[64] This makes international politics a sphere more likely to manifest the negative and destructive dimensions of politics rather than its positive possibilities. But judgement is essential if the negative dimensions of politics are not to be mistaken for politics as a whole, and if its negative expression in a politics of enmity is not to be erroneously taken as the inevitable outcome of the relational construction of collective identities. Responding to the dynamics of collective identity formation is indeed a choice, however much it must be located within historical structures and limitations. But it is essential that this choice is underpinned by an ethos, an ethos that Morgenthau seeks to ground in the nature of politics itself.

Seen in this light, Morgenthau's Realist analysis of the concept of politics is part of an attempt to generate the 'particular types of social practices' that might act to mitigate violent conflict and encourage non-violent engagement. The idea of politics as a positive value – yoked to a principled commitment to a social balance of power designed to foster that openness and offset its negative potential – is a strategy to defend the positive potential of politics as a practical ethos, and to defend the public sphere as an arena for critical, pluralistic engagement. Power can certainly be generated by enmity and division; indeed this may be one of the most effective tactics of all, and one of the key strategies of power is to foreclose the political sphere and to limit debate through the mobilisation of oppositional identities. But, for Morgenthau, one of the core commitments of a Realist theory of international politics lies in a resistance to this process, and the concept of politics correctly understood provides an ethical (fundamentally democratic) position from which,

[64] See Morgenthau's remarks on what a properly Realistic vision of international law – one accounting for the relationship between rules, 'social forces', and the definitional and decision-making role and capacity of the state – would look like. As he puts it: 'It is obvious that this double or triple guarantee has an important bearing upon the observance and validity of a given precept. When such a multiple guaranty exists, that is, when ethics, mores, and law co-operate to realize a certain order of things, there is a much greater likelihood that this order will be realized than when the law alone seeks it.' 'International Law', in *Politics in the Twentieth Century,* vol. I, p. 303.

and in the name of which, strategies of enmity can be resisted in both domestic and foreign policy.

At the heart of the relationship between conventional and critical constructivism, therefore, is the crucial question which Wendt asks in an impressive recent work: 'what is IR for?'[65] It was not enough for Hobbes, or Rousseau, or Morgenthau simply to explain how different visions of the world were structured and how they were related to specific possibilities for action. It was crucial to evaluate these different constructions (and their connection to diverse knowledge claims) in terms of their adequacy to a political standard, a standard that was, I have argued, essentially one of liberal autonomy. Morgenthau's Realism can thus be seen as emerging from a profound engagement *with* themes characteristic of contemporary constructivist thought, not in opposition to it. Indeed one could go further, and argue that Morgenthau's thought reflects a profound concern with questions of the social construction of *politics* in a way which goes beyond much of current constructivist thought, and which is of the greatest relevance for both contemporary constructivist theory and its opponents.

As both Jervis[66] and Mearsheimer have noted, constructivism has tended to shy away from the less positive implications of adopting a view of politics as socially constructed.[67] The wilful Realist tradition, by contrast, takes on these issues directly. All constructions of the social world are not equal; nor can they be studied wholly in a detached way. A 'moderate' constructivism that focuses only on the question of better methods of social scientific explanation is not, in this view, more responsible as a result of this moderation: it is potentially politically irresponsible in its unwillingness to address and evaluate the consequences of different social constructions.[68] The idea that the world consists of nothing but competing constructions, and that the sole

[65] Alexander Wendt, 'What is IR for?: Notes Toward a Post-Critical View', in *Critical Theory and World Politics*, ed. Richard Wyn Jones (Boulder: Lynne Rienner, 2001).

[66] Jervis, 'Realism in the Study of World Politics', p. 974.

[67] This charge itself reflects the dominance of 'conventional' constructivism, and the influence of cognitive liberalism, within the United States in particular. It would be less true if more critical positions were included.

[68] The commitment of Realism to criticism is demonstrated effectively in Rosenthal, *Righteous Realists*, pp. 151–76 especially. These issues are directly relevant to the debate between 'conventional' and 'critical' constructivists: for various discussions, see Emmanuel Adler, 'Seizing the Middle Ground: Constructivism in World Politics', *European Journal of International Relations*, 3:3 (1997); Hopf, 'Promise of Constructivism'; Price and Reus-Smit, 'Dangerous Liaisons?', and James Der Derian, 'The Art of War and the Construction of Peace: Toward a Virtual Theory of International Relations', in Morten Kelstrup and Michael C. Williams (eds.), *International Relations Theory and the Politics of European*

task of 'objective' analysis is to describe these as best it can, is not a stance that Morgenthau's Realism could support. It would mean that the question of whether those constructions and conventions are good or bad would be by definition unanswerable. There would, for example, be little reason why Carl Schmitt's mythological politics of enmity would in principle trouble a 'positivist' constructivism if a mirroring of the operation of such a politics is all that social constructivism entails. Without a critical, ethical, and evaluative dimension, a focus on the social construction of practices risks becoming politically irresponsible.[69]

The modern and the postmodern

Debates surrounding 'postmodernism' have been subject to even more intense forms of the same divisive dichotomisation as other aspects of theoretical debate in International Relations. Most commonly, 'postmodernism' has become the bogey-man of the field, the subject of a set of (largely undefined and inadequately articulated and argued) charges about how in challenging the canons of science and destroying the value of Truth (and the truth of Values), it disavows the entire Western rationalist tradition, and risks destroying the vision of political order, progress, and responsibility with which that tradition is associated. Yet despite clear attempts to distance themselves from questions raised by the relationship between modernity and postmodernity – part of the general tendency in rationalist International Relations to sideline the question of the dilemmas of modernity and politics more generally – the analysis above suggests that no aspect of contemporary International Relations theory can remain immune from their consideration via cosy self-assurances of social scientific legitimacy, or analytic and political responsibility.[70] Moreover, if an ironic conclusion of this

Integration (London: Routledge, 2000). For recent moves toward a clearer articulation of critical and normative concerns while still locating themselves within a broadly defined constructivist position see Christian Reus-Smit, *The Moral Purpose of the State* (Princeton University Press, 1999), and Heather Rae, *State Identities and the Homogenisation of Peoples* (Cambridge University Press, 2002).

[69] Nicholas Rengger has suggested that a similar set of concerns also confront the English School, see *International Relations, Political Theory and the Problem of Order*.

[70] At least this is true at the intellectual level; at the institutional level it is all too likely to succeed, and indeed there are worrying indications that it has already to a large extent done so within the institutional culture of large parts of academic International Relations in the United States. For a survey, see Ole Waever, 'The Sociology of a not so International Discipline: American and European Developments in International Relations', *International Organization*, 52:4 (1998).

reassessment of the Realist tradition is that the liberal–realist and rationalist–constructivist divides are fundamentally misleading, then an even more ironic conclusion is that the wilful Realist tradition has much in common with certain aspects of postmodern thinking.

That (what has often been termed 'classical') Realism and postmodern approaches have strong affinities is far from a novel claim.[71] Clearly, the sceptical sensibility, with its stress on contingency, concern with language and rhetoric, and focus on the social construction of practices, resonates in many ways with the themes which postmodern conceptions have stressed. The idea, therefore, that these themes are identifiably and particularly 'postmodern', and that they represent a complete rejection of prior traditions of analysis in International Relations or Western traditions of thought is quite misleading. It is in fact only the narrow identification of modernity and the Realist tradition with the liberal empiricism and rationalism which prevails in much of International Relations theory that makes them appear so. Seen from the perspective of the wilful Realist tradition, the concerns evinced by postmodern views can be seen as a working out of themes within the problematic of modernity, not as standing outside it.[72] And they resonate frequently with wilful Realist engagements with similar dilemmas.

This recognition also means that conventional framings of the modern–postmodern divide as being between responsible, constructive, modern social science and irresponsible, destructive, postmodern theory are also often misplaced. Indeed the entire way in which the rhetoric of responsibility has framed these controversies – of responsible rationalist and liberal-empiricist commitments versus irresponsible postmodern deconstructions – has tended to obscure the issues at stake. For if liberal-rationalist claims to represent an undifferentiated and unproblematic 'modern' tradition are false – if what is at stake in powerful aspects of the (sceptical) Realist tradition is precisely the status of modernity in its own terms and a rejection of liberal-rationalist claims to solve the question or exhaust its possibilities – then an engagement with the sceptical Realist tradition places questions

[71] Walker, *Inside/Outside*; James Der Derian, 'A Reinterpretation of Realism', in *Post-Realism: The Rhetorical Turn in International Relations*, ed. Robert Harriman and Francis A. Beer (East Lansing: Michigan State University Press, 1996). For a similar point, Guzzini, *Realism in International Relations*, p. 228.
[72] This argument has been clearly made by Ashley, and especially by Walker, for whom it has been at the centre of his consistent attempts to reorient International Relations' vision of its place in modernity. For a cogent overview of some of the issues involved, see Nicholas Rengger, *Political Theory, Modernity and Postmodernity* (Oxford: Blackwell, 1995).

of modernity/postmodernity at the heart of this theoretical lineage in International Relations theory, not at its margins.

Moreover, a critique of liberal rationalism does not involve a rejection of the Enlightenment tradition as either an historical legacy or, necessarily, as a set of practical political commitments to tolerant, liberal, democratic, or even liberal-democratic forms of politics. As even the most cursory glance at diverse contemporary articulations of 'post-foundational' liberal democratic theory (and their historical lineages) easily attests, the idea that liberal-rationalist commitments are the foundation of a liberal or democratic politics is both deeply challenged and often strongly rejected. From the 'agonistic liberalism' of Isaiah Berlin,[73] to the diverse forms of pragmatic liberalism represented by thinkers such as Richard Rorty, George Kateb, or Benjamin Barber,[74] to the 'radical democracy' of Chantal Mouffe, or the 'agonistic democracy' of William Connolly,[75] and through a further array of views too broad to canvass in this context, the idea that either liberalism, or democracy, or political order, or justice depends upon liberal-rationalist conceptions of politics, truth, or responsibility is explicitly challenged.

These views resonate strongly with many of the concerns of the wilful Realist tradition I have tried to outline here. There are, to be sure, important issues at stake and significant differences exist between divergent presentations of these issues, and the wilful Realist insistence on the importance of power and decision in politics often provides difficult challenges for these positions. But these possible engagements are precisely the issue, and the divergences should not be allowed to obscure the point that they take up common problematics surrounding the nature of politics in modernity. The scepticism toward foundationalism found in both postmodernism and wilful Realism does not necessarily imply the wholesale rejection of the Enlightenment tradition, of the importance of values, or of some vision of progress in a practical sense. The charge of 'mainstream' International Relations theory – sometimes explicit, usually implicit – that a scepticism toward cognitive liberalism is inherently irrational, anarchic, and irresponsible, often simply

[73] The identification of Berlin's liberalism as 'agonistic' belongs to John Gray in his *Isaiah Berlin* (London: HarperCollins, 1995), chapter 6 in particular. For a further exploration, see also Gray's *Post-Liberalism* (London: Routledge, 1993).
[74] Particularly in Richard Rorty, *Contingency, Irony, Solidarity* (Cambridge University Press, 1989); George Kateb, *The Inner Ocean* (Ithaca: Cornell University Press, 1992); Benjamin Barber, *Strong Democracy* (Princeton University Press, 1984).
[75] Mouffe, *The Return of the Political*; William Connolly, *Identity/Difference: Democratic Negotiations of Political Paradox* (Ithaca: Cornell University Press, 1991).

demonstrates a lamentable lack of engagement with the diverse workings out of the 'modern' tradition and some of its most significant contemporary expressions.

But if 'mainstream' International Relations theory has seen this connection too narrowly, postmodern positions have often been guilty of a corresponding myopia toward the Realist tradition, and have tended to reduce Realism to a naïve form of 'modernism' associated with rationalism (logocentrism, positivism, etc.) in both politics and method. Defining the issue this way has not only contributed to the general misrecognition of rationalism's status as an historically constituted theoretical practice; more importantly, in mistaking the practice of objectification for intellectual objectivism it has reduced substantial discussion and engagement to a series of caricatures. Claims to rediscover the problematic of subjectivity, the crucial question of identity, the question of 'the political', and the like are all important in the context of rationalist reifications of all these factors, and many more besides. But to contrast an awareness of these questions to a claim about their absence in the Realist tradition as a whole does little to advance either the relationship of these concerns to prior analyses in the field, or the potential contribution which an engagement with them can make to current theoretical dialogue and development.

As an illustration, consider the question of the relationship between identity and foreign policy. One of the most interesting and important aspects of post-structuralist analysis in International Relations has been to explore how the dilemmas of identity manifest themselves in a constitutive politics of opposition: of how, in short, foreign policy can be understood not only as an expression of state identity but as a central element in the construction and maintenance of collective identity. Consider, in this light, the following two analyses of the role which the peculiarities of American identity have played in the formulation of American foreign policy, and the importance of these themes in the rise of McCarthyism and American culture in the Cold War:

> No state possesses a prediscursive, stable identity, and no state is free from the tension between the various domains that need to be aligned for a political community to come into being, an alignment that is a response to, rather than constitutive of, a prior and stable identity. Yet for no state is this condition as central as it is for America. If all states are 'imagined communities', devoid of ontological being apart from the many practices that constitute their reality, America is the imagined community par excellence. Arguably more than any other state,

the imprecise process of imagination is what constitutes American identity. In this context, the practices of 'foreign policy' come to have special importance. If the identity of the 'true nationals' remains elusive and 'inorganic', it can only be secured by the effective and continual ideological demarcation of those who are 'false' to the defining ideals.

It [McCarthyism] sprang from an impulse that, as we have seen, has been endemic in American society: the primordial anxiety about its ability to survive, the fear of losing its reason for being, its identity, itself. Could a society so deprived of traditional foundations, so deliberately built upon nothing but the consensus to be equal in freedom in a spacious land – could such a society withstand, without losing its identity, a drastic influx of foreign people and alien ideas? Could the new and deliberately chosen loyalty to the American consensus compete successfully with the old-established loyalties – found and not chosen – to foreign governments and alien ideas? Those questions haunted American society from its very beginnings, and whenever the danger of alienation seemed to be particularly acute, a law was passed, the police were called out, a mob was formed, to enforce loyalty to the American consensus. McCarthyism belongs in that tradition of a typically American self-defense against alienation.

Each of these authors seeks to understand the role of identity in politics, and to link this issue to American Cold War politics. Indeed each is concerned centrally with dimensions of the Cold War, and with the ways in which what they regard as the specific nature of the American identity yields a politics in which charges of treason become linked to relations of enmity, and where claims of danger (both internal and external) are used to discipline citizens. Strikingly, each even illustrates their argument by referring to exactly the same policy document – Executive Order 10450 of the Eisenhower administration – as a demonstration of how claims of loyalty operated in an attempt to enforce and *secure* particular forms of legitimate identity and values within the specifically unstable or alienated nature of the American identity. Given the importance of claims about the relationship between identity, politics, and foreign policy in 'post-structural' International Relations theory, it is likely to come as little surprise that the first quotation is from a pioneering post-structuralist work, David Campbell's *Writing Security*, first published in 1993.[76] The

[76] The quote is from Campbell, *Writing Security*, p. 91. As he puts his point elsewhere, 'America is more than a good example of the logic of identity at work in the realm of the state. In many ways, America is an exemplification of this logic, for America is the imagined community par excellence. As with all republics, America has constantly confronted the dilemma of securing legitimacy and establishing authority in a culture that renders ontological guarantees suspect'; p. 131. The use of Executive Order 10450 is on p. 151.

identity of the second is perhaps more surprising: it is from *The Purpose of American Politics*, by Hans Morgenthau published in 1960.[77]

The use of limited pieces of text as a means of comparatively demonstrating a point is, of course, a tricky and intrinsically limited argumentative device. I am not claiming that there are not substantial differences between, for example, Campbell's and Morgenthau's analysis of the 'American identity' and its political consequences. And I am certainly not claiming that Morgenthau was a 'post-structuralist' all along (any more than such an anachronistic and essentially meaningless point would apply to Hobbes or Rousseau). What I am arguing, however, is that the idea that there are unbreachable chasms between post-structuralism and Realism is simply fallacious. Similarly, the idea (put about by both its purported defenders and its critics) that the 'Realist tradition' exemplified by someone like Morgenthau represents a 'modernist' stance unfamiliar with and untroubled by (for better or worse) issues such as the relational nature of identity and other themes often characterised as 'postmodern' is equally false. My goal here is simply to point to the extraordinary shared interests and insights that may exist, and above all to call for an acknowledgement of the diversity of thought and call for a greater degree of openness in its light.[78]

Taking the wilful Realist position more seriously also poses significant challenges to ways in which some forms of postmodern thinking have located their relationship to the practice of international politics. By identifying Realism as a form of modernist 'essentialism' comprising either a rationalist vision of subjectivity, an objectivist theory of knowledge, or both, some postmodern approaches have tended to present a non-objectivist, anti-essentialist, and primarily deconstructive theory as a *return* to practice, as an attempt to open up questions of practice and

[77] *Morgenthau, The Purpose of American Politics*, p. 146. The ideas expressed in this remarkable yet oft-ignored book challenge even further most prevailing views of Morgenthau in International Relations. The fact that Morgenthau (so often identified as the archetypal Realist with little or no understanding of such issues) was working with such ideas thirty years before 'identity' hit centre-stage in International Relations also speaks volumes about the contemporary categorisations in the field, and about its capacity for the reification of forgetting. For an important account of the cultural dimensions of Realism, see Rosenthal, *Righteous Realists*.

[78] A similar case could be made for the relationship between Rousseau, and particularly Morgenthau, and the forms of Critical theory associated with the Frankfurt School, or that have more recently been associated with, and advanced under, the name of E. H. Carr. The key initial text here is, of course, Robert Cox, 'Social Forces, States, and World Orders: Beyond International Relations Theory', *Millennium: Journal of International Studies,* 10:2 (1982). For a variety of interpretations of Carr and his legacy, see Michael Cox (ed.), *E. H. Carr: A Critical Appraisal.*

'the political' foreclosed by the Realist tradition.[79] While this argument has considerable merit in the context of the neo-neo debate, it does scarce justice to the engagements of wilful Realism. The constitution of 'the political' was hardly an unknown question for Morgenthau, for example, who as noted earlier devoted much of his early intellectual energy and a substantial portion of his second book to a sustained consideration of Carl Schmitt's 'concept of the political'. The revived influence of Schmitt discernible in many challenges to rationalist politics thus can hardly be viewed as a radical and novel challenge to this aspect of the Realist tradition.

Moreover, the links between sceptical realism and prevalent postmodern themes go more deeply than this, particularly as they apply to attempts by post-structural thinking to reopen questions of responsibility and ethics.[80] In part, the goals of post-structural approaches can be usefully characterised, to borrow Stephen White's illuminating contrast, as expressions of 'responsibility to otherness' which question and challenge modernist equations of responsibility with a 'responsibility to act'. A responsibility to otherness seeks to reveal and open the constitutive processes and claims of subjects and subjectivities that a foundational modernism has effaced in its narrow identification of responsibility with a 'responsibility to act'.[81] Deconstruction can from this perspective be seen as a principled stance unwilling to succumb to modernist essentialism which in the name of responsibility assumes and reifies subjects and structures, obscures forms of power and violence which are constitutive of them, and at the same time forecloses a consideration of alternative possibilities and practices.

Yet it is my claim that the wilful Realist tradition does not lack an understanding of the contingency of practice or a vision of responsibility to otherness. On the contrary, its strategy of objectification is precisely

[79] For an important treatment that does *not* make this mistake, see Walker, 'The Concept of the Political'.
[80] Notably in the Levinasian turn adopted by David Campbell in his *National Deconstruction* (Minneapolis: University of Minnesota Press, 1998). For an interesting perspective on this overtly ethical turn in post-structural International Relations, see Richard Wyn Jones, 'Introduction' to *Critical Theory and World Politics*, and for a broad survey, Chris Brown, *International Relations Theory, New Normative Approaches* (New York: Columbia University Press, 1992). For an interesting analysis of Levinas with connections to themes in this study, see Howard Caygill, *Levinas and the Political* (London: Routledge, 2002). The connection between classical Realism and the 'philosophy of the limit' often found in postmodern thought has been insightfully noted by Huysmans, 'Question of the Limit'. It could be pursued at great length, if one was so inclined.
[81] Stephen White, *Political Theory and Postmodernism* (Cambridge University Press, 1992).

an attempt to bring together a responsibility to otherness and a responsibility to act within a wilfully liberal vision. The construction of a realm of objectivity and calculation is not just a consequence of a need to act – the framing of an epistemic context for successful calculation. It is a form of responsibility to otherness, an attempt to allow for diversity and irreconcilability precisely by – at least initially – reducing the self and the other to a structure of material calculation in order to allow a structure of mutual intelligibility, mediation, and stability. It is, in short, a strategy of *limitation*: a wilful attempt to construct a subject and a social world limited – both epistemically and politically – in the name of a politics of toleration: a liberal strategy that John Gray has recently characterised as one of *modus vivendi*.[82]

If this is the case, then the deconstructive move that gains some of its weight by contrasting itself to a non- or apolitical objectivism must engage with the more complex contrast to a sceptical Realist tradition that is itself a constructed, ethical practice. This issue becomes even more acute if one considers Iver Neumann's incisive questions concerning postmodern constructions of identity, action, and responsibility.[83] As Neumann points out, the insight that identities are inescapably contingent and relationally constructed, and even the claim that identities are inescapably *indebted* to otherness, do not in themselves provide a foundation for practice, particularly in situations where identities are 'sedimented' and conflictually defined. In these cases, deconstruction alone will not suffice unless it can demonstrate a capacity to counter in practice (and not just in philosophic practice) the essentialist dynamics it confronts.[84] Here, a responsibility to act must go beyond deconstruction to consider viable alternatives and counter-practices.

To take this critique seriously is not necessarily to be subject yet again to the straightforward 'blackmail of the Enlightenment' and a narrow 'modernist' vision of responsibility.[85] While an unwillingness to move beyond a deconstructive ethic of responsibility to otherness for fear that an essentialist stance is the only (or most likely) alternative expresses a

[82] Gray, *Two Faces of Liberalism*.
[83] See especially the conclusion in Neumann's *The Uses of the Other*.
[84] It might, perhaps, be argued that the idea of an essentialist, modernist Realist tradition as the basis for the theory and practice of 'mainstream' International Relations provides the defining Other that makes some of the less reflective postmodern claims that deconstruction *is* political practice viable, thus insulating them from a fuller engagement with both the tradition and the dilemmas of practice.
[85] As Campbell might seem to imply in the Epilogue to the second edition of *Writing Security*.

legitimate concern, it should not license a retreat from such questions or their practical demands. Rather, such situations demand also an evaluation of the structures (of identity and institutions) that might *viably* be mobilised in order to offset the worst implications of violently exclusionary identities. It requires, as Neumann nicely puts it, the generation of compelling 'as if' stories around which counter-subjectivities and political practices can coalesce. Wilful Realism, I submit, arises out of an appreciation of these issues, and comprises an attempt to craft precisely such 'stories' within a broader intellectual and sociological analysis of their conditions of production, possibilities of success, and likely consequences. The question is, to what extent are these limits capable of success, and to what extent might they be limits upon their own aspirations toward responsibility? These are crucial questions, but they will not be addressed by retreating yet again into further reversals of the same old dichotomies.

There are certainly many different ways to assess what Robert Gilpin once called the 'richness of the tradition of political realism', and the treatment here makes no claims to having done more than scratch the surface of the questions involved. However, I do hope to have demonstrated that a fuller encounter with the sources, strengths, and limits of the Realist tradition requires that International Relations engage with a series of intellectual traditions and issues well beyond those that have recently tended to dominate discussion. It is insufficient to limit these debates to a contest between various forms of rationalism struggling over the legacy of the neo-neo debate, or to appeal to the essence of the Realist tradition as an undifferentiated tradition of anarchy, or to limit analytic debate through implicit claims about a responsible politics of knowledge. On the contrary, an engagement with the Realist tradition challenges directly many of the categorical distinctions that have come to structure – and to limit – the development of theoretical dialogues in the study of world politics.

The possibility of a 'dialogue' across divergent theoretical positions in International Relations has emerged as an issue of significant concern in recent discussions of the future development of the field. I have sought in this chapter to demonstrate some of the ways that taking seriously the wilful Realist tradition can provide an opening – and even a basis – for such a dialogue. Taking fuller account of the Realist tradition does more than clarify its historical status and its role in the evolution of International Relations theory: it places Realism within the orbit of some of the most vibrant debates in contemporary political science and social theory, ranging from the shifting nature of 'the political' in political theory, to the contribution of historical sociology to International Relations, to the relationship between the social construction of political action (and its analysis), to questions of political responsibility. Recovering the wilful Realist vision of politics demonstrates that these contemporary themes are not separated by a vast gulf from the Realist origins of the field. On the contrary, they take up issues that are at the heart of this tradition.

5 The ethic of responsibility

Over the course of the preceding chapters, I have attempted to show that questions of the construction of action, and its ethical and political evaluation, lie at the core of the wilful Realist tradition. This final chapter seeks to demonstrate how this is expressed in two key and continuingly controversial Realist concepts: the ethic of responsibility and the national interest. The relationship between these two concepts is at the heart of many understandings of Realist ethics. In its most straightforward form, the national interest is seen to provide the value to be pursued and defended, while a foreign policy limited to and by the pursuit of that national interest and a prudent consequentialism provides a responsible limit on state action. While this certainly captures important aspects of the Realist position, I will suggest that it fails to capture either the complexity or the continuing significance of wilful Realism's engagement with the question of responsibility and its ethic of the national interest.

In order to recover some of this complexity, I develop an understanding of the ethic of responsibility that reflects the sceptical and relational dimensions of wilful Realism. In this view, the concentration on consequences reflects more than simple prudence and calculations of instrumental efficiency; it is also a tactic that attempts to encourage self-reflection by actors about the values and interests they pursue, and to foster the construction of responsible selves and political orders. I then return to Morgenthau, to sketch an understanding of the national interest that reflects this ethic of responsibility. The national interest is more than an assumption about the sources of state action; it is a rhetorical device that seeks to use the political power of this concept to encourage critical reflection and dialogue about interests and their relation to identity – to how a society sees itself and wishes to be seen by others.

Bringing the concepts of interest and the nation into relation, wilful Realism thus attempts to construct a complex if deeply unstable practice of the national interest as an ethic of responsibility. This may seem a long way from understandings of Realism today, especially as it applies to debates dominated by the contemporary legacy of neorealism. But paradoxically it allows wilful Realism to engage directly with some of the most important controversies over foreign policy today. Nowhere is this clearer than in the rise of neoconservative visions of foreign policy in the United States, which demonstrate not only the continuing salience of the philosophical and political issues at the heart of wilful Realism, but also some of the most significant tensions within it and the continuing importance and limitations of its legacy of a politics of limits.

The ethic of responsibility

Few concepts are so closely associated with Realism as that of responsibility. In opposition to an idealist 'ethic of absolute ends', the story often goes, Realism stresses the importance of consequences and the need for political acts constantly to be viewed in light of their probable outcomes. In this concern, sophisticated Realists have accused idealism of more than just ethical naïveté; they have argued that an ethic of absolute ends actually subverts its own moral stance. Ethical universalism, to put the argument bluntly, either precludes less than morally pure actions on the grounds that the end can never justify the means – thus leaving itself practically disadvantaged or even impotent in the face of those who refuse such scruples – or it takes the form of a crusading universalism in which the value of the ultimate end brushes aside all scruples concerning responsible means.

These are powerful arguments, and from their paradigmatic formulation by Max Weber (at least) onward, they have been central to sophisticated articulations of Realist positions. Yet if accepted too readily, a crudely dualistic formulation of the ethic of responsibility in Realism leads both to distortion of its ethical dimensions, and ironically risks supporting forms of political naïveté and irresponsibility in the name of political Realism. Indeed to cast the question of responsibility solely within a straightforward contrast between absolute moral principles and consequential ethics is to miss much of the complexity of the Realist tradition and the difficult questions with which it struggles since, as R. B. J. Walker has nicely put it, even if one accepts a critique of idealist ethical universalism, the appeal to an ethic of responsibility begs a deceptively simple question: responsible to what?[1] Responsibility assumes both something to which one is responsible, and a self and political order capable of recognising, sustaining, and acting upon that responsibility. Without a consideration of what one is responsible to, appeals to an ethic of responsibility become little more than pale reflections of the idealism against which Realism has so long defined itself.

As I have argued over the past four chapters, the wilful Realist tradition does not take for granted the rational(ist) liberal self (in its Kantian or utilitarian guises) as the foundation toward which responsibility can be exercised. Nor does it assume that the state or the nation naturally occupies such a position. As Hobbes' struggle with competing religious claims to obligation in the seventeenth century, and Morgenthau's engagement with the clashing claims of state, nation, and class in twentieth-century Weimar clearly illustrate, political responsibility is a complex historical and ethical question in the wilful Realist tradition, not a postulate. This openness and indeterminacy is one of the great strengths of wilful Realism. But it is clearly also a challenge. For if there are no obvious foundations – no 'natural' or essential structures of either the self or the political order – then how is one to achieve a politics of responsibility? How is one to create order and value? How is one to call forth responsible actors at both the individual and collective levels when the problem is that they do not naturally exist? And to what or to whom should these actors be responsible?

Within International Relations, Realist ethics has frequently been accused of being a contradiction in terms. Two forms of argument have been at the forefront of these charges: first, that the Realist identification of responsibility with consequentialism as an ethic is parasitic upon commitments that it cannot justify; and second, that Realism's commitment to 'objectivity' enmeshes it in a fact–value dichotomy that effectively precludes ethical considerations. The core of the first charge is that an ethic of consequences takes for granted the values it claims to support. Thus, a consequentialist condemnation of irrational behaviour in a market (or a failure to pursue the national interest) is, by this argument, dependent on the prior valorisation of market (or national) values – it is incapable of reflecting upon these values in themselves. To judge consequences thus requires the initial acceptance of an ethic which consequentialism itself cannot provide, and upon which it cannot even

[1] Walker, 'Violence, Modernity, Silence: From Max Weber to International Relations'.

reflect. The second criticism holds that in its quest for objectivity, Realism effectively forecloses the question of ethics. Erecting a divide between the Real and the ideal in the name of social science and a commitment to understanding how the world is, Realism becomes equally committed to *not* pronouncing upon how the world ought to be, and is in fact rendered incapable of making such judgements by its vision of scientific objectivity.[2]

As discussed in the last chapter, in reference to much of International Relations theory (where the Realist tradition has been subsumed within an overarching social scientific rationalism) these criticisms are compelling, and I have no wish to demur from them in that context. However, I would like to suggest that the commitments to consequentialism and objectivism have a much different significance when seen through the lens of wilful Realism. The ways in which consequentialism and objectivity are deployed within this tradition are not a mark of the exclusion of deeper ethical questions, but instead represent an attempt to engage with questions of ethical practice and a politics of responsibility.

At the heart of the wilful Realist understanding of responsibility lies an attempt to foster individuals, political cultures, and institutions capable of critical self-reflection and self-limitation. Consequentialism, in this case, is an essential dimension of political ethics beyond its ability to encourage prudence; it is part of an attempt to foster self-reflection upon both the means and ends that actors pursue. In fact, objectivism and consequentialism need to be seen as *ethical strategies and moral practices* in wilful Realism. As deployed within this tradition, objectivism and consequentialism do not deny or ignore the question of the construction of responsible selves, moral choices, and political orders: they are essential elements of an attempt to *produce* those selves and political orders. It is within this enterprise that the Realist commitment to consequentialism, materialism, empiricism, and instrumentalism – often subsumed somewhat misleadingly under the rubric of 'objectivity' (or 'objectivism' to its critics) – can in part be understood.

Consequences and the construction of responsibility

If viewed simply as the consideration of likely outcomes, an ethic of consequences is without doubt deeply flawed. Not only is such a vision limited in its capacity to reflect upon the values it presupposes, but it

[2] For example, Jim George, 'Realist "Ethics", International Relations, and Post-Modernism: Thinking Beyond the Egoism-Anarchy Thematic', *Millennium: Journal of International Studies*, 24:5 (1995).

may become the basis of a patently irresponsible politics. Most simply, a reduction of ethics to consequences risks becoming irresponsible precisely by taking for granted the value of its ends and reducing all other actors – and indeed all actions – solely to the consideration of their efficiency as means to this end. The outcome of this could scarcely be more clearly expressed than in Edward Luttwak's definition of strategy; as he puts it: 'strategy is not a neutral pursuit and its only purpose is to strengthen one's own side in the contention of nations'.[3] In this case, the value of the end is placed beyond consideration, and it is only the consequences of actions which further the goals of this end (in this case, the nation) that are of concern. The difficulties here are obvious. One is left wondering, for example, what might be Luttwak's opinion of a strategist supporting a policy of global domination via genocidal extermination. Purely consequential calculation either assumes and leaves unexamined the values to which one is to be responsible (a given state, community, or creed), or (and perhaps at the same time) renders prudence the servant of an uncriticised and potentially purely irrational set of drives or commitments. It conspicuously, and damningly, avoids asking the question, 'responsible to whom or to what?'.

If this form of objectivity (instrumental calculation) and scepticism (uncriticised ends) were all that Realism entailed, it would indeed seem to support a form of pure decisionism or irrationalism, making for a quite sophisticated but extremely radical form of realpolitik – or a neutral 'policy science' – acting in the name of whatever ideology or institution, party or programme happened to prevail at a given moment. Yet despite the attempts of theorists of such a crude realpolitik to appropriate the title and tradition of 'Realism' for themselves, it seems clear that there is little in such a stance that the wilful Realists surveyed in this book would find compelling. For if all Realist ethics amounts to is just a consideration of consequences, then the fanaticist politics of religious faction so scathingly attacked by Hobbes, the model (and critique) of technical rationality that Morgenthau identified as central to understanding Nazism, or the logic of domination that Rousseau found and rejected in instrumental reason, would have little resonance in the Realist tradition.

[3] Edward Luttwak, *Strategy and History: Collected Essays*, vol. II (New Brunswick, NJ: Transaction Books, 1985), p. xiii. I owe awareness of this citation originally to its insightful discussion in Richard Wyn Jones, *Security, Strategy, and Critical Theory* (Boulder, Colo.: Lynne Rienner, 1999), p. 150. For a broader discussion of responsibility, see Daniel Warner, *An Ethic of Responsibility in International Relations* (Boulder, Colo.: Lynne Rienner, 1991).

A useful place to begin re-examining an ethic of consequences is to return to a brief consideration of the figure most often invoked in the context of an ethic of responsibility: Max Weber. For all that Weber's famous distinction between an ethic of responsibility and an ethic of conviction has been cited in support of dichotomous presentations of ethical alternatives in International Relations, it is precisely in his commitment to a more complex understanding of objectivity, consequentialism, and the ethic of responsibility that part of his more profound 'Realist' legacy can be found. For Weber, consequential analysis cannot in itself generate responsibility. But it can be a strategy which fosters reflection *on* responsibility. Consequentialism is not a blind attachment to existing structures. Nor should it be understood as restricted to a calculation of the likely outcomes of alternative courses of action – though Weber clearly sees this as essential. More substantially, the consequentialist aspect of the ethic of responsibility can be understood as an attempt to demonstrate how a consequential evaluation of particular actions can foster a sense of responsible self-reflection in the actor who undertakes them. This goal could scarcely be better evoked than it is by Weber himself; as he phrases it in his famous discussion of 'Science as a Vocation' and the goals of social analysis:

> if we are competent in our pursuit (which must be presupposed here) we can force the individual, or at least we can help him, to give *an account of the ultimate meaning of his own conduct*. This appears to me as not so trifling a thing to do, even for one's personal life. Again, I am tempted to say of a teacher who succeeds in this: he stands in the service of 'moral' forces; he fulfills the duty of bringing about self-clarification and a sense of responsibility.[4]

A commitment to an ethic of consequences reflects a deeper ethic of criticism, of 'self-clarification', and thus of reflection upon the values adopted by an individual or a collectivity. It is part of an attempt to make critical evaluation an intrinsic element of responsibility. Responsibility *to* this more fundamental ethic gives the ethic of consequences meaning.[5] Consequentialism and responsibility are here drawn into what Schluchter, in terms that will be familiar to anyone conversant with constructivism in International Relations, has called a 'reflexive

[4] Max Weber, 'Science as a Vocation', in *From Max Weber*, ed. H. H. Gerth and C. Wright Mills (New York: Free Press, 1970). For a thoughtful overview of these themes, see Owen, *Maturity and Modernity*.
[5] See Wolfgang Schluchter, *Paradoxes of Modernity: Culture and Conduct in the Thought of Max Weber*, trans. Neil Solomon (Stanford University Press, 1996), p. 87.

principle'.[6] In the wilful Realist vision, scepticism and consequentialism are linked in an attempt to construct not just a more substantial vision of political responsibility, but also the kinds of actors who might adopt it, and the kinds of social structures that might support it. A consequentialist ethic is not simply a choice adopted by actors: it is a means of trying to foster particular kinds of self-critical individuals and societies, and in so doing to encourage a *means* by which one can justify and foster a politics of responsibility. The ethic of responsibility in wilful Realism thus involves a commitment to both autonomy and limitation, to freedom and restraint, to an acceptance of limits and the criticism of limits. Responsibility clearly involves prudence and an accounting for current structures and their historical evolution; but it is not limited to this, for it seeks ultimately the *creation* of responsible subjects within a philosophy of limits.

Seen in this light, the Realist commitment to objectivity appears quite differently. Objectivity in terms of consequentialist analysis does not simply take the actor or action as given, it is a political practice – an attempt to foster a responsible self, undertaken by an analyst with a *commitment* to objectivity which is itself based in a desire to foster a politics of responsibility. Objectivity in the sense of coming to terms with the 'reality' of contextual conditions and likely outcomes of action is not only necessary for success, it is vital for self-reflection, for sustained engagement with the practical and ethical adequacy of one's views. The blithe, self-serving, and uncritical stances of abstract moralism or rationalist objectivism avoid self-criticism by refusing to engage with the intractability of the world 'as it is'. Reducing the world to an expression of their theoretical models, political platforms, or ideological programmes, they fail to engage with this reality, and thus avoid the process of self-reflection at the heart of responsibility. By contrast, Realist objectivity takes an engagement with this intractable 'object' that is not *reducible* to one's wishes or will as a necessary condition of ethical engagement, self-reflection, and self-creation.[7] Objectivity is not a naïve naturalism in the sense of scientific laws or rationalist calculation; it is a necessary engagement with a world that eludes one's will. A recognition of the limits imposed by 'reality' is a condition for a recognition of one's own limits – that the world is not simply an extension of one's

[6] Schluchter, *Paradoxes of Modernity*, p. 79.

[7] There are clear links here to ethical traditions of Otherness or alterity, though Realism's consistent focus on power, politics, and decision takes it some distance from the often pristinely philosophical formulation in ethical theory.

own will. But it is also a challenge to use that intractability as a source of possibility, as providing a set of openings within which a suitably chastened and yet paradoxically energised will to action can responsibly be pursued.

In the wilful Realist tradition, the essential opacity of both the self and the world are taken as limiting principles. Limits upon understanding provide chastening parameters for claims about the world and actions within it. But they also provide challenging and creative openings within which diverse forms of life can be developed: the limited unity of the self and the political order is the precondition for freedom. The ultimate opacity of the world is not to be despaired of: it is a condition of possibility for the wilful, creative construction of selves and social orders which embrace the diverse human potentialities which this lack of essential or intrinsic order makes possible.[8] But it is also to be aware of the less salutary possibilities this involves. Indeterminacy is not synonymous with absolute freedom – it is both a condition of, and imperative toward, responsibility.

From the wilful Realist position I have attempted to sketch here, consequentialism can be seen as an element of a multifaceted ethic centred around plurality, individuality, and limitation. Paradoxical as it may sound, for wilful Realists, the essence of responsibility is to be limited by one's responsibility to the sense of limits. The universality denied by scepticism at the level of determinate epistemic or moral principles (quite literally, clear self-knowledge about the limits of knowledge) is transformed into an ethic bearing responsibility for the freedom and plurality which scepticism yields, along with a commitment to act in the difficult contingent circumstances which will allow this diversity to flourish with a minimum degree of violence. This is supported by a consequentialist vision that stresses the destructive implications of not adopting a politics of limits at both the domestic and the international levels. These consequences are not themselves enough to ensure limitation, but they can support its wilful adoption.

Wilful Realism thus adopts what might be called an 'ethic of opacity'. The creative goal is to foster political understandings which appreciate

[8] As Flathman nicely puts it, 'Human action as strong voluntarists conceive and valorize it is only finally or ultimately, not entirely or unqualifiedly, mysterious and unpredictable . . . Will and willfulness as voluntarists conceive and especially as they promote them, are preeminently sources of self-command and self-control rather than means of commanding and controlling others. Will and willfulness, the at once animating and controlling sources of individuality and diversity, are essential to spirited, challenging, and hence engaging human lives.' *Willful Liberalism*, p. 11.

this ethic of opacity, recognise the sense of limits and the discipline required by it, and to construct political practices on their bases. Complete transparency is neither possible nor desirable, in either the domestic or the international realms; indeed the desire for transparency and certainty is seen as most likely destructive. To a significant extent, this ethic values the limited rationality of the world for its potentially positive contribution to diversity and creativity, and it seeks to construct practices of objectivism and instrumentalism as a way of both dealing with the limited reasonableness of the world *and* of achieving a maximum degree of positive development within it. What both Hobbes and Morgenthau seek, for example, is the foundation of a liberal politics which does not rely upon insupportable claims about objective knowledge or universal rationalism. Rather than fleeing from the consequences of their analyses of the limits of human knowledge to rest in the easy alternatives of a dogmatic rationalism or a facile scepticism, they seek to construct forms of political subjectivity, understanding, and practice that will make possible a political order in which liberal values of plurality, toleration, and diversity can exist in a situation of order and with a minimum of physical violence. An analysis of limits seeks a practice of limits, which paradoxically yields the greatest possibilities for personal and social autonomy. Since there is no absolute ground, the ethic of responsibility has to be toward the fostering of possibilities, of creating circumstances in which different possibilities can flourish, and of constructing political practices through which these can get along.

For Hobbes the construction of a materialist vision of the self, and of an understanding of self-interest based upon it, could be part of the foundation for stable and liberal political order within, and a stable international order without. For Morgenthau, as I shall discuss more fully in a moment, the construction of a responsible conception of the national interest provides a means for both the recognition of the claims of other states, and a mutual process of self-limitation on that basis. Rousseau, by contrast, stands as one of the most trenchant critics of the limits of opacity, and of its role in political domination and ethical diminution. Yet, despite the claims of both hagiographers and many critics in International Relations, neither Hobbes, nor Rousseau, nor Morgenthau believed that the position they espoused was a straightforward description of the world. Each provides an analysis of the conditions of political life with an appraisal of what ought to be done in those conditions. The goal of the strategy of opacity is to construct a form of practical reason in support of this project of limitation. A stress on the limits of knowledge and the limited rationality of the world is part of this process. The attempt to construct materialism and instrumentalism as practices is yet another. Yet to be successful each of these relies upon a political commitment and culture through which they can prevail, conditions that cannot themselves be grounded upon principles of materialism or instrumentality. Objectivity, in this sense, can be understood as a will to objectivism in the service of toleration. Value freedom in the sense of treating others as having interests that cannot be immediately reduced to mendacity or rejected out of hand as misguided or evil (as not reducible to one's own will or desire, or immediately subject to one's visions of good and evil) is a mark of *value*: a respect for their 'otherness' generated by a politics of responsibility and an ethic of opacity and limitation.

This commitment to the construction of an ethic of responsibility in a world without foundations is also illustrated in the very idea of objective enquiry. Why, for example, should analysts be committed to objectivity given wilful Realism's scepticism toward a science of international politics? Why, as Morgenthau so pointedly asked, should it be a 'calling' to seek 'truth' and not just 'power', when it is so often and so clearly advantageous to speak the truth which power wants to hear? Would not a Realist appreciation of power lead its most astute practitioners to tell power whatever it wanted to hear in order to gain power themselves? Within the wilful Realist tradition, this is again a question of responsibility and, importantly, of will. It is a responsible choice, itself beyond ultimate ground of objectivity. The capacity to recognise the lack of a naïvely 'objective' standpoint is necessary for an objective (realistic) understanding of the social world and, vitally, is a condition of the construction of an ethic of responsibility within it.[9] Responsibility in wilful Realism does *not* entail a simple support for, and acquiescence to, dominant political realities and a consequential analysis of their implications. On the contrary, it is a condition of responsible scepticism toward dominant political claims. Power, in this vision, wants continually to claim that there is no gap between its understandings and actions and truth. The commitment to objectivity in wilful Realism is to demonstrate the inevitably partial nature of these claims, to uncover the ethical and practical limitations and forms of domination that they seek to disguise, and to subject these to ruthless and ongoing criticism. If political success is a matter of continually ensuring that truth bends to the needs of power, responsibility entails consistently challenging this dynamic.

[9] Owen, *Maturity and Modernity*, p. 91.

The commitment to truth does not emerge from an external reality: it is a responsible element and expression of self-mastery, autonomy, and freedom. Rather than being the outcome of some naïve, disembodied, positivist ideal, or of the uncritical pursuit of some Modernist utopia, it is an expression of will, of creative self-assertion and moral commitment fully conscious of the limits of knowledge. To give oneself over fully to the demands of prevailing structures of power – in the form of either a servile ascription to dominant forms of knowledge or political obligation – or retreat wholly from such commitments in the name of the inescapability of some soporific 'relativism', is precisely to forfeit one's autonomy and to abdicate one's responsibility.[10]

The ethic of responsibility in wilful Realism is therefore, as Morgenthau clearly stated, inevitably antagonistic toward political power, and a Realist theory is in this regard inevitably 'subversive'.[11] Recognising the inevitability of 'perspectivism' and the historical situatedness of knowledge, the responsible analyst seeks always to demonstrate this partiality, and is thus in intrinsic conflict with those who seek to conceal or deny it. Whereas power seeks always to cloak itself in truth, responsibility demands that one demonstrate both the links and the tensions between structures of truth and power, and that these links be critically evaluated in the name of autonomy. The plurality of truth claims makes the claim to possess *the* truth a constant element in the quest for (and exercise of) power. It is the responsibility of wilful Realism to recognise this fact, to demonstrate its operation, and to provide a continual stimulus to ethical and political reflection upon the adequacy of particular resolutions to the problems of political life in an inherently uncertain world. This commitment is wilful in the sense that it requires an ethical choice. Its adoption requires a continual rebellion against the seductions of prevailing structures of power, identity, and knowledge.

It is in precisely this struggle that – in classical Weberian terms – Hans Morgenthau located the ethically responsible 'calling' of the theorist of international politics. And it was from this commitment that he launched

[10] For explorations of this essential Nietzschean theme, see Mark Warren, *Nietzsche and Political Thought* (Cambridge, Mass.: MIT Press, 1988), and Leslie Paul Thiele, *Friedrich Nietzsche and the Politics of the Soul* (Princeton University Press, 1994). In International Relations, the theme has been very perceptively explored by Der Derian in 'Post Theory: The Eternal Return of Ethics in International Relations' and 'A Reinterpretation of Realism'.

[11] See, most clearly, Morgenthau, 'The Commitments of a Theory of International Politics', in *Politics in the Twentieth Century*, vol. I: *The Decline of Democratic Politics*.

his most vitriolic attacks upon those who confused (often under the mistaken guise of 'objectivity') the need to engage with practical politics with the self-serving subordination to dominant political visions or actors.[12] Among his chief worries in this regard was not that academics will enter the world of politics, but that, once there, they will use their academic claims to justify their political actions. To do so, Morgenthau is crystal clear, is a betrayal of their calling; as he puts it, 'Their betrayal does not just consist in the exchange of one calling for another, which can be respectable and even worthwhile. It consists in the exploitation of one calling on behalf of another, in the false pretense of politicians, dedicated to the pursuit of power, who make it appear as though they were still intellectuals dedicated to the pursuit of truth.'[13] The tendency of academic claims to expertise to become closely connected with declarations of certainty as the basis of state policy involves a potentially dangerous abdication of responsibility on the behalf of intellectuals. As he puts it, 'For by making it appear as though the voice of the government were necessarily the voice of truth, it powerfully supports the trend toward consensus politics and the concomitant destruction of an autonomous private sphere already referred to. It also tends to obliterate the confrontation between truth and power from which stems the vitality of democratic pluralism.'[14] Nowhere was this need for contestation between competing claims more important than in consideration of Morgenthau's primary practical ethic: the national interest.

The national interest

The ethic of responsibility in wilful Realism attempts to straddle a difficult tension. The responsible end can never be sacrificed to the goal of political efficacy, although it must always account for the potential efficacy of actions in a context structured beyond the dictates of its own will. This is not just a playing out of the old dilemma of means and ends.

[12] See particularly Morgenthau's almost 'structural' view of his conflictual and acrimonious relationship with President Lyndon Johnson in *Truth and Power*.

[13] Morgenthau, *Truth and Power*, pp. 17–18. This does, however, reflect Morgenthau's tendency to reduce the political realm solely to power. This is one of the least compelling aspects of his thinking, since it risks completely dividing politics as other social spheres.

[14] Morgenthau, *Truth and Power*, p. 54. While some deconstructively inclined readers may be tempted to demur from this position on the grounds that it is too naïve a presentation of the power/knowledge nexus, it is interestingly and strikingly similar to many of the later formulations of Michel Foucault. For a good analysis of these themes in Foucault, see Beatrice Hanssen, *Critique of Violence* (London: Routledge, 2000), chapters 2 and 3 especially.

It goes right to the heart of the vision of theory and practice as adopted by wilful Realism. For in this commitment lies one of the tragic and difficult paradoxes of wilful Realism – that a commitment to the ethics of responsibility may very well stand in opposition to the levers (and corridors) of power through which responsibility might be effected. While wilful Realism relies on the construction of responsible limitation, it has to believe that individuals and societies are ultimately capable of such responsibility; if this belief is not viable, then the Realist tradition risks, ironically, being 'hopelessly utopian'.[15] It is in an attempt to address these questions that the concept of the national interest takes on a crucial significance, and once again it is Morgenthau who provides one of its most intriguing formulations.

As is well known, Morgenthau follows Weber in his advocacy of an ethic of consequences in opposition to an ethic of absolute ends. Yet the basis and implications of this position have been much less well understood. Often, the ethic of responsibility and the ethic of absolute ends are treated as polar opposites, with the latter – in which the dictum 'let right be done though the world perish' prevails – playing a consistent role in Realist assaults upon the destructive naïveté of an idealism that results either in a destructive crusade or a politically ineffectual passivity. Morgenthau frequently does invoke this opposition in precisely these terms,[16] but as he was well aware, to leave the question at this level was too simple since it left unaddressed the essential question of to what, or to whom, one is to be responsible.[17] As we have seen, in the intellectual and political context within which Morgenthau moved, the answers to these questions could not be assumed: indeed divergent answers to them were at the heart of political dispute. One could not assume the political object – the state, or nation, or class, or individual – on whose behalf one could act responsibly, because the question of to whom or to what one owed obligation and responsibility was at the heart of political conflict (as Weimar vividly illustrated). Nor could one assume the political object toward which individuals would

[15] As Flathman describes wilful liberalism, *Willful Liberalism*, p. 222. It thus operates within what in another context Connolly has called the powerful and yet 'fundamentally unstable' doctrine of responsibility, Connolly, *Identity/Difference*, p. 113. As Connolly notes, the roots of this position go back well beyond the context of modernity which I have stressed, providing a link to other 'traditions' (e.g. the 'West' as a whole) which are equally pertinent but beyond the purview of this study.

[16] See Michael J. Smith, *Realist Thought*, p. 24.

[17] I here differ from the common criticism that he *fails* to do so, as found for example in Michael J. Smith, *Realist Thought*, pp. 51–3; and Griffiths, *Realism, Idealism, and International Politics*, pp. 39–41 and 75–6.

relate in a form capable of effective and/or affective political mobilisation. Individual Reason alone was insufficient as a principle and object of responsibility, as the travails of liberalism demonstrated. Nor could one assume that acting in the name of power could be equated with responsibility. Certainly, both Weber and Morgenthau held that taking account of structures of power was essential in any responsible action. But responsible action could not be *reduced* to this, for if power was all that mattered in the calculation of action then the idea of responsibility as an *ethic* would be meaningless.[18] Correct political action would be defined simply as acquiescing and actively collaborating within the currently dominant structure of power, whatever it might be. It is clear that Weber did not accept this crude reading of responsibility, and even the most superficial examination of Morgenthau's views demonstrates his clear rejection of such a stance.

The essence of Morgenthau's response to this situation lies in his adoption and advocacy of a Realistic form of political knowledge which brings two of the dominant aspects of modern politics – rationalism and nationalism – into relation in order to minimise their individual pathologies and maximise their 'political' potential. Each of these dynamics is destructive when taken singularly.[19] What Morgenthau attempts to provide is a synthesis of the two in the service of an ethical politics of responsibility; the result is his paradoxical concept of the national interest.[20]

To uncover this vision of the national interest, it is helpful first to examine briefly the inadequacy of each element of this concept – interest and nation – as resolutions in themselves. In Morgenthau's eyes, the traditional linkages of interest and objective relations characteristic of the Westphalian epoch (which allowed it to declare what the national interest meant in concrete terms) are no longer viable.[21] Under absolutism, the problems of interest, calculation, and limits were resolved

[18] As Weber famously put it: 'there is no more harmful distortion of political power than . . . worship of power per se'. Weber, 'Politics as a Vocation' in *From Max Weber*, ed. H. H. Gerth and C. Wright Mills (New York: Free Press, 1970), p. 116. See also the good discussions in Michael J. Smith, *Realist Thought*, pp. 31 and 44–7; and Schluchter, *Paradoxes of Modernity*, p. 61. The moral themes in Morgenthau are strongly expressed in Murray, 'The Moral Politics of Hans Morgenthau'.

[19] One might also argue that when taken as an *exclusive* conceptual pair they yield Schmitt's concept of the political.

[20] For a good discussion of the national interest, see W. David Clinton, *The Two Faces of the National Interest* (Baton Rouge: Louisiana State University Press, 1994).

[21] In this area, Morgenthau's thinking clearly exhibits the influence of Meinecke's classic study of realpolitik in *Machiavellism: The Doctrine of Raison d'Etat and its Place in Modern History* (London: Routledge, 1957). On Morgenthau's early engagement with these issues,

by the reduction of interest to the personal interests of the monarch, the broad acceptance of the legitimacy of absolutist rule between them, and the calculation of foreign policy on this basis. Under classical liberalism, calculations were reduced to the material interests of the state, and the assumption of rational calculation and a shared epistemic objectivism provided an analogous basis for shared practices of foreign policy. As has often been noted, Morgenthau occasionally exhibits a wistful nostalgia for these periods, and for the ordering and limiting practices that they expressed. Yet he does not believe that they can be recovered.[22] Absolutism, he argues, liberated political space from feudalism, while nationalism liberated people from an absolutism which conspired against individual freedom. Classical liberalism endeavoured to make a politics of the free individual, but ended up with an inadequate understanding of that freedom which resulted in its constraint. The inadequacies of each – embodied sequentially in the classical liberal critique of absolutism and the democratic and nationalist critiques of classical liberalism – make any such return impossible and in many ways undesirable.[23]

As discussed in chapter three, despite Morgenthau's oft-cited formulation of the national interest as the calculation of 'interest defined as power', his vision of the national interest is not just a state-centred assumption yoked to an essentially rationalist understanding of action. To see it as such obscures the profoundly radical nature of his critique of rationalism and struggle with the question of an ethic of responsibility, not to mention his clear awareness of the difficulties of positing a unified interest in a pluralistic polity. To appeal to 'interest' alone (in rationalist terms) is to misunderstand how reason as pure instrumentality is linked to irrationality and violence. Reason, as he puts it, 'is carried by the irrational forces of interest and emotion to where those forces want it to move, regardless of what the inner logic of abstract reason would require. To trust in reason pure and simple is to leave the field to the stronger irrational forces which reason will serve.'[24] While some have seen this as an indication that Morgenthau 'argues that reason and morality are merely instruments for attaining and justifying power',[25]

and his decision to abandon a study of them on having discovered Meinecke's work, see Frei, *Hans Morgenthau*.

[22] For a very good treatment, see Koskenniemi, *Gentle Civilizer of Nations*, pp. 437–40.

[23] Morgenthau, *Politics in the Twentieth Century*, vol. I: *The Decline of Democratic Politics*, pp. 181–2 especially.

[24] Morgenthau, cited in Griffiths, *Realism, Idealism, and International Politics*, p. 40.

[25] Griffiths, *Realism, Idealism, and International Politics*, p. 40.

placing it within a broader Weberian context (and that of Rousseau's critique of instrumentality) shows how Morgenthau's views reflect not a simple rejection of reason, or its total subordination to more fundamental power dynamics, but an assertion about the political limits and dangers of instrumental reason in an age of rationalisation. Alone, universal rationalism is either 'decadently' weak, or universalising and destructive.[26] It is not just that the (liberal, objectivist) epoch of 'interest' has passed; unmoored from its foundations, 'interest' itself is remarkably dangerous.

Nor can nationalism alone provide the solution to the question of the national interest. For Morgenthau, nationalism is explicable as a manifestation of the need and desire for substantial community – a basis for the substantive determination of values and affective obligation. In this sense the particularistic claims of nationalism contain insights which abstract and universalist liberalism has ignored to its detriment. Despite this, the 'new nationalism' – a modern, universal ideology quite distinct from the rooted locality of premodern forms – is a politics without limits. Linked to universal conceptions of truth and goodness, this modern form of nationalism is a 'political religion', universally intolerant, crusading, and violent. As an exclusive principle of political order it is 'insufficient, self-contradictory, and self-defeating' and, most importantly, one that 'has no inherent limits . . . taken by itself, is both in logic and experience a principle of disintegration and fragmentation' prevented from creating anarchy only by countervailing political power that it inevitably engenders.[27] The nation of the 'new nationalism', he argues, has dissolved the tension between morality and power by subsuming both under its own universalising desire, and as a result, the 'nation, deeming itself intellectually and morally self-sufficient, threatens civilization and the human race with extinction'. Nationalism by itself, he argues, is no solution to the problem of political order and justice, as the post-Versailles world all too clearly demonstrates: 'How different that world is from the world our fathers thought they lived in! Nationalism, they thought, meant of necessity freedom, civilization and justice; we know now that it can also mean slavery, barbarism and death.'[28]

[26] On this key theme in both Schmitt and Morgenthau, see Koskenniemi, *Gentle Civilizer of Nations*, pp. 432–6 and 438–40.
[27] Morgenthau, 'Nationalism', in *Politics in the Twentieth Century*, vol. I: *The Decline of Democratic Politics*, pp. 184 and 187.
[28] Morgenthau, 'Nationalism', p. 194.

One of the most important tasks of a theory on international politics, accordingly, is to develop a strategy that can counter these dangers. In fact, Morgenthau argues, the successful accomplishment of such a task 'would constitute not only an intellectual and moral, but a political triumph as well. For it would indicate that at least the mind of man has succeeded in mastering that blind and potent monster which in the name of God or history is poised for universal destruction.'[29]

The national interest

Morgenthau's challenge does not therefore lie in a longing for a world of 'interest' irrecoverably lost, or in a reactionary conservatism.[30] He clearly does not believe that a return to either the politics of absolutism or classical liberalism, whatever their virtues, is possible or desirable. The difficulty he confronts is daunting: not only are previous forms of order no longer viable, their likely replacements constitute a series of dangerous paradoxes. Neither of the dominant political logics of modernity – liberal rationalism or nationalism – can provide a solid basis for a politics of limits. Both the politics of decadent liberalism and its antithesis, the mythological nationalism of Schmitt, for example, are destructive of the values he seeks to uphold. Rationalism devolves into the inadequacies of liberalism, while nationalism degrades into barbarism. Indeed the two are often linked in a dialectic of extraordinarily destructive potential. In response, Morgenthau undertakes a difficult and complex relational synthesis of the two concepts, reconstructing their relationship so that their positive and effective elements can be mobilised, and destructive potentials offset. The result is a reconfigured *ethical practice* of the national interest as the construction of a politics of limits.

To take first the concept of interest. As a purely instrumental concept, interest as a basis for order is a familiar theme throughout discussions of Realism. But Morgenthau's vision of interest goes beyond an instrumental understanding in two important ways. First, as we have seen, the construction of a limited, materially calculating conception of self-interest is itself an achievement; a dimension of the ethic of responsibility, not an assumption. Equally importantly, this is not just a tactical

[29] Morgenthau, 'The Commitments of a Theory of International Politics', in *Politics in the Twentieth Century*, vol. I: *The Decline of Democratic Politics*, pp. 60–1.

[30] The first is the basic claim of Griffiths in *Realism, Idealism, and International Politics*, the second is pursued by George Lichtheim, 'The Politics of Conservative Realism' in his *The Concept of Ideology and Other Essays* (New York: Random House, 1967), I here differ also from Koskenniemi's characterisation of Morgenthau's thinking as 'conservative through and through'. *Gentle Civilizer of Nations*, p. 440.

transformation. It is also a moral one. For Morgenthau, treating others as having interests, even if they are in conflict with one's own, grants them a form of moral status: a recognition that they are not reducible to one's own values and interests. Reflecting on the nature of historical justice, for example, he argues that the conflict that is inevitable in political life – the desire to reduce others to the objects of one's will – paradoxically requires that one 'put himself into the other man's shoes', and that as a result: 'Seeking to deprive the other of his worth as a person by using, diminishing, or destroying him, the political actor must assess him exactly as a person in his own right. Paradoxically, he must be just in judgment in order to be effectively unjust in action.'[31]

Alone this instrumental/moral understanding is inadequate. But if it is combined with a 'transcendent charity' that accepts plurality, constructs instrumentality as a response, and yet refuses to see instrumental relations as the absolute limit of political relations, it can be an essential ingredient in a politics of responsibility.[32] This ethical practice will only operate with full effectiveness so long as actors recognise that their construction of an objective, rationalistic world is precisely that – a politically committed construction: if they recognise in it the imperative of conscious and disciplined limitation, and make it a basis for mutual calculation while rejecting naïvely universalist conceptions of truth and morality,[33] and if they use it as a basis for more creative political practices whenever possible.[34]

This sceptical and relational view of interest is to be brought into an engagement with a relational and political view of the nation. The

[31] Morgenthau, 'The Limits of Historical Justice', in *Truth and Power*, p. 69. An ethic of opacity and relativity, and the limited pursuit of self-interest are not assumptions for Morgenthau, they are rationally derived *moral obligations*. In his view, 'The moralistic detractors are *guilty* of both error and moral perversion.' *In Defense of the National Interest*, p. 33; see also pp. 38–9, and *Scientific Man versus Power Politics*, p. 92. See also Michael J. Smith, *Realist Thought*, p. 156, who notes this position but does not pursue it.

[32] For another development of such a view, see Guzzini, *Realism in International Relations*, especially the Conclusion.

[33] As he puts it: 'Yet as the historical truth emerges from the dialectic of opposite extremes, qualified and tempered by transcendent charitable understanding, so sound political judgment requires both the recognition of extreme positions as inevitable and their transcendence through a morality as alien to the moralism of our political folklore as Thucydidean justice is to the compensatory justice of opposing schools.' Morgenthau, 'The Limits of Historical Justice', in *Truth and Power*, p. 83.

[34] Again, for Morgenthau this is raised to an imperative in the nuclear age. As he puts it in regard to nationalism in the nuclear age: 'Political imagination is indeed the key word. If the West cannot think of something better than nationalism, it may well lose the opportunity to think at all.' 'Nationalism' in *Politics in the Twentieth Century*, vol. I: *The Decline of Democratic Politics*, p. 194.

'national' provides a limit on too-easy a universalism by stressing the particularity of the nation, its contextually located interests, and the corresponding diversity of national interests comprising the international system. At the same time, it attempts to foster reflection on universality by placing the question of what the national interest *is* within a sphere of public debate. To ask what the nation's interests are, is to ask what the nation itself stands for. As a result, competing claims about the national interest are forced to articulate themselves in relation to what the nation is: to its values and principles – indeed to its very identity. The national interest is thus a critical category seeking to foster public discourse and reflection. This process draws upon ethical traditions that are morally embedded and affectively powerful. However, it also takes the in principle open-ended nature of these traditions as a starting point for their engagement with the interests of others in an open 'political' sphere.

In classic Weberian language, Morgenthau argues that nations 'meet under an empty sky from which the gods have departed', and that while 'the actions of states are subject to universal moral principles' these cannot be assumed as effective practical political restraints.[35] Yet like Weber, Morgenthau seeks not to destroy the liberal political order as a whole, but to construct mechanisms for its defence. The foundation of ethics, he declares, is the Kantian stance in which 'the test of a morally good action is the degree to which it is capable of treating others not as means to the actor's ends but as ends in themselves'.[36] For Morgenthau, the degree to which a culture, a society, and a state recognises these limits and extends an ethical relation and recognition to those who stand beyond or outside its vision and resolutions is the mark of its historical 'greatness'. Historical greatness is embodied in a particular 'national purpose', and this greatness is defined explicitly as the ability to move beyond narrow definitions of national interests. As he puts it, 'It is only necessary to consult the evidence of history as our minds reflect it. We know that a great nation worthy of our remembrance has contributed to the affairs of men more than the successful defense of its national interests . . . In order to be worthy of our lasting sympathy, a nation must pursue its interests for the sake of a transcendent purpose that gives meaning to the day-to-day operations of its foreign policy.'[37]

[35] Cited in Michael J. Smith, *Realist Thought*, p. 146.
[36] Morgenthau, *Scientific Man versus Power Politics*, p. 196. See also Murray, 'The Moral Politics of Hans Morgenthau', pp. 86–7.
[37] Morgenthau, *The Purpose of American Politics*, p. 8. A great deal thus rides on this basic hermeneutic claim if Morgenthau is not to be left with only an instrumental conception of

The idea of the national interest, and its undeniable power as a mobilising claim in modern politics,[38] is thus transformed into a spur to reflection: a question about what kind of nation one is a part of, and what kind of interests are the proper expression of such a community. As a rhetorical strategy, the national interest seeks to hold together the unstable aspects of responsibility. It requires both a robust, responsible national culture and political leadership based in self-conscious construction and limitation: an ethic of responsibility. The social balance of power within the state is a key dimension for the preservation of democratic *political* debate about what the nation *is* and what its values are, as well as a recognition of the particularity of those values, of the need to be conscious of the claims of others, and of the need to maintain the political awareness of the positive possibilities of that engagement. The contested nature of the national interest is a symbol of its openness.

In this difficult yet sophisticated synthesis, the nation will provide both the content – the socially and historically grounded 'national purpose' – and the affective solidarity for the pursuit of a collective politics of interest. However, the very indeterminacy and contestability of the national interest within the state demonstrates the partiality of any particular resolution. Since there is no fixed understanding of the national interest within the political community, there is no absolute divide between inside and outside. The influence of the international on the determination of the national interest is not limited to instrumental considerations of material power, since the views of others on the legitimacy of the values and interests adopted by a state can impact on that state's own deliberations. These external considerations are by no means determining, and Morgenthau goes to great lengths to demonstrate both their limits and need for careful analyses of the conditions under which they operate. However, neither are they irrelevant, and any Realistic understanding of the national interest must take them into account.

the national interest. This is perhaps one of the weakest – and certainly most contestable – dimensions of his thinking. But it is also notable how it potentially links with more recent thinking on discourse and dialogical ethics. See, for example, Thomas Risse, 'Let's Argue!: Communicative Action in World Politics', *International Organization*, 54:1 (2000), and especially Richard Shapcott, *Justice, Community, and Dialogue in International Relations* (Cambridge University Press, 2001).

[38] Though even this is qualified, since 'it has not always been so and it is likely not to be so forever'. Morgenthau, 'Commitments of a Theory of International Politics', in *Politics in the Twentieth Century*, vol. I, p. 58.

This helps to explain the paradox which many critics have identified in Morgenthau's thinking: that he portrays the national interest as something objective, and yet is continually frustrated by the fact that the views and actions of policymakers and the public fail to conform to this objective fact.[39] Despite its apparent appeal, this criticism largely misses the point. Morgenthau does not see his vision of the *rational* pursuit of the national interest as obvious in a straightforward, epistemically objective sense. Rather, he views it as the outcome of a process of rational thought (an understanding of the nature and limits of the political) and conscious social and political construction. For Morgenthau, the fact that his view of the national interest is so often not recognised strengthens his case, showing the need for a Realistic vision rather than simplistic visions of objective knowledge or assumptions of universal rationality or values.

I am not claiming that Morgenthau does not also have a materialist-instrumentalist view of the national interest. He does, and he is often blunt about the necessities of power politics in conflictual situations. Struggle and division will persist – they are the essence of politics, whatever the groupings involved and whatever interests they pursue. Morgenthau does not shy away from the conclusion that power and coercion may and will be necessary to maintain these orders. In the case of domestic politics his allegiance to this Hobbesian legacy is clear, and in his understanding of international order – particularly in the maintenance of the balance of power – it is bluntly overt. But this does not mean that politics are defined by Schmittian parameters of absolute decision and violent enmity. For Morgenthau, the recognition that all politics involves power does not mean that all politics is reducible to violence. Far from embracing a link between wilfulness and violence, Morgenthau advocates a politics of wilful limitation. Material calculation within a political community defined by the nation-state is a political strategy. It attempts to draw upon powerful social understandings and historical structures to provide a basis for (liberal) domestic political order, and to provide guiding parameters and mediating practices for International Relations. The sceptical and pluralist character of practice provides the possibilities for a chastening limitation, and universality and particularity can be mediated through ethical principles and practices characteristic of the wilful Realist tradition.

The national purpose can be moderated by the concept of interest, by the liberal principle that values are relative, and by an acceptance

[39] For example, Michael J. Smith, *Realist Thought*, pp. 159–61.

that they should be advanced instrumentally by actors. But as in a liberal-constitutional polity, this first step only functions so long as it is underlain by a broader ethical principle that gives meaning to its plurality. Democracy, he asserts outright, is based on a 'relativistic philosophy' and a 'relativistic ethos' which is paradoxically protected by 'certain absolute objective principles which legitimize majority rule but are not subject to change by it'.[40] This paradox does not recommend itself easily to those who view the essence of politics (and its relationship to knowledge) as residing in claims of certainty and, as I shall argue momentarily, its political weakness may lie precisely in this confrontation.

A key challenge for Morgenthau becomes the construction of a political culture capable of sustaining such a politics of plurality and limitation while maintaining itself as a robust political community. Much of the despair that characterises his thinking (particularly in his later years) emerges from these concerns, particularly as they apply to the United States. Indeed, one of the most overlooked facets of Morgenthau's work is his deep concern with the *domestic* aspects of American politics, and it has far too infrequently been recognised how critical he was of trajectories within American society.[41] Far from constructing an absolute divide between the domestic and the international, in a profound sense Morgenthau's vision of international politics *is* a theory of domestic politics – an understanding of international politics emerging from divergent conceptions and constitutions of the political within (and thus between) societies and states. His approach to foreign policy seeks to foster a wilfully liberal commitment to discipline, opacity, and plurality.

Crucial here is the future of liberal democracy. A central element of Morgenthau's Realism lies in the recognition that the pluralistic politics of limits which he espouses depends upon a political culture that supports such a vision, along with institutions and leadership capable of sustaining it. The difficulties in the creation and maintenance of such a culture are enormous, and again Weberian themes are prevalent in Morgenthau's assessment. Politics, Morgenthau argues, is increasingly defined by rationalisation and bureaucratisation. While political

[40] Morgenthau, *Truth and Power*, pp. 40–1. It would be hard to find a clearer expression of the kind of liberal democratic principles which could easily belong to Popper or Berlin.

[41] See the essays collected in *Truth and Power*, particularly chapter 2, 'What Ails America'. In ironic contrast to his status as a 'mainstream' thinker in the various hagiographies of International Relations, it is hard to think of a contemporary scholar of International Relations so characterised who has expressed anywhere near so radical a vision. Again, see the revealing treatment in Rosenthal, *Righteous Realists*.

leadership is essential, these developments mean that the logic of effective leadership tends toward rationalised manipulation and demagoguery rather than responsible mobilisation and limitation. As a result, great political leaders are as rare as they are invaluable. He has, by contrast, a greater faith in 'the people'; but the links between societal rationalisation and an increasing individualistic materialism and 'hedonism'[42] mean that the public sphere of democratic debate and engagement is contracting, while racial inequality remains the great tragedy of American society.[43]

Far from being guided by an automatic and rational pursuit of the national interest, Morgenthau believed that often 'the distribution of power in America favors the continuation of policies that we regard to be indefensible on rational and moral grounds'.[44] At risk of losing its 'purpose' of 'equality in freedom', he worries that America has become an indefensibly status-quo power both domestically and internationally.[45] These concerns were reinforced by the implications for domestic politics which he drew from the evolution of American foreign policy. Morgenthau expresses deep concern that the demands of international politics will translate – via the failures of liberal positions and policies – into an irrational reaction that will threaten American liberal democracy. A recognition of the inescapability of power in politics risks being naïvely transformed into a rationale for restricting the public, political sphere in the name of the necessities of power politics. Indeed, he does

[42] This aspect of Realism was far from unique to Morgenthau. It finds equally clear expression, for example, in George Kennan's *Memoirs: 1925–1950* (New York: Pantheon, 1983). For a very interesting analysis of Kennan's views on the relationship between American society, its European links, and International Relations, see John Lamberton Harper, *American Visions of Europe* (Oxford University Press, 1997). These views have often been read as conservative, but as Morgenthau's case illustrates, such a position overlooks the much more difficult questions of political modernity that lie beneath their concerns.

[43] 'This lack of interest in public issues leads of necessity to the contraction of the public sphere. It results in the cessation of genuine political activity by the citizen, the encroachment of private interests upon the public sphere, and the relative shrinkage of national resources, human and material, committed to public purposes.' Morgenthau, *The Purpose of American Politics*, p. 203. The shadow of 'decadent liberalism' and the fate of Weimar hang heavily over the whole of this analysis.

[44] Morgenthau, *Truth and Power*, p. 5.

[45] Consider the Epilogue to *Truth and Power*: 'Regardless of the libertarian and reformatory rhetoric, its policies, both at home and abroad, have served the defense of the *status quo*. Abroad the United States has become the antirevolutionary power *par excellence*, because our fear of Communism has smothered our rational insight into the inevitability of radical change in the Third World . . . At home, our commitment to making all Americans equal in freedom has been at war with our fear of change and our conformist subservience to the powers-that-be', pp. 438–9.

not believe that the main threat to American democracy lies in the rise of a new 'relativism', but that it may manifest itself in a renewed desire for certainty, and in the willingness of an 'academic-political complex' to satisfy that desire. In such a situation, he argues, claims to knowledge and claims of power may fuse to be wielded in new and dangerous ways. And here, the pressing issues of international politics, the desire for certainty, and the socially rationalised structures of expert knowledge, risk becoming the powerful adversaries of democracy and of a realistic (that is, wilful Realist) politics.

These recognitions provide insights into the pervasive sense of tragedy that has often been noted in Morgenthau's political vision. Realism, seen from this perspective, is tragic not only in the commonly acknowledged sense that the world is a less-than-perfect place,[46] or even in the ethical stance that all politics inevitably involves forms of imposition, manipulation, and domination that are 'evil'. It lies also in the more sophisticated sociological judgement that while a Realist vision of the national interest – a combination of disenchanted calculation and reflective public discourse on the nation's values – may provide the most realistic vision (the least self-illusional, least prone to conflict, and most likely to foster progress), those who adopt it must realise that to do so is in a very real sense politically *unrealistic* since it removes from one's disposal some of the most powerful tools of political persuasion and mobilisation (such as a jingoistic nationalism, abstract moralism, and/or the demonisation of enemies). Similarly, the 'national interest' is a notoriously unreliable construction – a rhetoric as likely to act in the service of an unlimited, exclusionary, violent, and destructive politics as it is to support the politics of limits which Morgenthau seeks. Ironically, therefore, Realism in this sense is *not* realistic as a means of successfully playing the domestic game of power politics within which foreign policy is formulated. Political power and the capacity for influence is generated only occasionally by rational positions and arguments. Usually, to play this card is to lose – but it is the only responsible one to play, and it is in this that perhaps the most deeply pessimistic – and ultimately tragic – cast of Morgenthau's thinking is to be found.[47]

[46] See, for example, Michael Spirtas, 'A House Divided: Tragedy and Evil in Realist Theory', *Security Studies*, 5:3 (Spring 1996). On the tragic theme in Weber, see John P. Diggins, *Max Weber: Politics and the Spirit of Tragedy* (New York: Basic Books, 1996).

[47] It is impossible to read Morgenthau's assessment of the Vietnam War, and especially his acrimonious assaults upon President Lyndon Johnson, without coming away with a clear sense of his own engagement with this tragic dilemma.

The dilemmas of Realism

This reconstruction of the national interest as a politics of responsibility has tried to demonstrate that both these concepts are more complex than Realism is often given credit for. The national interest is an attempt to foster a politics of social and political self-reflection and debate, a productive dialogue of instrumentality and identity, and to embed that reflection in a supportive political culture and set of commitments that overcome the limits of instrumentality alone. The reduction of action to material self-interest as a powerful political tactic that is at the same time conscious of its own limitations, and its own need for an ethical and affective basis beyond material self-interest, is at the heart of Morgenthau's politics. His rhetorical action moves within this paradox, and attempts to negotiate the tensions that it inevitably produces. However, it is precisely this tension that made Morgenthau's thinking so susceptible to reification – to its transformation into an 'objective' and thus unchastened pursuit of the national interest defined as power – that contravened his goals. The 'national interest' is thus particularly vulnerable to cooptation in service of the irresponsible forms of power politics that he sought to counter. Having sought to mobilise a delicate synthesis of interest and the nation, his politics of wilful limitation contained an inherent fragility, and it is not at all difficult to sense his understanding of this paradoxical and tragic outcome in his assessments of American policy in Vietnam, and American foreign policy in general.

Objectivism and instrumentality – what might broadly be termed 'rationalisation' – can be understood as tactics of wilful Realism, and as elements of a broader (and broadly) liberal strategy of political order and limitation at both the domestic and international levels. If this is the case, however, then it must also be clearly recognised that these tactics are subject to grave limitations and carry with them considerable dangers to the wilful Realist project as a whole. As Rousseau so powerfully argued, and as Frankfurt-inspired Critical theorists have examined in detail, the ethical objectivism of a practice of opacity is all too easily transformed into a manipulative and technological approach to politics and toward others.[48] In this guise, liberal reason becomes not

[48] This, of course, is the theme developed most powerfully by the Frankfurt School, particularly Max Horkheimer and Theodor Adorno. See their *Dialectic of Enlightenment* and Max Horkheimer's *The Eclipse of Reason* (New York: The Seabury Press, 1974). For recent explorations of this legacy in International Relations, see Wyn Jones, *Security, Strategy, and Critical Theory* and Wyn Jones (ed.), *Critical Theory and World Politics*. It is also studied

only – as Morgenthau's analysis illustrates – 'decadently' weak in its disconnection from values, it becomes positively, actively, destructive of them. The reduction of individuals to objects, and the disconnection of reason from questions of the common and the good, result in a condition where values are reduced to a calculus of efficiency driven only by the needs of those doing the calculating and having value only in terms of their ends. Rationalisation can easily become the antithesis of responsibility, not only in the sense of generating an irrational opposition to it, but also by reducing everything – including individuals – to pure calculation in the name of a given, intrinsically irrational, or purely bureaucratically determined end. The result is an apolitical, cold, irresponsible realpolitik in which judgement and values are overwhelmed by an abstract rationalism which has forgotten that it was supposed to be a means to an end, and which takes itself either as an unimpeachable 'reality' or as an end in itself.

The project of rationalisation thus stands in continual tension with the construction of a political culture and community of values upon which it depends for its own self-limitation. One of the clearest illustrations of this danger can be found in the balance of power. As a technique, a tactic, the balance of power can seek to provide a mediating context and 'culture' – a set of shared understandings based upon material interest and instrumental calculation. In Morgenthau's view, for example, the rise of the balance of power within nineteenth-century thinking illustrates this principle. But nineteenth-century liberalism relied upon an understanding of this balance as natural, as tied to a purportedly 'objective' or evolutionarily triumphant liberal-rationalist epistemology, culture, and politics in ways that wilful Realism views as unsustainable and historically anachronistic. With the failure of this naturalistic liberal project, the balance of power cannot be assumed to operate naturally: it must be chosen and *willed* in full consciousness of its tactical and ethical dimensions. The national interest represents not just a recognition of the contingent coalescence of political cultures and sovereign powers in a pluralistic world. It represents an attempt to construct a set of political understandings and practices which will foster both stability and self-reflection. A failure to accept the fuller consequences of responsibility results in the balance of power deteriorating

with great power by Zygmunt Bauman in his *Modernity and the Holocaust* (Ithaca: Cornell University Press, 1989). These themes are very well explored in the legal context of Weimar by William Scheuerman, *Between the Norm and the Exception: The Frankfurt School and the Rule of Law* (Cambridge, Mass.: MIT Press, 1994).

from an ethical technique of plurality and pacification to an ideology of domination.

The national interest and the balance of power as a wilful Realist construction is thus always susceptible to reification in the name of a rationalist search for a science of international politics, or becoming cast as a simple truth of nature, or as an expression of a self-heroic (but intrinsically conservative) will to order. In either case, the risk is that Realism loses the sense of a tension between theory and reality, and is reduced to a unified realm of theory and practice where responsibility for action is denied by an appeal to a supposedly natural necessity. If, due to these dynamics, the responsible *practice of objectivity* becomes subsumed under a *theory of objectivism*, the balance of power constantly risks becoming reified into a mechanistic calculus devoid of political insight, sensitivity, or limitation. Equally, responsibility in the name of disenchantment can become a justification for violence and domination. The creation and manipulation of an instrumental order becomes a justification for the domination of those who 'irrationally' – and thus irresponsibly and illegitimately – fail to act within the dictates 'objectively' demanded by the structures and strictures of a rational order.[49]

The dangers of rationalisation in wilful Realism are paradoxically mirrored in its appeal to a particular form of heroic politics. At first sight this can appear counter-intuitive: traditionally, visions of heroism are identified more with mythical identities, transcendent truths, and individual certainties seemingly far distant from the disenchanted and chastened politics of limits advocated by wilful Realism. But the situation is rather more complex, for one of the most paradoxical aspects of wilful Realism is the way in which it seeks to evoke a disenchanted heroism as a form of affective mobilisation in the service of a politics of limits.

Wilful Realism invokes a politics of tragic self-denial, a choice which, drawing upon Weber's legacy, Rosalyn Baugh has nicely captured as one between love and greatness.[50] In a world without foundations, the heroically responsible individual is one who overcomes the desire for such foundations, who creates political order as an act of will, and yet who does so within the limits prescribed by an ethic of responsibility. The *choice* of a politics of responsibility, of self-denial, of discipline,

[49] Thus the power of criticisms of Realism and neorealism as ideologies of domination.

[50] Rosalyn Baugh, *Love or Greatness: Max Weber and Masculine Thinking: A Feminist Inquiry* (London: Unwin Hyman, 1990). Indeed a critical interrogation of this theme is a particularly incisive avenue of feminist critique of the Realist tradition.

disenchantment, and limitation, and the capacity to embody values in a world lacking intrinsic meaning (and avoiding falling into nihilism as a result of this lack), become one of the most powerful tropes in the heroic vision of wilful Realism. The adoption of an ethic of responsibility is in this vision a *moral accomplishment* requiring self-knowledge and a form of self-denial, as well as demanding the political acumen to make such politics prevail in a world often unamenable to a politics of limits. Through this disenchanted heroism the affective weakness of a chastened politics is transformed into a resource, a form of rhetorical and affective mobilisation that helps to overcome the more uninspiring aspects of a politics of limits.

For all its strengths, however, this heroic vision also risks subverting the very goals it seeks. Perhaps the most obvious manifestation of this danger lies in the capacity of heroic responsibility to devalue those who fail to live up to its demands, and in a tendency for the heroic individual to equate responsibility with the need to act despite the objections of others. Here, themes of responsibility in the name of liberal freedom can easily mutate into irresponsibility as the heroic individual transcends the norms of a liberal polity in order to preserve it, and as such 'heroes' declare themselves and their means beyond the recall of those on whose behalf they claim to act – the irresponsible and non-heroic populace as a whole. In this all-too-familiar scenario, the admitted complexities of political action can become subsumed beneath a logic of heroic realpolitik increasingly severed from the values it purports to defend, and destructive of the values it claims to uphold.[51]

In both 'classical' and 'neo' forms, disenchanted Realist heroes have often shown a willingness to use their self-portrayal to fend off criticism, to denigrate other conceptions of subjectivity and action, and to deride other political possibilities. This is not to claim that difficult choices will not inevitably have to be made in politics, but it is to note how claims of heroic responsibility can too easily be used to insulate these choices from criticism on the grounds that they are irrefutably necessary. Justifying themselves by positing a potentially chaotic world held together only

[51] Echoing Stanley Hoffmann's insightful observation, Stefano Guzzini has noted that Henry Kissinger's foreign policy was 'self-consciously heroic and neoromantic'. In this, Kissinger is far from unique: the heroic and romantic self-image of a disenchanted Realism is one of the most powerful and seductive tropes of the tradition as a whole. Guzzini, *Realism in International Relations*, p. 95. On this rhetoric in Kissinger, see Robert Harriman, 'Henry Kissinger: Realism's Rational Actor', in *Post-Realism: The Rhetorical Turn in International Relations*, ed. Francis A. Beer and Robert Harriman (East Lansing: Michigan State University Press, 1996).

by acts of will, heroic Realists risk falling prey to their own rhetoric, and losing sight of the responsibility which is the purported foundation for their acts. The heroism of limits is used to justify acts in the name of responsibility, and to limit criticism of those acts through the invocation of heroic responsibility and tragedy.[52]

Within the more narrowly academic study of international politics, these dynamics can take on a slightly different form. Here, the 'theological' tragedy of classical Realism has often been supplanted by a trope of scientific heroism characteristic of neorealism. The hero is one willing to face up to the objective and 'structurally determined' realities of the situation, and who is willing tragically to acknowledge their inescapability when others flinch from doing so. Rather than treating objectification as a political strategy, within this vision rationalist knowledge (and the rationalist social scientist) is mythologised as the hero within an historical struggle between science and belief, between truth and wishful thinking, irrationalism, or ideology. As discussed in the previous chapter, in this vision the hard-headed triumph of 'objective' science is portrayed as a necessary condition for political order, stability, and perhaps even progress, and its achievement is equated with the heroic struggle and responsibility of the social scientist. Cool rationalist calculation and a scientistic heroism merge in a powerful vision of responsibility. The result is that rationalist claims of responsibility serve to limit analytic horizons, the discussion of political options, and an engagement with the broader view of responsibility characteristic of the wilful Realist tradition.

The neoconservative movement

Enquiring into the nature and dilemmas of political modernity is not an activity that has found much of a place in recent Realist thinking. However, recovering these concerns is not only important in providing a better understanding of the Realist tradition in International Relations, it is also essential in addressing the relationship between Realism and one of the most controversial forms of thinking about contemporary International Relations – and one that *does* take these questions seriously: neoconservatism.[53] Neoconservatism is, as its proponents rarely tire of declaring, a very broad position – often defined more as an 'intellectual tendency' than a clear school of thought. Taken as a whole, however,

[52] Morgenthau, it should be noted, was himself far from immune to this tendency.
[53] I provide a fuller appraisal of the neoconservative position in Michael C. Williams, 'What Is the National Interest?' (forthcoming).

neoconservatism's vociferous critique of liberal rationalism as a basis for political order and foreign policy, and strong (at times strident) claim about the necessity of a conception of 'national greatness', bear clear affinities with many of the concerns of wilful Realism that I have attempted to trace here.[54] Yet in neoconservatism, heroic virtue and national greatness have been recombined as elements of a post-Cold War vision of the American national interest, and have re-emerged as self-conscious, assertive, and highly politicised dimensions of foreign policy discourse that is distant indeed from the chastened politics of limits found within the wilful Realist tradition.

Paradoxically yet accurately described by Joshua Muravchik as 'Reaganite Wilsonianism',[55] neoconservatism frequently casts itself in direct opposition to Realism (often identified with Henry Kissinger),[56] which it presents as an immoral and manipulative form of realpolitik – a manifestation of a broader liberal decadence that erodes the moral fabric of domestic society while being at the same time incapable of generating the domestic support necessary for robust action abroad. In the neoconservative vision, the national interest can only be sensibly and compellingly defined – and gain popular support – if it reflects the values and identity of the nation, its particular 'greatness'. As one of the most powerful figures in this movement, Irving Kristol, put it: 'patriotism springs from love of the nation's past; nationalism out of hope for the nation's future, distinctive greatness . . . Neoconservatives believe . . . that the goals of American foreign policy must go well beyond a narrow, too literal definition of "national security". It is the national interest of a world power, as this is defined by a sense of national destiny . . . not a myopic national security.'[57] Similarly, in a ringing endorsement of then-Presidential candidate George W. Bush's foreign policy, Robert Kagan and William Kristol argued that: 'There is no shirking of America's world role; on the contrary, Bush clearly

[54] This is scarcely surprising, given the roots of neoconservatives such as Irving Kristol in the crises of early twentieth-century American liberalism. For a broad treatment of this general context, albeit with little reference to its neoconservative elements, see John P. Diggins, *The Promise of Pragmatism: Modernism and the Crisis of Knowledge and Authority* (University of Chicago Press, 1994).

[55] Joshua Muravchik, contribution to 'American Power – For What? A Symposium', *Commentary* (January 2000), p. 40.

[56] Indeed, their criticisms have sometimes had affinities to the charges of irresponsibility in Realism surveyed above. For a neoconservative criticism of Realism in general, and Morgenthau in particular, see Joshua Muravchik, *Exporting Democracy: Fulfilling America's Destiny* (Washington, DC: AEI Press, 1992), pp. 19–37.

[57] Irving Kristol, *Reflections of a Neoconservative* (New York: Basic Books, 1983), p. xiii.

recognizes that role as an essential part of America's national greatness. There is no hint of a pseudo-"Realist" notion that American principles have to be set aside in favor of exclusive concentration on America's "vital national interests".'[58]

Without a connection to the values and aspirations of the society, a foreign policy of 'interest' alone will fail to stir hearts and inspire political vision, and a state that fails to pursue its values and ideals internationally will not be able to sustain them either abroad *or* at home. The core of American foreign policy, neoconservatives argue, is democracy: a universal value that is embodied in the American ideals, and – via declarations of the democratic peace – that happens to dovetail nicely with its interests.[59] A national interest driven by the synthesis of national greatness and universal values can yield a foreign policy framework for the post-Cold War world, providing the foundation for an aggressively internationalist foreign policy. Lacking a conception of greatness to drive them on, a 'decadent' public might well call for 'deeper and deeper cuts in defense and foreign-affairs budgets and gradually decimate the tools of US hegemony'.[60] But by drawing on a vision of national interest as national greatness, this tendency can be countered and 'old' forms of Realism put to the sword. Michael Ledeen, for example, declares that America is an inherently dynamic and 'revolutionary' society, where traditional notions of Realism will crumble when confronted with the allure of greatness. Notions of 'stability', he argues, are

> for tired old Europeans and nervous Asians, not for us . . . We are not going overseas to fight foreign wars or send our money overseas merely to defend the status quo; we must have a suitably glorious objective. We are not going to stick by a government that conducts foreign policy on the basis of *Realpolitik*. Without a mission, it is only a matter of time before public opinion turns against any American administration that acts like an old-fashioned European nation-state. Just ask Henry Kissinger.
>
> That is why I find the realist position highly unrealistic. The only truly realistic American foreign policy is an ideological one that seeks to advance the democratic revolution wherever and whenever possible.[61]

[58] Robert Kagan and William Kristol, 'A Distinctly American Internationalism', *Weekly Standard*, 29 November 1999.
[59] Again, one of the fullest expressions of this view is Muravchik, *Exporting Democracy*.
[60] William Kristol and Robert Kagan, 'Toward a Neo-Reaganite Foreign Policy', *Foreign Affairs*, July/August 1996, p. 28.
[61] Michael Ledeen, contribution to 'American Power – For What? A Symposium', *Commentary* (January 2000), pp. 36–7. Secretary of Defense Donald Rumsfeld's widely reported disparagement of 'old' Europe emerges from a similar logic.

This appeal to national greatness has come hand in hand with a renewed appeal to a politics of virtue, and especially to heroism. In one of the most striking and influential illustrations of this tendency, Robert Kaplan has recently argued for the adoption of a self-consciously heroic American foreign policy willing to embrace the paradoxes of power politics and founded upon a recovery of the 'pagan virtues'.[62] Lionising Winston Churchill, he explicitly invokes the dangers of decadence and the importance of heroism in combating it. Of Churchill, for example, he writes:

> The man who celebrated his nation's colonialist enterprise and later roused it to war against a much stronger Germany was deeply immersed not only in the history of his own country and civilization, but also in ancient history: which teaches that without struggle – and the sense of insecurity that motivates it – there is decadence. In the first century B.C., Sallust writes 'The division of the Roman state into warring factions . . . had originated some years before, as a result of peace and of that material prosperity which men regard as the greatest blessing,' for 'the favorite vices of prosperity are license and pride . . .' Churchill's understanding of that helps account for his toughness, what the Greeks associated with 'manhood' and the 'heroic outlook'.[63]

We now, according to Kaplan, live in times of heroic necessity, and it is not difficult to detect the fears of decadence beneath his vision of the emergence of a new aristocracy of virtue. Dealing with the emerging global situation, he argues, will require a diminution of democratic accountability and an increased willingness to use violence against adversaries who are either irredeemably antagonistic or fundamentally irrational. In such a setting, the best that can be hoped for is an heroic leadership. As he puts it, 'Such conflict will feature warriors on one side, motivated by grievance and rapine, and an aristocracy of statesmen,

[62] While Kaplan does not fit the strict neoconservative mould or movement, his views demonstrate the pervasiveness of these contemporary concerns and their political resonance.

[63] Kaplan, *Warrior Politics*, p. 26. One of the most grievous aspects of Kaplan's treatment here involves his use of the 'historical' wisdom of Churchill's romantic account of the Battle of Omdurman in 1898 as a 'panoramic succession of cavalry charges' (p. 20). In military history, by contrast, Omdurman is likely best known as the first decisive and devastating use of the machine gun, where perhaps 11,000 Sudanese were killed while the British and their allies lost fewer than two dozen men. Heroic indeed. On Omdurman, see John Ellis, *A Social History of the Machine Gun* (Baltimore: Johns Hopkins University Press, 1986).

military officers, and technocrats on the other, motivated, one hopes, by ancient virtue.'[64]

It is not hard to detect in this declaration echoes of the Cold War – and a desire to recover the political solidarity of that period (at least for many on the Right) is one of its key attractions. In this process, the tendency to devalue others that is a consistent worry of the ethic of responsibility becomes ever more severe as great, virtuous, and heroic citizens can become cast as the alter-images of those who are either decadent (and thus unreliable allies in the struggle), or who are irrational, intrinsically dangerous, or lacking in virtue (and thus beyond the virtuous pale).[65] The need for heroic statesmen and warriors to take on the morally tragic but politically virtuous acts required by the logic of power politics is part of a general assault upon the twin dangers of irrationalism and decadence that haunt modern politics.

The affinities between the neoconservative and wilful Realist diagnoses of the dilemmas of modernity, and the divergence between their political sensibilities and foreign policy postures, demonstrate once again crucial dilemmas within the wilful Realist position. Kaplan's position reveals again how the history of heroic claims to defend the national interest continually threatens to overwhelm the more limited forms of social mobilisation which a wilful Realism seeks to support, slipping easily into a rhetoric of absolute necessity: an heroic choice to accept that there is no choice but to act decisively in conditions of emergency when others – or even society as a whole – have become too soft, too secure, too 'decadent' to recognise the imperatives of responsibility and power politics.[66]

[64] Kaplan, *Warrior Politics*, p. 121. In such situations, he holds, democracy will be 'an afterthought'.

[65] In this way, initial attempts to support and foster liberal virtues can become the spur for profoundly illiberal programmes. The paradoxical role that the aspirations to create liberal individuals played in the rise of authoritarian politics in the twentieth century is a theme insightfully pursued in Richard Bellamy, *Liberalism and Modern Society* (University Park, Penn.: University of Pennsylvania Press, 1992), and is one of the most important issues raised by postmodern thinkers such as Walker. For different views on how modern social structures challenge or facilitate a politics of virtue, see Berkowitz, *Virtue and the Making of Modern Liberalism*, and Connolly, *Identity/Difference*. In International Relations, important treatments include James Der Derian, *Virtuous War* (Boulder, Colo.: Westview, 2001).

[66] Kaplan, *Warrior Politics*, pp. 25–6. For an influential recent analysis which also bears overtones of this theme, see Kagan, *Of Paradise and Power*.

The appeal to virtue is not an exclusively ancient phenomenon.[67] As I have tried to demonstrate, it is also a key dimension of the form of liberalism that underlies wilful understandings of Realism. From Hobbes' attempt to foster enlightened individuals, to Rousseau's conception of the citizen, to Morgenthau's vision of a robust democratic polity, a politics of virtue is central to wilful Realism. And it is precisely here that some of the most acute ambivalences of this tradition lie. Calls for virtue, and definitions of national greatness within its terms, can easily lead to perceptions of decadence and decline – a cultural crisis calling for a concerted reinvigoration and reassertion of heroic individual and national virtue. The attraction of such calls is heightened by appeals to international politics as a realm of danger and emergency, and the neoconservative movement has shown an affinity for older visions of heroic virtue combined with a self-conscious mythologisation of the American 'purpose' as a mission. Here, the martial virtues that have often characterised the Machiavellian tradition of civic republicanism – or, for the followers of Leo Strauss, the appeal of the virtues of the Ancients in contrast to the shallow 'interests' and corruption of the Moderns[68] – can appear tremendously attractive as mechanisms for overcoming a supposedly debilitating malaise in domestic politics, solving the difficulty of the national interest in an era of uncertainty, and meeting the exigencies of power politics through a robust assertion of the universal values underlying a particular form of national greatness.[69]

While wilful Realism evinces many of the same concerns as neoconservatism, it also provides powerful resources for a critique of the neoconservative position. Wilful Realism advocates a chastened vision of virtue; indeed, placing a limit on one's claim *to* virtue was an essential element of the restraint and self-reflection of the ethic of responsibility.

[67] For an argument that virtue has always been an essential aspect of modern liberalism, see Berkowitz, *Virtue and the Making of Modern Liberalism*.

[68] As Malcolm importantly points out, this (Machiavellian, civic republican) response is one that Hobbes would have steadfastly opposed, precisely because of its potential for conflict. A sustained valorisation of Machiavelli can be found in Michael Ledeen, *Machiavelli on Modern Leadership: Why Machiavelli's Iron Rules Are as Timely and Important Today as Five Centuries Ago* (New York: St Martin's Press, 1999). Here, a recovery of Hobbes may yet again be of value today. Similarly, examining the engagement between Strauss and Schmitt would provide another way of reading important dimensions of the broader evolution of power politics in the twentieth century, with their contrasting views of Hobbes a key starting point.

[69] Muravchik accuses Realism of damagingly undermining exactly this claim: 'In emphasizing the absence of universally recognized moral standards, realists are eager to disabuse Americans of any notion that one nation stands on a higher plane than others.' *Exporting Democracy*, p. 23.

As I have tried to show, an appeal to the pagan virtues, to the martial virtues of Machiavelli's civic republicanism, or to conceptions of destiny is something Hobbes would roundly have opposed. Similarly, to speak of an 'aristocracy' of virtue with its distinctly Straussian overtones is scarcely an understanding of virtue that Morgenthau would have been comfortable with, while his understanding of the dilemmas of contemporary American society emerges from a deeply critical and Realistic assessment of the limits of the United States to live up to its own ideals at home, not to mention its capacity to spread them abroad. The vision of virtue is not a transcendental one, but one much more imbued with self-questioning: scepticism is a defence against self-certainty. Equally importantly, national greatness is not an inherited possession, nor is a particular history to be uncritically idealised or idolised as of uniquely universal value. In wilful Realism, virtue and greatness are *relational* recognitions – something developed through an engagement with the views of others, both at home and abroad.[70] One of the most striking things about neoconservatism is its extraordinary lack of self-questioning, its remarkable – and from a wilful Realist perspective, hubristic – certainty, both morally and politically.

The neoconservative view of Realism again trades on a very narrow understanding of the Realist tradition – its reduction to forms of realpolitik – as part of its case. However, wilful Realism can also be seen as challenging the neoconservative position in a direct and sophisticated manner, and as arguing for a very different politics of moderation in response. Yet the neoconservative reformulations of virtue and national greatness are also expressions of important ambivalences and potentials in wilful Realism. Morgenthau's appeal to the 'purpose of American politics' and his declaration of the limits of a rationalist liberalism seek to address similar issues, but to do so while retaining a politics of self-restraint and limitation, and avoiding a messianic stance. This is a difficult balance to maintain theoretically and, if anything, perhaps a more difficult stance to propagate politically – especially in an era where the chastening effects of a material balance of power are less available to support a policy of restraint. Can a rhetoric of self-limitation prevail in politics? This paradox haunts the wilful Realist position, bringing with it the continual worry that it may well be tragically unrealistic.

[70] In this regard, the recent re-stressing, by Kagan in particular, of the importance of legitimacy in the wake of the second Iraq War marks a revealing trend in neoconservative thinking. For a criticism along these lines, see John Ikenberry, 'The End of the Neoconservative Moment', *Survival*, 46:1 (2004).

After anarchy

Anarchy, of course, remains the core concept of most understandings of political Realism in International Relations. As I have tried to demonstrate, however, the understanding of the meaning, sources, and consequences of anarchy within the tradition of wilful Realism often diverges dramatically from their formulations within contemporary International Relations theory. This divergence can to a significant degree be traced to the influence of an uncritical rationalism in contemporary thinking, an influence that contributes to the markedly limited – and mutually reinforcing – understandings of both sovereignty and anarchy that prevail within much of the field. At the core of this limitation is the way in which the sociological, ethical, practical, and competing dimensions of the wilful Realist tradition have been systematically obscured by the adoption of a rationalist and narrowly contractualist understanding of sovereignty.

By taking the limited *construction* of the individual as an *assumption*, the political strategy of wilful Realism has been reduced by rationalist approaches to an unreflective basis for narrowly contractarian visions of political order. If atomistic, instrumentally rational individuals are taken as the basis for political analysis – as the ultimate 'units' comprising a state of nature – then it follows that political obligation, authority, and order are *a priori* circumscribed by the contractual authority (a rationalist view of the Hobbesian Leviathan or, alternatively, some anodynely utilitarian rendition of Locke[71]) that provides a structure allowing rational cooperation between these self-interested individuals. This vision emerges neither from a theory of the state, nor of the international structure, but from an implicit theory of the subject in the sense of the individual person: the modern representation of the individual as an autonomous rational actor confronted by an environment filled with other like actors. These others are a source of insecurity: hence the classic security dilemma and the popularity of state of nature analogies supposedly drawn from Hobbes or Rousseau. Whether this situation arises from the nature of the actors or from the situation in which they find themselves (the traditional categories of debate between first, second, and third image explanations) is here less important than recognising the common foundation from which both possibilities spring: an

[71] For an excellent antidote to such a view of Locke, and for an analysis that engages a number of themes raised in this study, see Tully, *An Approach to Political Philosophy: Locke in Contexts*, in particular chapter 5, 'Governing Conduct'.

assumption of methodological individualism in which all social action (cooperation and conflict) is strictly the product of the interaction of wholly self-contained, instrumentally rational, subjects.[72]

The state accordingly becomes the primary locus of security, authority, and obligation, and contractual obligations between citizens represent the limit (underwritten by the authority of the state) of effective coordination of collective action (or of community). The security of citizens is identified with (and guaranteed by) that of the state and, by definition, those who stand outside it represent potential or actual threats. Relations between states are thereby rendered purely strategic (or contractual) in the instrumental sense of the word, and this foundation provides the basis for claims about international anarchy and the possible variations on world orders. The declaration that the state is the subject of security, and anarchy the eternal condition of International Relations, is thus premised not upon objective facts, or structural determinations, but is grounded in a deeper set of claims about the nature of political subjects and their relationship to sovereignty. The fact of anarchy is based upon an *a priori* claim about autonomous (liberal-rationalist) individuals and the kind of contractarian political order that these subjects necessarily require. At the international level, the essence of this conception is not simply a world of self-regarding states operating under the security dilemma, but the assumption of a particular form of individual rationality in state action as both the source and outcome of that anarchy.

In this form of Realism, the strategic political engagement of wilful Realism's politics of limits is reduced to an abstraction in which contractual sovereignty, defined by the limits of the state, becomes the defining condition and limit of politics. In mistaking the strategy and tactics of wilful Realism as a political and ethical *practice* of ordering, narrowly contractual visions of sovereignty become identified as the limit of political order in its essence. For all their claims to hard-headed Realism, it must be clearly recognised that theorists of anarchy along these lines are pre-eminently liberal rationalists.[73] Abstracting an *a priori* logic of sovereignty from its concrete historical and practical-strategic

[72] See also, R. B. J. Walker, 'The Subject of Security', in *Critical Security Studies* ed. Keith Krause and Michael C. Williams (Minneapolis: University of Minnesota Press, 1997). This point is also made by Ringmar, *Identity, Interest and Action*, and Onuf, *The Republican Legacy in International Thought*, p. 13.

[73] Elements of these practices – in particular the link between a materialist vision of power and a contractual view of government – as attempts to secure the basic practices of liberalism and democracy, rather than as simple-minded assumptions, are nicely discussed in Held, *Democracy and the Global Order*, chapter 1.

contexts, they accept essentialised contractarian politics as a foundation, and deduce 'anarchy' from this basis. The claim that the resolution to the problem of anarchy in the state of nature via the sovereign state simply recreates the logic of anarchy at a higher (international) level is little more than the expression of this abstract logic in operation. Sovereignty is transformed from an historical practice into an abstract deduction, and international politics is reduced to a structure of anarchy on the basis of this abstraction. The consistent reductions of both Hobbes' and Rousseau's understandings of politics are a consequence of, and contribution to, this basic dynamic in International Relations theory. Sovereignty, defined in rational-actor contractualist terms, becomes the precondition of order, and the only logical options allowed by this principle are either particular Leviathans (and international anarchy) or a global Leviathan. A consciously limited vision of subjectivity and political order becomes transformed into an unconscious reification which presents a practical judgement and strategy as an 'objective' (in the naïve sense) necessity and limit.[74]

But this is not the stance or the form of liberalism characteristic of the wilful Realist tradition. In this tradition, the construction of a limited subjectivity and a correspondingly limited and bounded understanding of the political are twin aspects of an attempt to *produce* a responsible modern politics. In contrast to contractual abstractions which tend to force debate into questions of whether the state is obstinate or obsolete, whether sovereignty is eroding or strengthening, this view holds that political order has always been shifting and contingent, and it continues to be so now. The crucial issue for Realism is not whether the state is necessarily withering away in this period, or that states are here to stay; it is that in an important sense 'the state' as some kind of stable, fixed entity was never here in the first place. This is one of the key insights of the wilful Realist tradition: that political orders must be created, and that the ethical and practical contexts and consequences which this entails must be central to a Realistic analysis.[75] It is one of the greatest weaknesses of rationalist appropriations of the Realist tradition that

[74] An issue most interestingly expressed in the ongoing debates between international historians and rationalist theorists of international relations. For an analysis that is interesting both for how it challenges the assumption of sovereignty and yet exemplifies the preceding commitments to it, see Stephen Krasner, *Organized Hypocrisy* (Princeton University Press, 1999).

[75] See, for example, Ashley, 'Untying the Sovereign State'; R. B. J. Walker, 'Realism, Change and International Political Theory', *International Studies Quarterly*, 31:1 (1988); and most extensively, Bartelson, *A Genealogy of Sovereignty*.

these questions – central to wilful Realism, and central to the analysis of contemporary world politics – have been largely lost in International Relations, smothered as they are beneath a thick theoretical blanket of abstractions.

One of the most common criticisms of Realism is that in an era of increasing interdependence and globalisation of social flows, environmental dynamics, and economic and communications structures, a purely territorial and contractual understanding of political community simply cannot capture the concrete dynamics and practical challenges of contemporary politics or deliver effectively upon the goals of autonomy and security which wilful Realists sought. A materialist ontology and a stress on the territorial state and a public sphere coterminus with that territory are simply increasingly unrealistic as a way of comprehending these shifts, structures, and the political challenges which they entail.[76] Contractual understandings of political authority, and of democracy in particular, which remain limited to territoriality simply cannot meet the demands of responsibility either to their own citizens or to the broader humanity which wilful Realism has always sought to accommodate.

As challenging as these dynamics are for the resolutions of materialism, rationalism, and state sovereignty put forth by powerful elements of the wilful Realist tradition, this tradition can be seen as calling not for their marginalisation but for a more serious reconsideration of a 'realistic' understanding of world politics. Crucial here is the claim at the heart of this study: that the Realist tradition has always been defined by a concern with the construction of political orders, both ethically and sociologically. The concerns of wilful Realism with contingency, historical transformation, and the construction of political practices make it considerably better-placed for a consideration of these contemporary dynamics than its rationalist alternatives. Questions of how structures of legitimacy, authority, loyalty, and power are generated and shifting, coalescing, and conflicting are necessarily central for a Realist theory of international politics today. This is hardly a revolutionary idea, since they have been at the core of the tradition throughout. But a contemporary Realist theory cannot be blinkered by misleading historical reifications that systematically denude that tradition of its historical and political sensitivity, or that reify its political and ethical engagements

[76] James Der Derian has provided some of the most incisive and imaginative investigations of these issues at both the theoretical and sociological levels. See 'A Reinterpretation of Realism' and *Virtuous War*.

into little more than an ossified form of immoralist realpolitik or abstract rationalism.

If we treat Realism as defined by rationalism, then it certainly looks in trouble.[77] But if we regard the Realist tradition in its wilful form, and see it as comprising not a philosophy of fixed and insuperable limits, but rather as one which attempts to generate *practices* of order, toleration, and engagement, then the scenario is more interesting. In this case, the limits of rationalist liberalism, themselves *constructions* of wilful liberalism, become susceptible to assessment. Forms and relations of authority, order, and value do not disappear into a meaningless chaos; they reappear from beneath their too narrow identification with rationalist, statist structures. Taking the philosophy of limits as a process of construction, in other words, allows us to assess its strengths and limits. If the sense of limits is a conscious construction, it is capable of rearticulation. If its goal is to maximise autonomy, then it must consider its current adequacy and be systematically critical of its own limitations and shortcomings.

Nor is wilful Realism without considerable resources for contemporary thinking. In this tradition, for example, basic, formal rights – security of the person, freedom of thought and association, etc. – do not emerge from a transcendental foundation, but from a principled pragmatism and scepticism. The lack of foundations becomes the basis for a principled openness, an ethical imperative of mutual respect, and a commitment to individual*ity* rather than an assumption of individual*ism*. What is now often taken as a commitment to basic human rights engages with some of the most powerful formulations within this tradition, though in its constant questioning of the *content* of those rights, and the socially viable processes for their determination and administration, and the processes whereby claims of right become transformed into logics of domination, wilful Realism provides a strong analytic and ethical challenge to too-easy an appeal to universalist 'rights' in world politics.

Instead of seeking permanent foundations for, or resolutions to, the dilemmas of international politics, wilful Realism combines a principled commitment to autonomy with the practical search for a *modus vivendi* and engagement between contrasting values and forms of life.[78]

[77] cf. Legro and Moravcsik, 'Is Anybody Still a Realist?'

[78] The concept of *modus vivendi* as the core of this form of liberalism is argued in Gray, *Two Faces of Liberalism*, though my usage here is somewhat different from his. Again, see Shapcott, *Justice, Community, and Dialogue* for a thoughtful set of reflections with possible affinities with this view of Realism.

Freedom and order do not depend on certainty, but on a pluralism which is in a deep sense unavoidable and which depends upon a pluralistic political system, tolerance, and a valuing of diversity. However, a recognition of openness and plurality as inescapable conditions of political life does directly translate into their operation as practices of political order. Nor does a vision of the essentially constructed nature of social and international orders necessitate or license a belief that progress will follow. Indeed, the adoption of such perspectives may contribute toward a considerable pessimism, as it has often done throughout the tradition of wilful Realism. This ethos cannot be sociologically naïve. It requires an engagement with the conditions under which certain forms of legitimacy, stability, values, and authority operate. While malleable, these conditions provide the parameters within which practices will be successful. Nor is it necessarily anti-statist. In the context of simultaneous fragmentation and integration, of interconnected processes of regionalisation and globalisation, the state remains central. As a structure for the mediation of politics in modernity, as a provider of order and guarantor of formal rights, the state, for all its imperfections and with all its inadequacies and potential abuses, is likely to remain a limit of political life and a vital provider of political order. As John Dunn once nicely phrased it, 'mere plurality is not itself the solution to the riddle of modern history. For it to aid and not impede such a solution we will always need peace. And to have peace, it is always perfectly possible that we may well need Leviathan, and need it very urgently.'[79]

Liberal democratic institutions in this sense possess 'foundations' clearly related to some of the most powerful themes in the wilful Realist tradition. Indeed, as I have tried to argue, the questions at the heart of liberal democracy are also at the core of Realism. Moreover, it is important to note that the state remains *a* limit – not *the* limit of political community. A recognition of the continuing centrality of the state in no way precludes the development – and the analytic recognition – of other forms of order, institutions, transversal solidarities, and transformations beyond boundaries. In the best wilful Realist sense, Michel Foucault once stated that: 'I do not think that a society can exist without power relations, if by that one means the strategies by which individuals try to direct and control the conduct of others. The problem, then, is not to try to dissolve them in the utopia of completely transparent communication but to acquire the rules of law, the management techniques,

[79] John Dunn, *Interpreting Political Responsibility* (Cambridge University Press, 1996), p. 88.

and so the morality, the *ethos*, the practice of the self, that will allow us to play these games of power with as little domination as possible.'[80] As a statement of an ethic of responsibility, it seems to me, these words stand as a challenge which any claim upon the Realist tradition must live up to. The task of international political theory worthy of that tradition is to confront these difficult ethical and practical questions, to enquire into the multiple and shifting structures of power and possibility in contemporary world politics, and to engage with limits in the dual sense of fostering limits upon the worst excesses and challenging limits which make those excesses possible.

[80] Michel Foucault, 'The Ethics of Concern for the Self as a Practice of Freedom', in *Michel Foucault: Ethics, Subjectivity and Truth, Essential Works of Foucault*, vol. I, ed. Paul Rabinow (New York: Free Press, 1997), p. 298. See also the excellent discussion of this same passage in James Tully, 'The Agonic Freedom of Citizens', *Economy and Society*, 28:2 (1999), p. 175.

Bibliography

Adler, Emmanuel, 'Seizing the Middle Ground: Constructivism in World Politics', *European Journal of International Relations*, 3:3 (1997), 319–63.

Amstrup, Niels, 'The "Early" Morgenthau: A Comment on the Intellectual Origins of Realism', *Cooperation and Conflict*, 13 (1978), 163–75.

Ashley, Richard, 'The Poverty of Neorealism', *International Organization*, 38:2 (1984), 225–86.

'Untying the Sovereign State: A Double Reading of the Anarchy Problematique', *Millennium: Journal of International Studies*, 17:2 (1988), 227–62.

Baldwin, David A., *Neorealism and Neoliberalism: The Contemporary Debate* (New York: Columbia University Press, 1993).

Barber, Benjamin, *Strong Democracy* (Princeton University Press, 1984).

'Foundationalism and Democracy', in Seyla Benhabib (ed.), *Democracy and Difference* (Princeton University Press, 1996), 348–59.

Barkawi, Tarak, 'Strategy as a Vocation: Weber, Morgenthau and Modern Strategic Studies', *Review of International Studies*, 24:2 (1998), 159–84.

Bartelson, Jens, *A Genealogy of Sovereignty* (Cambridge University Press, 1995).

Baugh, Rosalyn, *Love or Greatness: Max Weber and Masculine Thinking: A Feminist Inquiry* (London: Unwin Hyman, 1990).

Bauman, Zygmunt, *Modernity and the Holocaust* (Ithaca: Cornell University Press, 1989).

Beitz, Charles, *Political Theory and International Relations* (Princeton University Press, 1979).

Bell, Duncan S. A., 'Political Theory and the Functions of Intellectual History: A Response to Emmanuel Navon', *Review of International Studies*, 29:1 (2003), 151–60.

Bellamy, Richard, *Liberalism and Modern Society* (University Park, Penn.: University of Pennsylvania Press, 1992).

Berki, R. N., *On Political Realism* (London: Dent, 1982).

Berkowitz, David, *Virtue and the Making of Modern Liberalism* (Princeton University Press, 2000).

Berlin, Isaiah, *The Crooked Timber of Humanity* (Princeton University Press, 1998).

Blits, Jan J., 'Hobbesian Fear', *Political Theory*, 17:3 (1989), 417–31.

Boucher, David, *Political Theories of International Relations: From Thucydides to the Present* (Oxford University Press, 1998).

Bourdieu, Pierre, *Language and Symbolic Power* (Cambridge: Polity Press, 1992).

Brooks, Stephen G., 'Dueling Realisms', *International Organization*, 51:3 (1997), 445–77.

Brown, Chris, *International Relations Theory, New Normative Approaches* (New York: Columbia University Press, 1992).

Bull, Hedley, 'Hobbes and the International Anarchy', *Social Research*, 48:4 (1977), 717–38.

Burch, Kurt, 'Constituting IPE and Modernity', in Kurt Burch and Robert A. Denemark (eds.), *Constituting International Political Economy* (Boulder, Colo.: Lynne Rienner, 1997), pp. 21–40.

'Property' and the Making of the International System (Boulder, Colo.: Lynne Rienner, 1999).

Burnyeat, M., *The Skeptical Tradition* (Berkeley: University of Calfornia Press, 1983).

'The Sceptic in His Time and Place', in Richard Rorty, J. B. Schneewind, and Quentin Skinner (eds.), *Philosophy in History* (Cambridge University Press, 1984).

Butler, Judith, *Excitable Speech* (London: Routledge, 1996).

Buzan, Barry, 'From International System to International Society: Structural Realism and Regime Theory Meet the English School', *International Organization*, 47:3 (1993), 327–52.

'The Timeless Wisdom of Realism?', in Steve Smith, Ken Booth, and Marysia Zalewski (eds.), *International Theory: Positivism and Beyond* (Cambridge University Press, 1996), 47–65.

Campbell, David, 'Political Prosaics, Transversal Politics, and the Anarchical World', in Hayward Alker and Michael Shapiro (eds.), *Challenging Boundaries: Global Flows, Territorial Identities* (Minneapolis: University of Minnesota Press, 1995), 7–31.

National Deconstruction (Minneapolis: University of Minnesota Press, 1998).

Writing Security: United States Foreign Policy and the Politics of Identity (2nd edn), (Minneapolis: University of Minnesota Press, 1998).

Carr, E. H., *The Twenty Years Crisis* (London: Macmillan, 1977).

Cassirer, Ernst, *Rousseau, Kant, Goethe: Two Essays* (Princeton University Press, 1945).

The Question of Jean-Jacques Rousseau, trans. and ed. Peter Gay (Bloomington: Indiana University Press, 1963).

The Philosophy of the Enlightenment (Princeton University Press, 1968).

Caygill, Howard, *Levinas and the Political* (London: Routledge, 2002).

Checkel, Jeff, 'The Constructivist Turn in International Relations', *World Politics*, 50:2 (1998), 324–48.

Clark, Ian, *The Hierarchy of States: Reform and Resistance in the International Order* (Cambridge University Press, 1981).

'Traditions of Thought and Classical Theories of International Relations', in Ian Clark and Iver B. Neumann (eds.), *Classical Theories of International Relations* (Basingstoke: Macmillan, 1996), 1–19.
Claude, Inis L., *Power and International Relations* (New York: Random House, 1962).
Clinton, W. David, *The Two Faces of the National Interest* (Baton Rouge: Louisiana State University Press, 1994).
Colletti, Lucio, *From Rousseau to Lenin,* trans. J. Merrington and J. White (New York: Monthly Review Press, 1972).
Connolly, William, *Political Theory and Modernity* (Oxford: Basil Blackwell, 1988).
Identity/Difference: Democratic Negotiations of Political Paradox (Ithaca: Cornell University Press, 1991).
Copeland, Dale, 'The Constructivist Challenge to Structural Realism', *International Security*, 25:2 (2000), 187–212.
Cox, Michael (ed.), *E. H. Carr: A Critical Appraisal* (London: Palgrave, 2000).
Cox, Robert, 'Social Forces, States, and World Orders: Beyond International Relations Theory', *Millennium: Journal of International Studies*, 10:2 (1982).
Cox, Robert (with Timothy Sinclair), *Approaches to World Order* (Cambridge University Press, 1996).
Crawford, Robert M. A., and Jarvis, Daryl S. L. (eds.), *International Relations – Still an American Social Science?* (Albany: State University of New York Press, 2001).
Der Derian, James, 'A Reinterpretation of Realism', in Francis A. Beer and Robert Harriman (eds.), *Post-Realism: The Rhetorical Turn in International Relations* (East Lansing: Michigan State University Press, 1996), 277–304.
'The Value of Security: Hobbes, Marx, and Baudrillard', in R. Lipschutz (ed.), *On Security* (New York: Columbia University Press, 1996), 24–45.
'Post-Theory: The Eternal Return of Ethics in International Relations', in Michael Doyle and John Ikenberry (eds.), *New Thinking in International Relations* (Boulder, Colo.: Westview), 1998, pp. 54–76.
'The Art of War and the Construction of Peace: Toward a Virtual Theory of International Relations', in Morten Kelstrup and Michael C. Williams (eds.), *International Relations Theory and the Politics of European Integration* (London: Routledge, 2000), 72–105.
Virtuous War (Boulder, Colo.: Westview, 2001).
Deudney, Daniel, 'Regrounding Realism: Anarchy, Security, and Changing Material Contexts', *Security Studies*, 10:1 (2000), 1–42.
Diggins, John P., *The Promise of Pragmatism: Modernism and the Crisis of Knowledge and Authority* (University of Chicago Press, 1994).
Max Weber: Politics and the Spirit of Tragedy (New York: Basic Books, 1996).
Dillon, Michael, *The Politics of Security* (London: Routledge, 1996).
Donnelly, Jack, *Realism in International Relations* (Cambridge University Press, 2000).
Doyle, Michael, *Ways of War and Peace* (New York: Norton, 1997).

Dunn, John, 'Political Obligation', in David Held (ed.), *Political Theory Today* (Stanford: Polity Press, 1991), 23–47.

Interpreting Political Responsibility (Cambridge University Press, 1996).

Dunne, Tim, 'Methodology or Mythology?: Traditions in International Relations', *Review of International Studies*, 19 (1993), 305–18.

Inventing International Society: A History of the English School (London: Macmillan, 1998).

Dyzenhaus, David, *Legality and Legitimacy: Carl Schmitt, Hans Kelsen and Hermann Heller in Weimar* (Oxford: Clarendon Press, 1997).

Ebata, Michi and Neufeld, Beverly (eds.), *Confronting the Political in International Relations* (London: Palgrave, 2000).

Edkins, Jenny, *Poststructuralism and International Relations: Bringing the Political Back In* (Boulder, Colo.: Lynne Rienner, 1999).

Ellis, John, *A Social History of the Machine Gun* (Baltimore: Johns Hopkins University Press, 1986).

Elshtain, Jean Bethke, *Augustine and the Limits of Politics* (Notre Dame, Ind.: Notre Dame University Press, 1995).

Feaver, Peter, *et al.*, 'Correspondence: Brother Can You Spare a Paradigm (Or, Was Anybody Ever a Realist?)', *International Security*, 25:1 (2000), 165–93.

Flathman, Richard, *Toward a Liberalism* (Ithaca: Cornell University Press, 1989).

Willful Liberalism (Ithaca: Cornell University Press, 1992).

Thomas Hobbes: Scepticism, Individuality and Chastened Politics (London: Sage, 1993).

Forde, Stephen, 'International Realism and the Science of Politics: Thucydides, Machiavelli, and Neorealism', *International Studies Quarterly*, 39:2 (1995), 141–60.

Foucault, Michel, *Discipline and Punish*, trans. Alan Sheridan (New York: Vintage Books, 1979).

'Two Lectures', in M. Foucault, *Power/Knowledge*, ed. Colin Gordon (New York: Pantheon, 1980).

'The Ethics of Concern for the Self as a Practice of Freedom', in Paul Rabinow (ed.), *Michel Foucault: Ethics, Subjectivity and Truth, Essential Works of Foucault*, vol. I (New York: Free Press, 1997), 281–301.

Frei, Christophe, *Hans Morgenthau: An Intellectual Biography* (Baton Rouge: Louisiana State University Press, 2001).

Gallie, W. B., *Philosophers of Peace and War* (Cambridge University Press, 1978).

Garst, Daniel, 'Thucydides and Neo-Realism', *International Studies Quarterly*, 33:2 (1989), 3–28.

Gaubatz, Kurt T., 'The Hobbesian Problem and the Microfoundations of International Relations Theory', *Security Studies*, 11:2 (2001/2), 164–86.

Gauthier, David, *The Logic of Leviathan* (Oxford: Clarendon Press, 1969).

George, Jim, *Discourses of Global Politics* (Boulder, Colo.: Lynne Rienner, 1994).

'Realist "Ethics", International Relations, and Post-Modernism: Thinking Beyond the Egoism-Anarchy Thematic', *Millennium: Journal of International Studies*, 24:5 (1995), 195–223.

Gilpin, Robert, 'The Richness of the Tradition of Political Realism', in Robert Keohane (ed.), *NeoRealism and its Critics* (New York: Columbia University Press, 1986), 301–21.

Goldstein, Judith and Keohane, Robert (eds.), *Ideas and Foreign Policy: Beliefs, Institutions, and Political Change* (Ithaca: Cornell University Press, 1993).

Goodnight, G. Thomas, 'Hans J. Morgenthau *In Defense of the National Interest*: On Rhetoric, Realism, and the Public Sphere', in Francis A. Beer and Robert Harriman (eds.), *Post-Realism: The Rhetorical Turn in International Relations* (East Lansing: Michigan State University Press, 1996), 143–65.

Gray, John, *Post-Liberalism* (London: Routledge, 1993).

Isaiah Berlin (London: HarperCollins, 1995).

Two Faces of Liberalism (Cambridge: Polity Press, 2000).

Grieco, Joseph M., 'Realist International Theory and the Study of World Politics', in Michael Doyle and John Ikenberry (eds.), *New Thinking in International Relations* (Boulder, Colo.: Westview, 1997), 163–201.

Griffiths, Martin, *Realism, Idealism, and International Politics* (New York: Routledge, 1992).

Gunnell, John G., *Political Theory: Tradition and Interpretation* (Cambridge, Mass.: Winthrop, 1979).

Between Philosophy and Politics (Amherst: University of Massachusetts Press, 1986).

Guzzini, Stefano, *Realism in International Relations and International Political Economy: Continuing Story of a Death Foretold* (London: Routledge, 1998).

Hacking, Ian, *The Emergence of Probability* (Cambridge University Press, 1984).

Hall, John A., *International Orders* (Cambridge: Polity Press, 1996).

Hanson, Donald, 'Thomas Hobbes's "Highway to Peace"', *International Organization*, 38:2 (1984), 329–54.

Hanssen, Beatrice, *Critique of Violence* (London: Routledge, 2000).

Harper, John Lamberton, *American Visions of Europe* (Oxford University Press, 1997).

Harriman, Robert, 'Henry Kissinger: Realism's Rational Actor', in Francis A. Beer and Robert Harriman (eds.), *Post-Realism: The Rhetorical Turn in International Relations* (East Lansing: Michigan State University Press, 1996), 35–53.

Haslam, Johnathan, *No Virtue Like Necessity: Realist Thought in International Relations since Machiavelli* (New Haven: Yale University Press, 2002).

Held, David, *Democracy and the Global Order* (Cambridge: Polity Press, 1995).

Hellmann, Gunther (ed.), 'Are Dialogue and Synthesis Possible in International Relations?', *International Studies Review*, 5:1 (2003), 123–53.

Herzog, Don, *Happy Slaves* (University of Chicago Press, 1989).

Hindess, Barry, *Discourses of Power: Hobbes to Foucault* (Oxford: Basil Blackwell, 1996).

Hinsley, F. H., *Power and the Pursuit of Peace* (Cambridge University Press, 1963).

Hirschman, Albert O., *The Passions and the Interests: Political Arguments for Capitalism Before its Triumph* (Princeton University Press, 1977).

Hobbes, Thomas, *Behemoth or the Long Parliament*, ed. F. Tonnies (New York: Barnes and Noble, 1969).
De Cive (Indianapolis: Hackett, 1993).
Leviathan (Indianapolis: Hackett, 1993).
Three Discourses, ed. Noel B. Reynolds and Arlene W. Saxonhouse (University of Chicago Press, 1996).
Hobden, Steven, 'Historical Sociology: Back to the Future in International Relations?', in Steven Hobden and John M. Hobson (eds.), *Historical Sociology and International Relations* (Cambridge University Press, 2002).
Hobson, John M. and Seabrooke, Leonard, 'Reimagining Weber: Constructing International Society and the Social Balance of Power', *European Journal of International Relations*, 7:2 (2001), 239–74.
Hoffmann, Stanley, *The State of War* (New York: Praeger, 1965).
Duties beyond Borders (Syracuse, NY: Syracuse University Press, 1981).
Holden, Gerard, 'Who Contextualizes the Contextualizers? Disciplinary History and the Discourse about IR Discourse', *Review of International Studies*, 28:2 (2002), 253–70.
Holmes, Stephen, *Passions and Constraint: On the Theory of Liberal Democracy* (University of Chicago Press, 1995).
Holsti, K. J., *The State, War, and the State of War* (Cambridge University Press, 1997).
Holsti, Ole, 'Models of International Relations: Realist and Neoliberal Perspectives on Conflict and Cooperation', in Charles W. Kegley and Eugene Wittkopf (eds.), *The Global Agenda* (5th edn) (New York: McGraw-Hill, 1998), 131–44.
Honig, Bonnie, *Political Theory and the Displacement of Politics* (Ithaca: Cornell University Press, 1993).
Honig, Jan Willem, 'Totalitarianism and Realism: Hans Morgenthau's German Years', in Benjamin Frankel (ed.), *Roots of Realism* (London: Frank Cass, 1996), 283–313.
Hooykaas, R., *Religion and the Rise of Modern Science* (Edinburgh: Scottish Academic Press, 1972).
Hopf, Ted, 'The Promise of Constructivism in International Relations Theory', *International Security*, 23:1 (1998), 171–200.
Horkheimer, Max, *The Eclipse of Reason* (New York: The Seabury Press, 1974).
Horkheimer, Max and Adorno, Theodor, *Dialectic of Enlightenment* (New York: Continuum, 1972).
Horowitz, Asher, *Rousseau, Nature and History* (University of Toronto Press, 1987).
Horowitz, Gad and Horowitz, Asher, *Everywhere They Are in Chains* (Toronto: Macmillan, 1990).
Huysmans, Jef, 'The Question of the Limit: Desecuritization and the Aesthetics of Horror in Political Realism', *Millennium: Journal of International Studies*, 27:3 (1998), 569–89.

'Know your Schmitt: A Godfather of Truth and the Spectre of Nazism', *Review of International Studies*, 25:2 (1999), 323–8.

Ikenberry, John, 'The End of the Neoconservative Moment', *Survival*, 46:1 (2004), 7–22.

Inayatullah, Naeem and Rupert, Mark, 'Hobbes, Smith, and the Problem of Mixed Ontologies in Neorealist IPE', in Steven Rostow, *et al.* (eds.), *The Global Economy as Political Space* (Boulder, Colo.: Lynne Rienner, 1994), 61–86.

Jay, Martin, *The Dialectical Imagination* (Boston: Little, Brown, 1973).

Jervis, Robert, 'Hans Morgenthau, Realism, and the Scientific Study of International Politics', *Social Research*, 61:4 (1994), 853–76.

'Realism in the Study of World Politics', *International Organization*, 52:4 (1998), 971–91.

Johnston, David, *The Rhetoric of Leviathan: Thomas Hobbes and the Politics of Cultural Transformation* (Princeton University Press, 1986).

Jones, Charles, *E. H. Carr and International Relations: A Duty to Lie* (Cambridge University Press, 2000).

Kagan, Robert, *Of Paradise and Power* (London: Atlantic Books, 2003).

Kagan, Robert and Kristol, William, 'A Distinctly American Internationalism', *Weekly Standard*, 29 November 1999.

Kahler, Miles, 'Inventing International Relations: International Relations Theory after 1945', in Michael Doyle and John Ikenberry (eds.), *New Thinking in International Relations* (Boulder, Colo.: Westview, 1997), 20–53.

Kaplan, Robert, *Warrior Politics: Why Leadership Demands a Pagan Ethos* (New York: Vintage Books, 2002).

Kateb, George, *The Inner Ocean* (Ithaca: Cornell University Press, 1992).

Katzenstein, Peter J. (ed.), *The Culture of National Security* (New York: Columbia University Press, 1996).

Katzenstein, Peter J., Keohane, Robert O., and Krasner, Stephen D., '*International Organization* and the Study of World Politics', *International Organization* 52:4 (1998), 645–85.

Kegley, Charles and Wittkopf, Eugene, *World Politics: Trend and Transformation* (7th edn) (New York: St Martin's Press, 1999).

Kennan, George, *Memoirs: 1925–1950* (New York: Pantheon, 1983).

Keohane, Robert and Nye, Joseph, *Power and Interdependence* (2nd edn) (Glenview, Ill.: Scott, Foreman, 1989).

'Ideas Part-way Down', *Review of International Studies*, 26:1 (2000), 125–30.

Koselleck, Reinhart, *Critique and Crisis: The Enlightenment and the Pathogenesis of Modern Society* (Oxford: Berg, 1988).

Koskenniemi, Martti, *The Gentle Civilizer of Nations: The Rise and Fall of International Law 1870–1960* (Cambridge University Press, 2001).

Krasner, Stephen, 'The Accomplishments of International Political Economy', in Steve Smith, Ken Booth, and Marysia Zalewski (eds.), *International Theory: Positivism and Beyond* (Cambridge University Press, 1996).

Organized Hypocrisy (Princeton University Press, 1999).

'Wars, Hotel Fires, and Plane Crashes', *Review of International Studies*, 26:1 (2000), 131–6.

Kratochwil, Friedrich, 'The Monologue of "Science"', *International Studies Review*, 5:1 (2003), 124–8.

Kratochwil, Friedrich and Lapid, Yosef, 'Culture's Ship: Returns and Departures in International Relations Theory', in Yosef Lapid and Friedrich Kratochwil (eds.), *The Return of Culture and Identity in International Relations* (Boulder, Colo.: Lynne Rienner, 1996).

Kristol, Irving, *Reflections of a Neoconservative* (New York: Basic Books, 1983).

Kristol, William and Kagan, Robert, 'Toward a Neo-Reaganite Foreign Policy', *Foreign Affairs*, 75:4 (July/August 1996), pp. 18–32.

Laffey, Mark and Weldes, Jutta, 'Beyond Belief: Symbolic Technologies in International Relations', *European Journal of International Relations*, 3:2 (1998), 193–237.

Lebow, Richard Ned, 'Thucydides the Constructivist', *American Political Science Review*, 95:3 (2001), 547–60.

The Tragic Vision of Politics (Cambridge University Press, 2003).

Ledeen, Michael, *Machiavelli on Modern Leadership: Why Machiavelli's Iron Rules Are as Timely and Important Today as Five Centuries Ago* (New York: St Martin's Press, 1999).

Contribution to 'American Power – For What? A Symposium', *Commentary*, January 2000, 36–7.

Legro, Jeffrey W. and Moravcsik, Andrew, 'Is Anybody Still a Realist?', *International Security*, 24:2 (1999), 5–55.

Lichtheim, George, 'The Politics of Conservative Realism', in G. Lichtheim, *The Concept of Ideology and Other Essays* (New York: Random House, 1967), 129–50.

Linklater, Andrew, *Men and Citizens in the Theory of International Relations* (London: Macmillan, 1982).

The Transformation of Political Community (Cambridge: Polity Press, 1998).

Liska, George, *In Search of Poetry in the Politics of Power* (Lanham, Md: Lexington Books, 1998).

Little, Richard, 'Historiography and International Relations', *Review of International Studies*, 25:2 (1999), 291–9.

Long, David and Wilson, Peter, *Thinkers of the Twenty Years' Crisis: Interwar Idealism Reassessed* (Oxford: Clarendon Press, 1995).

Lovejoy, A. O., 'The Supposed Primitivism of Rousseau's Discourse on the Origins of Inequality', in A. O. Lovejoy, *Essays on the History of Ideas* (Baltimore: Johns Hopkins University Press, 1952).

Luttwak, Edward, *Strategy and History: Collected Essays*, vol. II (New Brunswick, NJ: Transaction Books, 1985).

McCormick, John M., 'Fear, Technology and the State: Carl Schmitt, Leo Strauss and the Revival of Hobbes in Weimar and National Socialist Germany', *Political Theory*, 22:4 (1994), 619–52.

Carl Schmitt's Critique of Liberalism: Against Politics as Technology (Cambridge University Press, 1997).
Malcolm, Noel, *Aspects of Hobbes* (Oxford: Clarendon Press, 2002).
'Hobbes's Theory of International Relations', in Noel Malcolm, *Aspects of Hobbes* (Oxford: Clarendon Press, 2002).
Manicas, Peter, *A History and Philosophy of the Social Sciences* (London: Routledge, 1984).
Mearsheimer, John, 'The False Promise of International Institutions', *International Security*, 19:3 (1994/5), 5–49.
'A Realist Reply', *International Security*, 20:1 (1995), 82–93.
The Tragedy of Great Power Politics (New York: Norton, 2001).
Meinecke, Friedrich, *Machiavellism: The Doctrine of Raison d'Etat and its Place in Modern History* (London: Routledge, 1957).
Mercer, Johnathan, 'Anarchy and Identity', *International Organization*, 49:2 (1995), 229–52.
Moon, Donald, *Constructing Community: Moral Pluralism and Tragic Conflicts* (Princeton University Press, 1995).
Moravcsik, Andrew, 'Theory Synthesis in International Relations: Real not Metaphysical', *International Studies Review*, 5:1 (2003), 131–6.
Morgenthau, Hans J., *La Notion du 'Politique' et la théorie des différends internationaux* (Paris: Librairie du Recueil Sirey, 1933).
'Nazism', in J. Roucek (ed.), *Twentieth-Century Political Thought* (New York: Philosophical Library, 1946).
Scientific Man versus Power Politics (University of Chicago Press, 1946).
In Defense of the National Interest (New York: Knopf, 1951).
The Purpose of American Politics (New York: Knopf, 1960).
Politics in the Twentieth Century, vol. I: *The Decline of Democratic Politics* (University of Chicago Press, 1962).
Politics in the Twentieth Century, vol. II: *The Impasse of American Foreign Policy* (University of Chicago Press, 1962).
Politics in the Twentieth Century, vol. III: *The Restoration of American Politics* (University of Chicago Press, 1962).
'Four Paradoxes of Nuclear Strategy', *American Political Science Review*, 58:1 (1964), 23–35.
Politics among Nations (4th edn) (New York: Knopf, 1967).
Truth and Power: Essays of a Decade (New York: Praeger, 1970).
Science: Servant or Master? (New York: New American Library, 1972).
'Fragment of an Intellectual Autobiography: 1904–1932', in Kenneth W. Thompson (ed.), *Truth and Tragedy: A Tribute to Hans Morgenthau* (Washington, DC: New Republic Books, 1977), 1–17.
Mouffe, Chantal, *The Return of the Political* (London: Verso, 1993).
Muravchik, Joshua, *Exporting Democracy: Fulfilling America's Destiny* (Washington, DC: AEI Press, 1992).

Contribution to 'American Power – For What? A Symposium', *Commentary*, January 2000.
Murray, A. J. H., 'The Moral Politics of Hans Morgenthau', *Review of Politics*, 58:1 (1996), 81–108.
Reconstructing Realism (Edinburgh: University of Keele Press, 1997).
Navari, Cornelia, 'Knowledge, the State and the State of Nature', in Michael Donelan (ed.), *The Reason of State* (London: George Allen and Unwin, 1978), 102–21.
Neufeld, Mark, *The Restructuring of International Relations Theory* (Cambridge University Press, 1995).
Neumann, Iver B., *The Uses of the Other: The 'East' in European Identity Formation* (Minneapolis: University of Minnesota Press, 1999).
Oakeshott, Michael, *Rationalism in Politics* (London: Methuen, 1962).
Oestreich, Gerhard, *Neostoicism and the Early Modern State* (Cambridge University Press, 1982).
Onuf, Nicholas G., *World of Our Making* (Columbia: University of South Carolina Press, 1989).
The Republican Legacy in International Thought (Cambridge University Press, 1998).
Owen, David, *Maturity and Modernity: Nietzsche, Weber, Foucault and the Ambiguity of Reason* (London: Routledge, 1994).
Pedersen, Vibeke Schou and Williams, Michael C., 'Between Europe and America: Hans Morgenthau and the Rhetoric of a Republican Peace', forthcoming.
Petersen, Ulrik Enemark, 'Breathing Nietzsche's Air: New Reflections on Morgenthau's Concepts of Power and Human Nature', *Alternatives*, 24 (1999), 83–118.
Philpott, Daniel, *Revolutions in Sovereignty: How Ideas Shaped Modern International Relations* (Princeton University Press, 2001).
Pichler, H.-K., 'The Godfathers of "Truth": Max Weber and Carl Schmitt in Morgenthau's Theory of Power Politics', *Review of International Studies*, 24:2 (1998), 185–200.
Pocock, J. G. A., *The Machiavellian Moment: Florentine Political Thought and the Atlantic Republican Tradition* (Princeton University Press, 1975).
Virtue, Commerce, History (Cambridge University Press, 1985).
Polanyi, Karl, *The Great Transformation* (Boston: Beacon Press, 1944).
Popkin, Richard, *The History of Skepticism from Erasmus to Spinoza* (Berkeley: University of California Press, 1979).
Price, Richard and Reus-Smit, Christian, 'Dangerous Liaisons?: Critical International Theory and Constructivism', *European Journal of International Relations*, 4:3 (1998), 259–94.
Rabb, Theodore, *The Struggle for Stability in Early Modern Europe* (Oxford University Press, 1975).
Rae, Heather, *State Identities and the Homogenisation of Peoples* (Cambridge University Press, 2002).

Rapaczynski, Andrzej, *Nature and Politics: Liberalism in the Philosophy of Hobbes, Locke, and Rousseau* (Ithaca: Cornell University Press, 1987).

Rengger, Nicholas, *Political Theory, Modernity and Postmodernity* (Oxford: Blackwell, 1995).

International Relations, Political Theory and the Problem of Order (London: Routledge, 2000).

Reus-Smit, Christian, *The Moral Purpose of the State* (Princeton University Press, 1999).

Ringmar, Erik, *Identity, Interest and Action* (Cambridge University Press, 1997).

Risse, Thomas, 'Let's Argue!: Communicative Action in World Politics', *International Organization*, 54:1 (2000), 1–39.

Risse-Kappen, Thomas, 'Democratic Peace, Warlike Democracies?: A Social Constructivist Approach to the Democratic Peace', *European Journal of International Relations*, 1:4 (1995), 491–527.

Rorty, Richard, *Contingency, Irony, Solidarity* (Cambridge University Press, 1989).

Rose, Gideon, 'Neoclassical Realism and Theories of Foreign Policy', *World Politics*, 51:2 (1998), 144–72.

Rosecrance, Richard, 'Has Realism Become Cost-Benefit Analysis?', *International Security*, 26:2 (2001), 132–54.

Rosenberg, Justin, *The Empire of Civil Society: A Critique of the Realist Theory of International Relations* (London: Verso, 1994).

Rosenthal, Joel, *Righteous Realists: Political Realism, Responsible Power, and American Culture in the Nuclear Age* (Baton Rouge: Louisiana State University Press, 1991).

Ross, Dorothy, *The Origins of American Social Science* (Cambridge University Press, 1991).

Rousseau, Jean-Jacques, '"Abstract" and "Judgement" on St Pierre's *Project for Perpetual Peace*', in M. G. Forsyth, H. M. A. Keans-Soper, and P. Savigear (eds.), *The Theory of International Relations* (London: George Allen and Unwin, 1970).

The Government of Poland, ed. W. Kendall (New York: Bobbs-Merrill, 1972).

The Indispensable Rousseau, comp. John Hope Mason (New York: Quartet Books, 1979).

The Social Contract and Discourses, trans. and intro. G. D. H. Cole, rev. J. M. Brumfitt and John C. Hall (London: Dent, 1983).

Ruggie, John G., *Constructing the World Polity* (New York: Routledge, 1998).

Russell, Greg, *Hans Morgenthau and the Ethics of American Statecraft* (Baton Rouge: Louisiana State University Press, 1990).

Scheuerman, William, *Between the Norm and the Exception: The Frankfurt School and the Rule of Law* (Cambridge, Mass.: MIT Press, 1994).

Carl Schmitt: The End of Law (New York: Rowan and Littlefield, 1999).

Schluchter, Wolfgang, *Paradoxes of Modernity: Culture and Conduct in the Thought of Max Weber*, trans. Neil Solomon (Stanford University Press, 1996).

Schmidt, Brian, *The Political Discourse of Anarchy* (Albany: State University of New York Press, 1998).

Schmitt, Carl, *Political Romanticism*, trans. Guy Oakes (Cambridge, Mass.: MIT Press, 1986).

The Crisis of Parliamentary Democracy, trans. Ellen Kennedy (Cambridge, Mass.: MIT Press, 1988).

Political Theology: Four Chapters on the Concept of Sovereignty, trans. George Schwab (Cambridge, Mass.: MIT Press, 1988).

The Concept of the Political, trans. George Schwab (University of Chicago Press, 1996).

The Leviathan in the State Theory of Thomas Hobbes: Meaning and Failure of a Political Symbol, trans. and ed. G. Schwab and E. Hilfstein (Westport, Conn.: Greenwood Press, 1996).

Schweller, Randall, *Deadly Imbalances: Tripolarity and Hitler's Strategy of World Conquest* (New York: Columbia University Press, 1998).

Shapcott, Richard, *Justice, Community and Dialogue in International Relations* (Cambridge University Press, 2001).

Shapin, Steven, *A Social History of Truth: Civility and Science in Seventeenth-Century England* (University of Chicago Press, 1994).

Shapin, Steven and Shaeffer, Simon, *Leviathan and the Air Pump: Hobbes, Boyle and the Experimental Life* (Princeton University Press, 1985).

Shapiro, Barbara, *Probability and Certainty in Seventeenth-Century England* (Princeton University Press, 1983).

Shimko, Keith L., 'Realism, Neorealism, and American Liberalism', *Review of Politics*, 54:1 (1992), 281–301.

Shklar, Judith, *Political Thought and Political Thinkers*, ed. Stanley Hoffmann (University of Chicago Press, 1998).

Skinner, Quentin, *Reason and Rhetoric in the Philosophy of Hobbes* (Cambridge University Press, 1996).

Liberty before Liberalism (Cambridge University Press, 1998).

Visions of Politics, vol. III: *Hobbes and Civil Science* (Cambridge University Press, 2002).

Slagstad, Rune, 'Liberal Constitutionalism and its Critics: Carl Schmitt and Max Weber', in Jon Elster and Rune Slagstad (eds.), *Constitutionalism and Democracy* (Cambridge University Press, 1988), 103–29.

Smith, Michael J., *Realist Thought from Weber to Kissinger* (Baton Rouge: Louisiana State University Press, 1986).

Smith, Steve, 'Positivism and Beyond', in Steve Smith, Ken Booth, and Marysia Zalewski (eds.), *International Theory: Positivism and Beyond* (Cambridge University Press, 1996), 11–44.

Somerville, Johann, *Thomas Hobbes: Political Ideas in Historical Context* (New York: St Martin's Press, 1992).

Spirtas, Michael, 'A House Divided: Tragedy and Evil in Realist Theory', *Security Studies*, 5:3 (Spring 1996), pp. 385–423.

Starobinski, Jean, *Jean-Jacques Rousseau: Transparency and Obstruction*, trans. Arthur Goldhammer (University of Chicago Press, 1988).

Sterling-Folker, Jennifer, 'Realism and the Constructivist Challenge: Rejecting, Reconstructing, or Rereading', *International Studies Review*, 4:1 (2002), 73–97.

Strong, Tracy, *Jean-Jacques Rousseau: The Politics of the Ordinary* (Thousand Oaks, Calif.: Sage, 1994).

Tellis, Ashley, 'Reconstructing Political Realism: The Long March to Scientific Theory', in Benjamin Frankel (ed.), *Roots of Realism* (London: Frank Cass, 1996), 3–94.

Thayer, Bradley A., 'Bringing in Darwin: Evolutionary Theory, Realism, and International Politics', *International Security*, 25:2 (2000), 124–51.

Thiele, Leslie Paul, *Friedrich Nietzsche and the Politics of the Soul* (Princeton University Press, 1994).

Thomas, Keith, 'The Social Origins of Hobbes's Political Thought', in K. C. Brown (ed.), *Hobbes Studies* (Cambridge, Mass.: Harvard University Press, 1965).

Todorov, Tzvetan, *Imperfect Garden: The Legacy of Humanism* (Princeton University Press, 2002).

Toulmin, Steven, *Cosmopolis: The Hidden Agenda of Modernity* (New York: Free Press, 1990).

Tuck, Richard, 'Optics and Sceptics: The Philosophical Foundations of Hobbes's Political Thought', in Edmund Leites (ed.), *Conscience and Casuistry in Early Modern Europe* (Cambridge University Press, 1988), 235–63.

Hobbes (Oxford University Press, 1989).

Tully, James (ed.), *Meaning and Context: Quentin Skinner and his Critics* (Cambridge: Polity Press, 1989).

Tully, James, *An Approach to Political Philosophy: Locke in Contexts* (Cambridge University Press, 1993).

'The Agonic Freedom of Citizens', *Economy and Society*, 28:2 (1999), 161–82.

Turner, Steven P. and Factor, R. A., *Max Weber and the Dispute over Reason and Value* (London: Routledge, 1984).

Underhill, Geoffrey, 'Conceptualizing the Changing Global Order', in Richard Stubbs and Geoffrey Underhill (eds.), *Political Economy and the Changing Global Order* (Oxford University Press, 1999), 3–24.

Vasquez, John, *The Power of Power Politics: From Classical Realism to Neotraditionalism* (Cambridge University Press, 1998).

Vincent, John, 'The Hobbesian Tradition in Twentieth-Century International Thought', *Millennium: Journal of International Studies*, 10:2 (1981), 91–101.

Viotti, Paul R. and Kauppi, Mark V., *International Relations Theory: Realism, Pluralism, Globalism* (New York: Macmillan, 1993).

Wæver, Ole, 'The Rise and Fall of the Inter-Paradigm Debate', in Steve Smith, Ken Booth, and Marysia Zalewski (eds.), *International Theory: Positivism and Beyond* (Cambridge University Press, 1996), 149–85.

'The Sociology of a not so International Discipline: American and European Developments in International Relations', *International Organization*, 52:4 (1998), 687–728.

Walker, R. B. J., 'Realism, Change and International Political Theory', *International Studies Quarterly*, 31:1 (1988), 65–86.
'Violence, Modernity, Silence: from Max Weber to International Relations', in David Campbell and Michael Dillon (eds.), *The Political Subject of Violence* (Manchester University Press, 1993), 137–60.
Inside/Outside: International Relations as Political Theory (Cambridge University Press, 1993).
'International Relations and the Concept of the Political', in Ken Booth and Steve Smith (eds.), *International Political Theory Today* (Cambridge: Polity Press, 1995), 306–27.
'The Subject of Security', in Keith Krause and Michael C. Williams (eds.), *Critical Security Studies* (Minneapolis: University of Minnesota Press, 1997).
Walt, Steven, 'The Renaissance of Security Studies', *International Studies Quarterly*, 35:2 (1991), 211–39.
Waltz, Kenneth, *Man, the State and War* (New York: Columbia University Press, 1959).
Theory of International Politics (Reading, Mass.: Addison-Wesley, 1979).
'Realist Thought and Neorealist Theory', in Robert L. Rothstein (ed.), *The Evolution of Theory in International Relations* (Columbia: University of South Carolina Press, 1991), 21–38.
Warner, Daniel, *An Ethic of Responsibility in International Relations* (Boulder, Colo.: Lynne Rienner, 1991).
Warren, Mark, 'Max Weber's Liberalism for a Nietzschean World', *American Political Science Review*, 82:1 (1988), 31–50.
Nietzsche and Political Thought (Cambridge, Mass.: MIT Press, 1988).
Weber, Max, *The Protestant Ethic and the Spirit of Capitalism*, trans. by Talcott Parsons (New York: Scribners, 1958).
'Politics as a Vocation', and 'Science as a Vocation', in H. H. Gerth and C. Wright Mills (eds.), *From Max Weber* (New York: Free Press, 1970).
Weldes, Jutta, *Constructing National Interests* (Minneapolis: University of Minnesota Press, 1999).
Wendt, Alexander, 'Anarchy is What States Make of it: The Social Construction of Power Politics', *International Organization*, 46:2 (1992), 391–425.
'Collective Identity Formation and the International State', *American Political Science Review*, 88:2 (1994), 384–96.
'Constructing International Politics', *International Security*, 20:1 (1995), 71–81.
Social Theory of International Politics (Cambridge University Press, 1999).
'What is IR for?: Notes Toward a Post-Critical View', in Richard Wyn Jones (ed.), *Critical Theory and World Politics* (Boulder, Colo.: Lynne Rienner, 2001), 205–24.
White, Stephen, *Political Theory and Postmodernism* (Cambridge University Press, 1992).
Wight, Martin, *International Relations: Three Traditions* (London: Holmes and Meier, 1992).

Williams, Michael C., 'Reason and Realpolitik: Kant's "Critique of International Politics"', *Canadian Journal of Political Science*, 25:1 (1992), 99–119.
'Identity and the Politics of Security', *European Journal of International Relations*, 4:2 (1998), 207–28.
'The Discipline of the Democratic Peace: Kant, Liberalism and the Social Construction of Security Communities', *European Journal of International Relations*, 7:4 (2001), 525–53.
'What Is the National Interest?', forthcoming.
Wittgenstein, Ludwig, *Philosophical Investigations* (Oxford: Basil Blackwell, 1958).
Wohlforth, William, *The Elusive Balance: Power and Perceptions during the Cold War* (Ithaca: Cornell University Press, 1993).
'Realism and the End of the Cold War', in Sean Lynn-Jones (ed.), *The Perils of Anarchy* (Cambridge, Mass.: MIT Press, 1995), 3–41.
Wolin, Richard, 'Carl Schmitt: The Conservative Reactionary Habitus and the Aesthetics of Horror', *Political Theory*, 20:3 (1992), 424–47.
Wong, Benjamin, 'Hans Morgenthau's Anti-Machiavellian Machiavellianism', *Millennium: Journal of International Studies*, 29:2 (2000), 389–410.
Wyn Jones, Richard, *Security, Strategy, and Critical Theory* (Boulder, Colo.: Lynne Rienner, 1999).
(ed.), *Critical Theory and World Politics* (Boulder, Colo.: Lynne Rienner, 2001).
Zakaria, Fareed, 'Realism and Domestic Politics: A Review Essay', *International Security*, 17:1 (1992), 177–98.
'Is Realism Finished?', *The National Interest* (Winter 1992–3).
From Wealth to Power: The Unusual Origins of America's World Role (Princeton University Press, 1998).

Index

CAMBRIDGE STUDIES IN INTERNATIONAL RELATIONS

88 *Susan Sell*
Private Power, Public Law
The Globalization of Intellectual Property Rights

87 *Nina Tannenwald*
The Nuclear Taboo
The United States and the Non-use of Nuclear Weapons since 1945

86 *Linda Weiss*
States in the Global Economy
Bringing Domestic Institutions Back in

85 *Rodney Bruce Hall and Thomas J. Biersteker (eds.)*
The Emergence of Private Authority in Global Governance

84 *Heather Rae*
State Identities and the Homogenisation of Peoples

83 *Maja Zehfuss*
Constructivism in International Relations
The Politics of Reality

82 *Paul K. Huth and Todd Allee*
The Democratic Peace and Territorial Conflict in the Twentieth Century

81 *Neta C. Crawford*
Argument and Change in World Politics
Ethics, Decolonization and Humanitarian Intervention

80 *Douglas Lemke*
Regions of War and Peace

79 *Richard Shapcott*
Justice, Community and Dialogue in International Relations

78 *Phil Steinberg*
The Social Construction of the Ocean

77 *Christine Sylvester*
Feminist International Relations
An Unfinished Journey

76 *Kenneth A. Schultz*
Democracy and Coercive Diplomacy

75 *David Houghton*
US Foreign Policy and the Iran Hostage Crisis

74 *Cecilia Albin*
Justice and Fairness in International Negotiation

73 *Martin Shaw*
Theory of the global state
Globality as an Unfinished Revolution

72 *Frank C. Zagare and D. Marc Kilgour*
Perfect Deterrence

71 *Robert O'Brien, Anne Marie Goetz, Jan Aart Scholte and Marc Williams*
Contesting Global Governance
Multilateral Economic Institutions and Global Social Movements

70 *Roland Bleiker*
Popular Dissent, Human Agency and Global Politics

69 *Bill McSweeney*
Security, Identity and Interests
A Sociology of International Relations

68 *Molly Cochran*
Normative Theory in International Relations
A Pragmatic Approach

67 *Alexander Wendt*
Social Theory of International Politics

66 *Thomas Risse, Stephen C. Ropp, and Kathryn Sikkink (eds)*
The Power of Human Rights
International Norms and Domestic Change

65 *Daniel W. Drezner*
The Sanctions Paradox
Economic Statecraft and International Relations

64 *Viva Ona Bartkus*
The Dynamic of Secession

63 *John A. Vasquez*
The Power of Power Politics
From Classical Realism to Neotraditionalism

62 *Emanuel Adler and Michael Barnett (eds.)*
Security Communities

61 *Charles Jones*
E. H. Carr and International Relations
A Duty to Lie

60 *Jeffrey W. Knopf*
Domestic Society and International Cooperation
The Impact of Protest on US Arms Control Policy

59 *Nicholas Greenwood Onuf*
The Republican Legacy in International Thought

58 *Daniel S. Geller and J. David Singer*
Nations at War
A Scientific Study of International Conflict

57 *Randall D. Germain*
The International Organization of Credit
States and Global Finance in the World Economy

56 *N. Piers Ludlow*
Dealing with Britain
The Six and the First UK Application to the EEC

55 *Andreas Hasenclever, Peter Mayer, and Volker Rittberger*
Theories of International Regimes

54 *Miranda A. Schreurs and Elizabeth C. Economy (eds.)*
The Internationalization of Environmental Protection

53 *James N. Rosenau*
Along the Domestic–Foreign Frontier
Exploring Governance in a Turbulent World

52 *John M. Hobson*
The Wealth of States
A Comparative Sociology of International Economic and Political Change

51 *Kalevi J. Holsti*
The State, War, and the State of War

50 *Christopher Clapham*
Africa and the International System
The Politics of State Survival

49 *Susan Strange*
The Retreat of the State
The Diffusion of Power in the World Economy

48 *William I. Robinson*
Promoting Polyarchy
Globalization, US Intervention, and Hegemony

47 *Roger Spegele*
Political Realism in International Theory

46 *Thomas J. Biersteker and Cynthia Weber (eds.)*
State Sovereignty as Social Construct

45 *Mervyn Frost*
Ethics in International Relations
A Constitutive Theory

44 *Mark W. Zacher with Brent A. Sutton*
Governing Global Networks
International Regimes for Transportation and Communications

43 *Mark Neufeld*
The Restructuring of International Relations Theory

42 *Thomas Risse-Kappen (ed.)*
Bringing Transnational Relations Back in
Non-state Actors, Domestic Structures and International Institutions

41 *Hayward R. Alker*
Rediscoveries and Reformulations
Humanistic Methodologies for International Studies

40 *Robert W. Cox with Timothy J. Sinclair*
Approaches to World Order

39 *Jens Bartelson*
A Genealogy of Sovereignty

38 *Mark Rupert*
Producing Hegemony
The Politics of Mass Production and American Global Power

37 *Cynthia Weber*
Simulating Sovereignty
Intervention, the State and Symbolic Exchange

36 *Gary Goertz*
Contexts of International Politics

35 *James L. Richardson*
Crisis Diplomacy
The Great Powers since the Mid-Nineteenth Century

34 *Bradley S. Klein*
Strategic Studies and World Order
The Global Politics of Deterrence

33 *T. V. Paul*
Asymmetric Conflicts: War Initiation by Weaker Powers

32 *Christine Sylvester*
Feminist Theory and International Relations in a Postmodern Era

31 *Peter J. Schraeder*
US Foreign Policy Toward Africa
Incrementalism, Crisis and Change

30 *Graham Spinardi*
From Polaris to Trident: The Development of US Fleet Ballistic Missile Technology

29 *David A. Welch*
Justice and the Genesis of War

28 *Russell J. Leng*
Interstate Crisis Behavior, 1816–1980: Realism versus Reciprocity

27 *John A. Vasquez*
The War Puzzle

26 *Stephen Gill (ed.)*
Gramsci, Historical Materialism and International Relations

25 *Mike Bowker and Robin Brown (eds.)*
From Cold War to Collapse: Theory and World Politics in the 1980s

24 *R. B. J. Walker*
Inside/Outside: International Relations as Political Theory

23 *Edward Reiss*
The Strategic Defense Initiative

22 *Keith Krause*
Arms and the State: Patterns of Military Production and Trade

21 *Roger Buckley*
US–Japan Alliance Diplomacy 1945–1990

20 *James N. Rosenau and Ernst-Otto Czempiel (eds.)*
Governance without Government: Order and Change in World Politics

19 *Michael Nicholson*
Rationality and the Analysis of International Conflict

18 *John Stopford and Susan Strange*
Rival States, Rival firms
Competition for World Market Shares

17 *Terry Nardin and David R. Mapel (eds.)*
Traditions of International Ethics

16 *Charles F. Doran*
Systems in Crisis
New Imperatives of High Politics at Century's End

15 *Deon Geldenhuys*
Isolated States: A Comparative Analysis

14 *Kalevi J. Holsti*
Peace and War: Armed Conflicts and International Order 1648–1989

13 *Saki Dockrill*
Britain's Policy for West German Rearmament 1950–1955

12 *Robert H. Jackson*
Quasi-States: Sovereignty, International Relations and the Third World

11 *James Barber and John Barratt*
South Africa's Foreign Policy
The Search for Status and Security 1945–1988

10 *James Mayall*
Nationalism and International Society

9 *William Bloom*
Personal Identity, National Identity and International Relations

8 *Zeev Maoz*
National Choices and International Processes

7 *Ian Clark*
The Hierarchy of States
Reform and Resistance in the International Order

6 *Hidemi Suganami*
The Domestic Analogy and World Order Proposals

5 *Stephen Gill*
American Hegemony and the Trilateral Commission

4 *Michael C. Pugh*
The ANZUS Crisis, Nuclear Visiting and Deterrence

3 *Michael Nicholson*
Formal Theories in International Relations

2 *Friedrich V. Kratochwil*
Rules, Norms, and Decisions
On the Conditions of Practical and Legal Reasoning in International Relations and Domestic Affairs

1 *Myles L. C. Robertson*
Soviet Policy Towards Japan
An Analysis of Trends in the 1970s and 1980s